VOLUME THREE:
TRADEMARKS & SYMBOLS OF THE WORLD

PICTOGRAM & SIGN DESIGN

by Yasaburo Kuwayama

Rockport Publishers • Rockport, Massachusetts

Distributed by North Light Books
Cincinnati, Ohio

Copyright © 1989 by Rockport Publishers

All rights reserved. No part of this
work may be reproduced in any form
without written permission of the
publisher.

Printed in Japan

First printing 1989

First published in the United States
of America in 1989 by:
Rockport Publishers
5 Smith Street
Rockport, MA 01966
TEL: (508)546-9590
FAX:(508)546-7141

For distribution by:
North Light, an imprint of
F&W Publications
1507 Dana Avenue
Cincinnati, Ohio 45207

First published in Japan as
TRADEMARKS & SYMBOLS OF
THE WORLD by Kashiwashobo

Library of Congress cataloging in
publication data:

Kuwayama, Yasaburo
Trademarks & Symbols of the World
Volume Three:
Pictogram & Sign Design

ISBN: 0-935603-30-1

Table of Contents

The contents of Pictograms and Signs data
are as follows:

1) Applicable Industries

2) Art Director

3) Designer

4) Client

5) Year Produced (Place Produced)

6) Data on Color

All the works in this book were produced between 1970 and 1983.

Note

The Pictograms and Signs contained in this book are the exclusive property of the designers and copyright holders. Some works are registered Pictograms and Signs and are Protected by law. All works represented in this book may not be reproduced or published without prior approval from the individual designers and copyright holders.

Contents

Table of Contents ——————————— 3
Note ——————————— 4
Pictogram and Sign Design——————— 6
Pictogram Classification/Data on Each Pictogram ———— 7
Pictograms and Their Applications——————— 8
Types and Functions of Pictograms ————— 9
Artists and Their Works——————— 10

Man ——————————— 13
Woman——————————— 20
Little One ——————————— 23
Person in Action——————————— 26
Person at Work ——————————— 32
Person Taking Exercise ——————— 35
Both Sexes ——————————— 42
Persons——————————— 44
Face——————————— 50
Eye or Ear——————————— 57
Mouth or Nose ——————————— 59
Limbs——————————— 61
Internal——————————— 68
Animal——————————— 70
Bird——————————— 80
Fish——————————— 83
Insect——————————— 86
Flower or Tree——————————— 88
Fruit——————————— 91
Celestial Body——————————— 96
Mountain or Land——————————— 98
Fire ——————————— 100
Water ——————————— 102
Vehicle——————————— 105

Building——————————— 114
Vessel ——————————— 119
Instrument ——————————— 129
Precision Machine——————————— 146
Communication——————————— 149
Equipment——————————— 154
Electricity——————————— 157
Sound or Reflex ——————————— 160
Medical Care——————————— 162
Stationery——————————— 164
Cigarette or Goods——————————— 168
Life ——————————— 171
Arrow ——————————— 178
Hearts ——————————— 180
Cross ——————————— 181
Numerial ——————————— 182
Romaji ——————————— 184
Traffic ——————————— 186
Transportation/Laboratory・Training School ——————— 191
Library/Medical Care ——————————— 192
Public Health ——————————— 193
Resort ——————————— 195
Physical Mass Meeting ——————————— 196

Index ——————————— 199
About The Editor ——————————— 236
Appendix ——————————— 237
Infomation About Forthcoming Edition(1985-91) ———— 238

Pictogram And Sign Design

Pictograms are often refered to as "Signs" or "isotypes."An "isotype" is, in fact, the name of a particular kind of pictogram designed by Mr. Otto Noilart of Australia. "Signs" have a more multifacefed meaning in that they convey sound, character, movement, and color. What then is a Pictogram ? Pictograms combine the visual language of signs with pictures to communi- cate with the viewer. Pictures can be enhaved enhanced letters, colors, sounds, etc. making them more effective at communicat- ing ideas. In some respects pictograms are similar in form to marks, symbols, and simple illustration. However, the collection in this book reveals that the applications of pictograms are distinct from those of other marks.

There are fewer applications for pictograms than there are for marks, symbols, and logotypes. A large measure of this is due to the fact that there are fewer pictograms in use. Another plausible explanation is that the word "pictogram"is not as well established in the design world. In Japan, pictograms were widely used during the Tokyo Olympics of 1964. Outside of Japan, however, they do not seem to be as popular, although many European traffic signs are designed with Pictograms. In fact, traffic sign pictograms originated in Europe. Japan quickly followed the European example. Although the majority of traffic signs in the United States are still lettered, pictogroms are becom- ming more widely used. It is increasingly evident that pictograms are evolving into an important aspect of visual communication and design throughout the world.

The pictograms presented in this book vary considerably from those published in the edition 20 years ago. In this older edition pictograms for public use were common place, such as those used for events and traffic signs. This all new edition reveals a wider range of uses : companies, resort facilities, books, and much more. The reader will also be impressed by how much more complex, colorful, and sophisticated the designs in use today are.

Pictogram Classification

The pictograms in this edition have been classified according to their shape and form. Naturally, both shape and form vary according to content as well as to the designer's personality and aesthetic sense. Despite these variations, we have arranged the pictogroms for easy reference, For clarity we have classified the pictograms into roughly three catagories: 1) Realistic Images 2) Letters and Signs 3) Abstract Images. Within each catagory a number of motifs are presented. A minimun of 8 pictograms per motif are included and are arranged from simple to complex designs.

Explanation of Classifications and Motifs

* Human Forms
* Active People (eg. working, running, bathing)
* Sports Themes (eg. bicycling, swimming, skiing, dancing)
* Groups of People
* Faces (including frontal views and profiles).
* Hands (eg. directions, grip, work situations, activities involving hands)
* Internal Organs
* Animals (eg. wildlife, birds, mammals, etc.)
* Fish (including other sea animals such as whales, shrimp, octopus)
* Insects
* Planets (eg. sun, moon, earth, stars)
* Mountains and other natural objects (stones, jewels)
* Water (eg. drops, waves, snow, steam)
* Tools (eg. Knives, forks, keys, scissors)
* Communication Devices (eg. telephones, mail, signals)
* Facilities (eg. fire extinguishers, gasolinepumps)
* Stationery & Related Materials (eg. typewriters, pens, pencils, paper)
* Everyday Life (eg. food, clothing, furniture)
* Directions
* Crosses
* Figures (eg. currency symbols)
* Alphabet (including letters from A to Z and punctuation marks)

Data on Each Pictogram

1) Applicable Industries
2) Art Director
3) Designer
4) Client
5) Year Produced
6) Data on Color

Footnotes:

1) Applicable Industries - Some pictograms do not have a corresponding industry and therefore in some cases they are not indicated.
2) Art Director - Some pictograms were submitted without the art directors name. In other cases the pictograms were co-designed.
3) Designer - often the designer and the art director are the same person, and in such cases we indicate this. If a third designer is invclved along with the art director and designer, they are indicated separately.
4) Client - If the client is Japanese then he, she, or it (the company) is presented in an abbreviated form.
5) Year Produced - Some pictograms required two years for production because they were a collaboration of more than one designer. When the letter "R" appears, this is an indication that the pictogram was redesigned from a previous form. We have also included the place where the pictograms are produced as an indication as to where they are actively being used.
6) Colors - We have noted the color number and its maker. The color companies include :
Pantone / Pms (U.S.A.)
DIC - Dai Nippon Ink (Tokyo)
Toyo Ink (Tokyo.)

Pictograms And Their Applications

As aforementioned, pictograms are similar to marks, symbols, and illustrations. The visual language of pictograms has evolved into a communication system with diverse applications.

1) Traffic Signs - airpots, stations, ports, timetables, vehicles, etc.
2) Transportation and Communication - package warnings, product instructions, counter instructions.
3) Education - schools, libraries, museums, book reference sections, etc.
4) Medical Facilities - hospitals, clinics, medicine use instructions, etc.
5) Office - entrance & exit╱signs, directions, etc.
6) Parks - zoos, water fountains, flower gardens, garbage areas, etc.
7) Events - Athletic╱meets and games, special event pictograms, etc.
8) Hotels and other Businesses - banks, markets, malls, directions, instructions etc.
9) Everyday Life - instructions for : eating foods, playing games, pet care, household appliances,etc.
10) Advertisments - newspapers, posters, magazines.
11) Art - sculpture, wall paintings, posters, etc.

Types And Functions of Pictograms

Types of Pictograms	Functions	Examples
Names	Enables the observer to distinguish between different things, products, and ideas	Product names, places, business names, facilities, jobs, animals, plants.
Directions	To make it easier to understand location.	Arrows, Hands, Lines Letters.
Information	To provide an overview as well as specific information.	Maps of buildings, floor plans, service counters.
Explanatory	To provide explanatory information on content, etc.	Displays, facilities, education history, instructions, etc.
Rules & Regulations	To Maintain safety and order.	Warning labels, restrication instructions.
Art	To provoke a thoughtful reflection on society and to beautify the environment.	Painting, Sculpture

Artists and Their Works

A

Aoki Seiko （Japan） 37,101,133,418,446,447,448, 471,522,911,928,1165,1183,1198,1201,1230,1281

B

Baba Yuji （Japan） 472,487,1742,1763
Benenti, Beppe （Italy） 1256,1362,1378,1397,1397, 1401,1402,1645,1646,1651,1652,1654

C

Canovas, Eduardo A. （Argentina） 703,804,1235, 1294,1774,1779,S9
Cauduro, Joao Carlos （Brazil） 598,603,628, 728
Chillemans, A. G. （Holland） 330,382,1210, 1541
Ćirić, Miloš （Yugoslavia） 30,31,98,171,307,365,366, 402,403,404,423,424,429,430,468,784,785,1241, 1748,S11

D

Dacosta, Rey R. （Venezuela） 805,1053,1080, 1083,1084,1161
Dieter, Joe （U.S.A.） 114,146,458,1567,1578,1599
Dradi, Massimo （Italy） 196,280,360,1711
Duncan, Mace （U.S.A.） 1094,1313,1325,1426

F

Feller, Ludvik （West Germany） 333,379,379,438, 441,449,462,479,496,516,566,840,863,864,868,936, 1046,1055,1059,1060,1062,1086,1095,1113,1127,1132, 1291,1389,1410,1428,1488,1538,1539,1550,1556,1585, 1593,1594,1595,1622,1623,1725,1728,S7,S8
Fernandez, Jorge （Mexico） 13,62,92,148,162, 163,186,306,318,334,469,511,520,531,548,697,788, 876,966,974,986,990,997,1034,1035,1111,1124,1219, 1335,1337,1338,1440,1452,1473,1483,1493,1499,1569, 1633,1638,1640,1722,1738,1739,1780,S1
Forman, J. （U.S.A.） 354
Friedland, Michael （Canada） 807,837,1002, 1018,1019,1025,1039,1065,1348,1429,S3
Frutiger, Adrian （France） 497,874,996,1041,1100, 1120,1212,1243,1433,1460,1555,1699,1761
Fujimoto Tomoko （Japan） 663
Fujishige Teruo （Japan） 663
Fukuda Masaaki （Japan） 950,959,960
Fukuda Narumi （Japan） 950,959,960
Fukuda Shigeo （Japan） 4,53,79,149,159,164,173, 361,540,547,1006,1103,1221,1438,1498,1731,1792
Fukushima Hiroshi （Japan） 764,769,774,778, 875,888,1187,1188,1414,1417,1519,1525

G

Gallardo, Francisco （Mexico） 13,62,92,148,162, 163,186,306,318,334,469,511,520,531,548,697,788, 876,966,974,986,990,997,1034,1035,1111,1124,1219, 1335,1337,1338,1440,1452,1473,1483,1493,1499,1569, 1633,1638,1640,1722,1780,S1

H

Hasegawa Yutaka （Japan） 249,505,518,677, 707,767,1114,1323,1600,1698

Himi Masanari （Japan） 793,794
Hiramatsu Motoki （Japan） 636,646,741,760,770, 772,773
Hirata Akira （Japan） 45,46,50,51,55,193,241,332, 358
Horimto Hiroko （Japan） 1790
Hoshi Miyuki （Japan） 19,67,68,93,152,182,305, 427,467,488,492

I

Ichikawa Masami （Japan） 719
Igarashi Takenobu （Japan） 3,89,140,147,169, 337,355,485,1300,1344,1625,1729,S9
Ikeda Hajime （Japan） 23,25,43,49,97,109,112, 137,142,143,198,216,364,484,624,825,954,972,1004, 1014,1021,1043,1052,1069,1070,1089,1162,1168,1171, 1172,1185,1312,1320,1324,1327,1464,1520,1577,1590
Ikeda Norio （Japan） 23,25,43,97,109,112,137,142, 143,216,364,378,484,706,825,830,867,954,1004,1026, 1052,1079,1122,1152,1156,1162,1168,1171,1172,1184,1312, 1320,1324,1327,1590
Ikeda Shigeo （Japan） 378,706,830,867,1026, 1079,1122,1152,1156,1184
Ikeda Tadashi （Japan） 32,188,207,209,229,234, 238,242,253,255,260,265,270,353,545,925,968,1051, 1221,1332,1474,1563,1642
Inoue Chikako （Japan） 596,604,608,610,613,616, 617,634,637,644,647,685,699,752
Inoue Fumio （Japan） 596,604,608,610,613,616, 617,634,637,644,647,685,699,752
Iseya Hiroshi （Japan） 808,1257,1260,1299,1404, 1710,1762
Ishida Yuko （Japan） 110,131,694,742,786,896, 975,976,978,1047,1049,1112,1146,1166,1167,1176,1178, 1200,1218,1258,1261,1267,1365,1370,1374,1431, 1540,1587,1659,1660,1661,1662,1719,1753
Ishikawa Tadashi （Japan） 1766,1790
Ishikawa Teruo （Japan） 737,937,945,1071,1232, 1315,1563,1485,1692,1783,1788
Ito Katsuichi （Japan） 295,565,592,672,714,756, 766,790,800,803,870,877,878,880,901,917,970,1009, 1030,1038,1058,1244,1614,1718,1771,1777,1781

K

Kalderon, Asher （Israel） 21,24,61,63,64,65,66, 84,282,345,425,428,450,493,754,872,984,1467,1487, S5,S13
Kamano Minoru （Japan） 100,204,599,680,1543
Kataoka Hisako （Japan） 37,101,133,418,446,447, 448,471,522,911,928,1165,1183,1198,1201,1230,1281
Kato Yoshimitsu （Japan） 245,1399
Katsumi Masaru （Japan） 5,48,57,77,106,139, 144,172,181,203,208,210,356,509,551,639,969,998, 1012,1013,1024,1105,1211,1239,1289,1297,1314,1318, 1319,1330,1406,1439,1451,1453,1477,1531,1565,1732, 1754,1778
Kishimoto Yoshihiro （Japan） 524,534,1603
Klose, Stanton （U.S.A.） 761,763,765,781,782, 795,796,831,834,859
Kobayashi Shigeji （Japan） 595,687,758,1155, 1390,1409
Kobayashi Yoko （Japan） 37,101,133,418,446, 447,448,471,522,911,928,1165,1183,1198,1201,1230, 1281
Kohn, Judy （U.S.A.） 269,296
Komazawa Keiko （Japan） 482,521,554,708,739, 746,813,817,820,824,829,920,921,926,927,1118,1163, 1164,1182,1195,1196,1197,1202,1203,1207,1228,1236,

1351,1709,1715
Konno Toru （Japan） 482,521,554
Kudo Tsuyokatsu （Japan） 359,1564,1583
Kunito Teruyuki （Japan） 5,48,57,77,106,139,144, 172,181,203,208,210,356,509,551,639,969,998,1012, 1013,1024,1105,1211,1239,1289,1297,1314,1318,1319, 1330,1406,1439,1451,1453,1477,1531,1565,1732,1754, 1778
Kurihara Hideko （Japan） 482,521,554,708,739, 746,813,817,820,824,829,920,921,926,927,1118,1163, 1164,1182,1195,1196,1197,1202,1203,1207,1228,1236, 1351,1709,1715
Kurose Norihisa （Japan） 1776
Kuroyone Akira （Japan） 5,48,57,77,106,139,144, 172,181,203,208,210,356,509,551,639,969,998,1012, 1013,1024,1105,1211,1239,1289,1297,1314,1318,1319, 1330,1406,1439,1451,1453,1477,1531,1565,1732,1754, 1778
Kuwayama Yasaburo （Japan） 8,23,25,33,36, 38,43,49,58,97,100,109,112,113,136,137,142,143,197, 198,204,216,219,294,338,340,364,384,390,401,463, 480,483,484,503,561,563,574,599,600,602,605,611, 615,618,619,624,625,641,642,643,657,675,676,680, 681,684,691,692,693,702,712,716,721,724,727,733, 735,750,757,771,775,802,806,825,869,871,883,886, 889,890,898,924,935,954,972,977,995,1004,1014, 1020,1021,1023,1042,1043,1045,1048,1052,1063,1066, 1069,1070,1077,1089,1138,1140,1159,1162,1168,1170, 1171,1172,1174,1185,1231,1241,1254,1269,1304,1306, 1307,1312,1317,1320,1324,1327,1347,1350,1356,1360, 1376,1391,1421,1430,1432,1434,1436,1464,1479,1486, 1489,1520,1542,1543,1553,1577,1590,1610,1613,1615, 1621,1647,1648,1706,1707,1712,1720,1730,1760,1784

L

Lehfeld, Ernest （Mexico） 13,62,92,148,162,163, 186,306,318,334,469,511,520,531,548,697,788,876, 966,974,986,990,997,1034,1035,1111,1124,1219,1335, 1337,1338,1440,1452,1473,1483,1493,1499,1569,1633, 1638,1640,1722,1780
Linkhorn, F. （U.S.A.） 1435,1566

M

Mabuchi Tetsuharu （Japan） 882,1364,1369, 1373,1379,1385,1392,1395,1400,1655,1658
Malerba, Carlo （Italy） 233,237,248,263,367,291, 292,293
Martino, Ludovico Antonio （Brazil） 598, 603,628,728
Masubuchi Kuniharu （Japan） 808,1299,1404, 1762
Masuike Seiji （Japan） 32,188,207,209,229,234, 238,242,253,255,160,365,270,535,545,925,968,1051, 1220,1332,1474,1563,1642
Miyata Kenichi （Japan） 32,188,207,209,229,234, 238,242,253,255,260,265,170,353,545,925,968,1051, 1220,1332,1474,1563,1642
Mizuguchi Hiroshi （Japan） 1067
Mizui Tadashi （Japan） 704,718,722,732,768,777, 791,792,950,959,960,1298,1301,1522,1749
Morikami Satoshi （Japan） 52,60,115,132,195, 206,213,214,218,228,232,240,247,251,272,277,300, 315,369,370,477,478,620,648,649,650,651,652,653, 654,655,656,979,980,991,994,1334,S16
Moroishi Yoichi （Japan） 667,674,690,736,744, 747,748,751,783,798,811,818,821,827,835,842,847, 851,852,853,855,856,866,1119,1135,1179,1191,1192, 1208,1229,1568,1575,1665,1667,1668,1669,1674,1677,

1680,1682,1684,1693
Murphy, Harry (U.S.A.) 269,296,383,761,763,
765,781,782,795,796,826,834,859

N
Nagasaki Kumiko (Japan) 1644
Nagata Katsumi (Japan) 1432,1434,1436,1553
Nakagawa Kenzo (Japan) 52,60,115,132,190,191,
192,195,206,213,214,218,228,232,240,247,259,272,
277,300,301,315,369,370,395,477,478,620,648,649,
650,651,652,653,654,655,656,711,723,779,809,979,
980,991,994,1334,1393,1418,1644,S16
Nakajima Akiteru (Japan) 3,5,6,16,37,44,48,54,
57,74,77,78,86,89,101,106,133,134,138,139,140,144,
147,155,169,170,179,180,181,184,185,194,203,208,210,
220,221,230,257,284,288,289,297,302,303,329,337,
339,355,356,362,363,372,377,380,381,385,386,387,
389,391,394,396,407,418,437,442,443,444,446,446,
447,448,456,457,466,471,473,474,482,485,486,491,
494,501,509,521,522,529,533,543,551,554,556,557,
568,572,580,588,590,594,638,639,645,664,667,668,
674,690,708,734,736,738,739,743,744,746,747,748,
751,776,683,798,811,813,817,818,820,821,824,827,
829,835,842,847,851,852,853,855,856,865,866,873,
881,897,902,904,905,909,911,920,921,922,923,926,
927,928,932,938,940,941,948,963,964,965,969,981,
985,987,992,998,1007,1011,1012,1013,1024,1032,1040,
1054,1056,1075,1081,1082,1085,1098,1104,1105,1115,
1118,1119,1122,1130,1134,1135,1139,1141,1160,1163,1164,
1165,1173,1175,1179,1182,1183,1191,1195,1196,1197,1198,
1201,1202,1203,1207,1208,1211,1215,1223,1228,1229,
1230,1236,1237,1239,1248,1253,1274,1275,1281,1289,
1290,1296,1297,1300,1308,1314,1318,1319,1329,1330,
1344,1346,1351,1355,1357,1359,1361,1366,1368,1375,
1387,1406,1424,1427,1437,1439,1441,1451,1453,1454,
1455,1468,1477,1484,1490,1491,1492,1511,1512,1513,
1515,1516,1521,1524,1526,1528,1531,1565,1568,1575,
1582,1584,1589,1596,1597,1612,1624,1625,1636,1639,
1650,1653,1656,1657,1664,1665,1667,1668,1669,1670,
1674,1675,1677,1678,1680,1682,1684,1685,1688,1689,
1670,1691,1693,1702,1704,1709,1714,1715,1717,1729,
1732,1743,1744,1751,1754,1769,1778,1786,1795,S4,S9,
S15
Nakamura Hajime (Japan) 23,25,43,97,109,112,
137,142,143,216,364,484,825,954,1004,1052,1162,1168,
1171,1172,1185,1312,1320,1324,1327,1590
Nakamura Isato (Japan) 636,646,741,760,770,
772,773
Nakamura So (Japan) 378,706,830,867,1026,
1079,1122,1152,1156,1184
Nara Ken (Japan) 134,185,381,437,444,456,474,
501,529,533,568,572,645,897,902,904,905,909,922,
923,965,1081,1082,1141,1160,1164,1171,1274,1275,1308,
1329,1346,1355,1357,1359,1492,1515,1516,1526,1528,
1582,1597,1702
Niinomi Syunji (Japan) 882,1364,1469,1373,1386,
1392,1395,1400,1655,1658
Nikolov, Nikola (Bulgaria) 1591,1608,1785
Nishimura Koichi (Japan) 508,536,537,573,
1548,1549,1552
Nobuyama Hiroyasu (Japan) 52,60,115,132,190,
191,192,195,206,213,214,218,228,232,240,147,159,272,
277,300,301,315,369,370,395,648,649,650,651,652,
653,654,655,656,711,723,779,809,979,980,991,9941,
1334,1394,S16

O
Ogawa Osamu (Japan) 793,794

Ogawa Takeshi (Japan) 86,220,221,302,329,
372,482,521,554,708,739,746,813,817,820,824,829,
920,921,926,927,1118,1163,1164,1182,1195,1196,1197,
1202,1203,1207,1228,1236,1351,1709,1715
Ogura Michio (Japan) 236,250,251,258,290
Oka Yasumasa (Japan) 69,70,71,72,73,405,406,
498,500,569
Okamoto Kazunori (Japan) 1257,1260,1710
Onoe Takashi (Japan) 452,453,454
Ota Yukio (Japan) 5,48,57,77,106,139,144,172,
181,203,208,210,356,509,551,639,969,998,1012,1013,
1024,1105,1211,1239,1289,1297,1314,1318,1319,1330,
1406,1439,1451,1453,1477,1531,1565,1732,1754,1778

P
Patiwael, Donald (Netherland) 885,1057,1064,
1470,1757
Petrov, Velizar (Bulgaria) 1448,1449,1461,1462,
1510,1734
Prüssen, Eduard (West Germany) 39,762,
1061,1068,1245,1407,1414
PVDI (Brazil) 1,2,20,29,88,90,91,99,135,212,283,
323,325,331,426,435,436,455,502,512,550,571,591,
593,601,606,609,614,622,626,627,630,640,682,713,
720,725,726,729,730,899,900,903,910,934,951,988,
989,999,1005,1015,1017,1022,1044,1101,1110,1117,1123,
1125,1129,1213,1214,1227,1233,1240,1262,1263,1265,
1266,1271,1272,1276,1277,1279,1292,1316,1349,
1363,1367,1377,1380,1382,1445,1447,1456,1457,1471,
1472,1475,1476,1480,1481,1482,1495,1496,1497,1504,
1505,1507,1508,1551,1571,1630,1631,1632,1723,1724,
1752,1755,1756,1793,S6,S12

Q
Quon, Mike (U.S.A.) 354,1094,1313,1325,1423,
1435,1566

R
Rajlich, Jan (Czechoslovakia) 56,85,308,343,
344,346,495,1099,1142,1225,1283,1303,1441,1450,1618,
1686,1727,1736,1750,1758
Rajlich, Jan Jr. (Czechoslovakia) 56,85,308,
495,1099,1142,1225,1283,1303,1450,1618,1686,1727,
1736,1750
Rathousky, Jiri (Czechoslovakia) 1354,1422,
1518,1523,1532,1554
Rüegg, Ruedi (Switzerland) 18,35,87,104,105,
153,154,157,158,140,167,176,310,324,327,328,341,535,
546,579,696,698,931,967,973,1000,1001,1016,1031,
1033,1037,1106,1109,1126,1136,1143,1148,1226,1333,
1339,1340,1341,1342,1343,1345,1446,1629,1637,1643,
1673,1676,1713,1787,1789,S2
Ruiz, Guillermo Gonzales (Argentina)
111,120,121,122,123,124,126,127,128,130,145,200,202,
215,224,225,276,312,319,322,326,347,348,349,350,
351,352,392,393,397,398,399,400,409,410,411,412,
413,414,415,416,420,422,451
Rzepecki, Stefan (Poland) 962

S
Saito Ichiro (Japan) 19,67,68,93,152,182,305,374,
427,467,488,492,1108,1180,1222,1443
Sakado Hideko (Japan) 1766
Sanchez, Manuel (Mexico) 13,62,92,148,162,
163,186,306,318,334,469,511,520,531,548,697,788,
876,966,974,986,990,997,1034,1035,1111,1124,1219,
1335,1337,1338,1440,1452,1473,1483,1493,1499,1569,
1633,1638,1640,1722,1780,S1

Sasaki Shin (Japan) 110,131,694,742,786,896,
975,976,978,1047,1049,1112,1146,1166,1167,1176,1178,
1200,1218,1234,1238,1261,1267,1365,1370,1374,1431,
1540,1587,1659,1660,1661,1662,1719,1753
Schmitt-Siegel, M, Helmut (West Germany)
449,513,514,519,528
Segawa Yoshimi (Japan) 508-536,573,1549
Shakespear Design Studio (Argentina)
10,11,95,96,165,166,175,178,273,275,320,321,375,408,
421,432,433,434,439,440,461,465,489,490,506,544,
576,582,585,586,587,673,731,810,832,915,916,933,
943,944,947,983,1072,1073,1074,1097,1102,1116,1128,
1133,1144,1145,1147,1150,1151,1249,1302,1326,1328,
1371,1372,1381,1383,1384,1385,1388,1398,1403,1419,
1420,1506,1570,1572,1573,1576,1579,1580,1581,1592,
1602,1606,1635,1672,1681,1683,1687,1696,1697,1700,
1701,1708,1726,1745,1746,1759,1794,1796,1797,S14
Shakespear, Raul (Argentina) 10,11,95,96,
165,166,175,178,273,275,320,321,375,408,421,432,
433,434,439,440,461,465,489,490,506,544,567,582,
585,586,587,673,731,810,832,915,916,933,943,944,
947,983,1072,1073,1074,1097,1102,1116,1128,1133,1144,
1145,1147,1150,1151,1249,1302,1326,1328,1371,1372,
1381,1383,1384,1385,1388,1398,1403,1419,1420,1506,
1570,1572,1573,1576,1579,1580,1581,1592,1602,1606,
1635,1672,1681,1683,1687,1696,1697,1700,1701,1708,
1726,1745,1746,1759,1794,1796,1797,S14
Shakespear, Ronald (Argentina) 10,11,95,
96,165,166,175,178,273,275,320,321,375,408,421,432,
433,434,439,440,461,465,489,490,506,544,576,585,
586,587,673,731,810,832,915,916,933,934,944,947,
983,1072,1073,1074,1097,1102,1116,1128,1133,1144,
1145,1147,1150,1151,1249,1302,1326,1328,1371,1372,
1381,1383,1384,1385,1388,1398,1403,1419,1420,1421,
1570,1572,1573,1576,1579,1580,1581,1592,1602,1606,
1635,1672,1681,1683,1687,1696,1697,1700,1701,1708,
1726,1745,1746,1747,1794,1796,1797,S14
Shibukawa Yasuhiko (Japan) 658,659,660,661,
662,697,749,814,929
Shimazu Goryo (Japan) 1548
Shimizu Yoshitaka (Japan) 222,367,376
Shimooka Shigeru (Japan) 9,26,34,47,75,76,
94,103,156,183,201,357,417,419,459,504,523,552,953,
1107,1181,1224,1255,1285,1288,1358,1426,1442,1494,
1503,1509,1529,1628,1747
Shirahama Kumi (Japan) 3,6,16,44,54,78,86,
89,134,138,140,147,155,169,170,170,180,185,194,220,
221,230,302,303,329,337,355,362,372,377,381,437,
444,456,474,485,501,529,533,556,568,572,645,667,
674,690,736,744,747,748,751,783,798,811,818,821,
827,835,842,847,851,852,853,855,856,866,897,902,
904,905,909,922,923,965,981,992,1040,1081,1082,
1098,1119,1130,1135,1141,1160,1179,1191,1192,1208,1215,
1229,1248,1253,1274,1275,1290,1300,1308,1329,1344,
1346,1355,1357,1359,1427,1437,1441,1454,1468,1490,
1492,1511,1515,1516,1526,1528,1568,1575,1582,1597,
1624,1625,1665,1667,1668,1669,1674,1677,1680,1682,
1684,1693,1702,1729,1786,1795,S9,S15
Shirahama Yumi (Japan) 363,385,387,389,391,
442,443,473,594,738,743,873,948,963,965,985,987,
1007,1011,1075,1076,1104,1134,1139,1173,1175,1223,
1237,1361,1366,1368,1375,1387,1424,1455,1484,1491,
1512,1513,1521,1524,1584,1589,1596,1612,1636,1639,
1650,1653,1656,1657,1664,1670,1675,1678,1685,1688,
1689,1690,1691,1704,1714,1717,1743,1751,1769
Siple, Greg (U.S.A.) 955,956,957,961
Sonohara Toshio (Japan) 623,710
Steiner, Peter (Canada) 807,837,930,1002,
1018,1019,1025,1039,1065,1348,1429,S3

Suehiro Nobuyuki（Japan）190,191,192,301

Sugiyama Kunihiko（Japan）22,34,117,118,119,
129,226,227,252,299,313,314,335,368,371,388,464,
470,481,507,515,517,526,527,538,539,558,559,560,
562,564,567,575,577,578,581,583,584,589,665,666,
683,709,715,717,74..,755,780,787,789,799,801,812,
815,816,822,823,828,833,836,838,843,844,845,846,
848,850,854,857,858,861,879,884,887,891,892,893,
894,895,906,907,908,912,913,914,918,919,939,942,
958,971,1027,1028,1029,1036,1050,1078,1087,1088,
1090,1091,1092,1093,1096,1131,1153,1154,1158,1169,
1177,1186,1194,1204,1205,1206,1209,1246,1264,1293,
1305,1309,1310,1311,1352,1353,1394,1405,1412,1413,
1415,1416,1469,1514,1527,1530,1533,1534,1535,1537,
1545,1546,1547,1574,1586,1598,1601,1607,1611,1616,
1617-1619,1649,1666,1694,1695,1703,1705,1716,1770,
1776,1782,1773,1775

Szekeres, István（Hungary）621,669,671,678,
686,689,700,705,797,819,839,841,860,862,1121,1247,
1250,1251,1258,1259,1517,1544,1604,1609

T

Tachiyama Emiko（Japan）808,1299,1404,1762

Takahara Shinichi（Japan）753,1408,1663

Takeuchi Tamio（Japan）230,363,385,387,389,
391,442,443,473,594,738,743,873,948,963,964,985,
987,1007,1011,1075,1076,1104,1134,1139,1173,1175,
1223,1237,1361,1366,1368,1375,1387,1424,1455,1484,
1491,1512,1513,1521,1524,1584,1589,1596,1612,1636,
1639,1650,1653,1656,1657,1664,1670,1675,1678,1685,
1688,1689,1690,1691,1704,1714,1717,1743,1751,1769

Tamura Noriaki（Japan）107,510,946,1010,1588,
1764

Tanifuji Yuichi（Japan）1466,1557,1558,1559,
1560,1561,1562,1620

Tasaka Koji（Japan）1067

Tatsuzawa Mikado（Japan）1067

Tokyo Shibaura Denki Design Department
（Japan）17,80,223,311,445,476,532,542,553,
1268,1270,1273,1278,1280,1282,1284,1268,1287

Torigoe Syuji（Japan）7,15,28,41,42,81,83,108,
116,150,161,168,205,211,309,317,460,525,541,549,949,
982,993,1008,1216,1217,1331,1336,1458,1459,1478,
1500,1502,1626,1641,1721,1733,1737,1791,S18

Travagliati, Aldo（Italy）196,360,1711

Tsuchiya Wataru（Japan）648,649,650,651,652,
653,654,655,656,979,980,991,994,1334,S16

Tsutani Sumiko（Japan）711

V

Van Der Wal, Julien（Switzerland）231,235,239,
243,244,246,254,256,261,262,264,266,268,271,274,
278,279,281,285,286,287,S17

W

Wada Yoshiko（Japan）737,937,945,1071,1232,
1315,1463,1485,1692,1783,1788

Wallen, Arvid（U.S.A.）187

Watanabe Masanobu（Japan）9,26,34,47,75,
76,94,103,156,183,201,357,417,419,459,504,523,552,
953,1107,1181,1224,1255,1285,1288,1358,1426,1442,
1494,1503,1509,1529,1628,1747

Wiens, Duane（U.S.A.）187

Wood, Bill（U.S.A.）59,177,199,298,316,342,S10

Wyser, Hans（Switzerland）189

Y

Yagi Akira（Japan）482,521,554,708,739,746,813,
817,820,824,829,920,921,926,927,944,1163,1164,1182,
1195,1196,1197,1202,1203,1207,1228,1236,1351,1709,
1715

Yamada Ryoichi（Japan）134,185,381,437,444,
456,474,501,529,533,568,572,645,897,902,904,905,
909,922,923,965,1081,1082,1141,1160,1248,1253,1274,
1275,1308,1329,1346,1355,1357,1359,1492,1515,1516,
1526,1528,1582,1597,1702

Yamada Yonefusa（Japan）110,131,694,742,786,
896,975,976,978,1047,1049,1112,1146,1166,1167,1176,
1178,1200,1218,1234,1238,1261,1267,1365,1370,1374,
1431,1540,1587,1659,1660,1661,1662,1719,1753

Yamaguchi Iwao（Japan）1137,1605

Yoguchi Takao（Japan）12,27,40,82,125,141,151,
160,174,304,336,373,452,453,454,530,631,632,670,
692,693,695,740,759,826,849,952,1003,1149,1157,
1189,1190,1193,1199,1321,1322,1425,1444,1501,1627,
1634,1671,1679

Yoshida Yoshihiro（Japan）14,102,597,607,612,
629,633,635,701

1

2

3

4

5

Man

6

10

14

7

11

15

8

12

16

9

13

17

18

19

20

21

22

23

24

25

26

27

28

29

30

34

38

31

35

39

32

36

40

33

37

41

42

46

50

43

47

51

44

48

52

45

49

53

Man

54

58

62

55

59

63

56

60

64

57

61

65

18

66

70

74

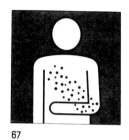

67

71

75

68

72

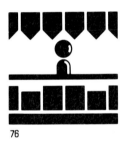

76

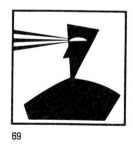

69

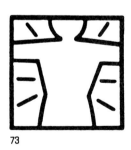

73

77

78

79

80

81

82

86

90

83

87

91

84

88

92

85

89

93

94

98

102

95

99

103

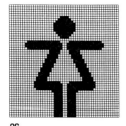

96

100

104

97

101

105

106

107

108

109

110

Little one

111

115

119

112

116

120

113

117

121

114

118

122

123

127

131

124

128

132

125

129

133

126

130

Person in action

134

135

136

137

138

139

143

147

140

144

148

141

145

149

142

146

150

Person in action

151

155

159

152

156

160

153

157

161

154

158

162

163

167

171

164

168

172

165

169

173

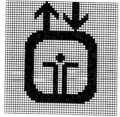

166

170

174

Person in action

175

179

183

176

180

184

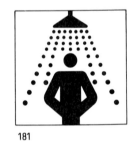

181

185

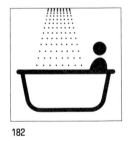

182

186

177

178

187

191

195

188

192

196

189

193

197

190

194

198

199

200

201

202

203

204

208

212

205

209

213

206

210

214

207

211

215

216

220

224

217

221

225

218

222

226

219

223

227

228

229

230

231

232

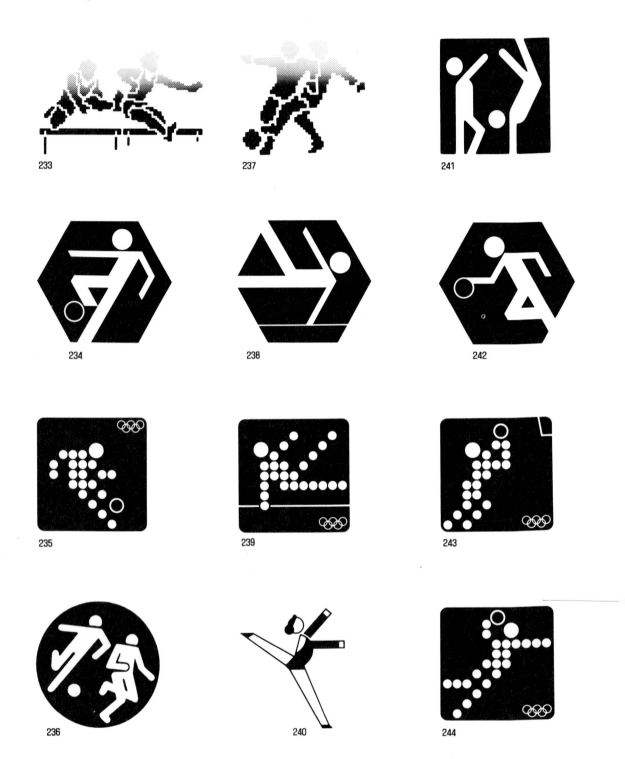

233

237

241

234

238

242

235

239

243

236

240

244

245

249

253

246

250

254

247

251

255

248

252

256

Person taking exercise

257

258

259

260

261

262

263

264

265

266

267

268

269

273

277

270

274

278

271

275

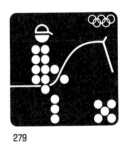

279

272

276

280

Person taking exercise

281

285

289

282

286

290

283

287

291

284

288

292

293

297

301

294

298

295

299

296

300

302

303

304

305

306

307

311

315

308

312

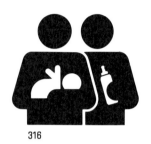

316

309

313

317

310

314

318

319

320

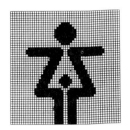

321

322

323

324

328

332

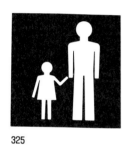

325

329

333

326

330

334

327

331

335

Persons

336

340

344

337

341

345

338

342

346

339

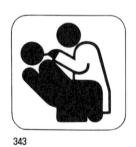

343

347

348

352

356

349

353

357

354

358

351

355

359

350

360

364

368

361

365

369

362

366

370

363

367

371

372

376

380

373

377

381

374

378

382

375

379

383

384

385

386

387

388

389

393

397

390

394

398

391

395

399

392

396

400

401

405

409

402

406

410

403

407

411

404

408

412

413

417

421

414

418

422

415

419

423

416

420

424

Face

425

429

433

426

430

434

427

431

435

428

432

436

437

441

445

438

442

446

439

443

447

440

444

448

449

450

451

452

453

454

455

456

457

458

459

460

461

462

463

464

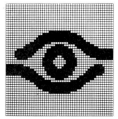

465

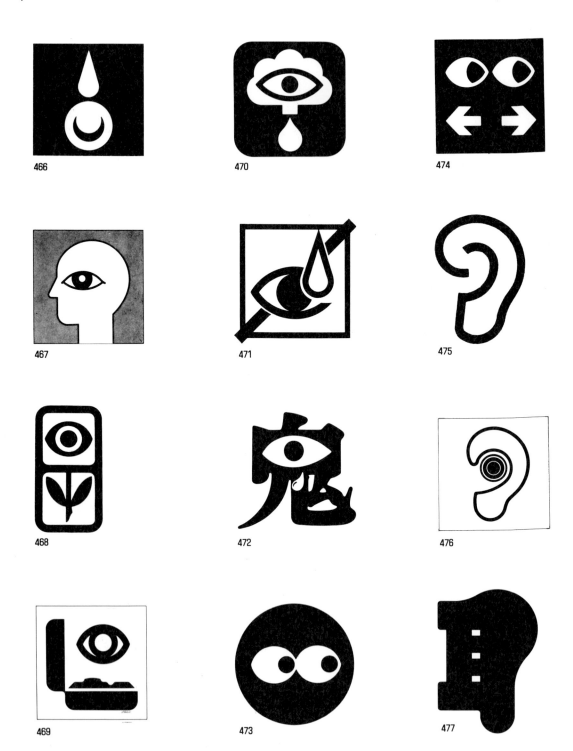

466

470

474

467

471

475

468

472

476

469

473

477

478

479

480

481

482

483

487

491

484

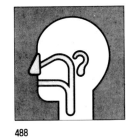

488

492

485

489

486

490

494

493

496

495

497

498

499

500

504

508

501

505

509

502

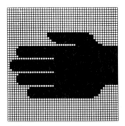

506

510

503

507

511

512

516

520

513

517

521

514

518

522

515

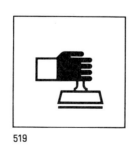

519

523

524

528

532

525

529

533

526

530

534

527

531

535

536

540

544

537

541

545

538

542

546

539

543

547

548

552

556

549

553

557

550

554

558

551

555

559

560

564

568

561

565

569

562

566

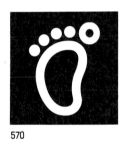

570

563

567

571

572

573

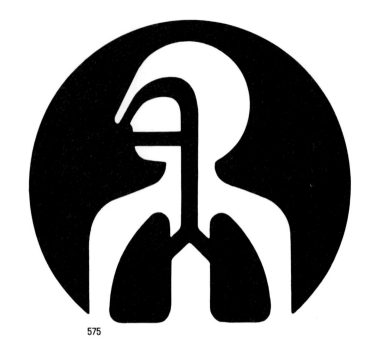

575

574

576

580

584

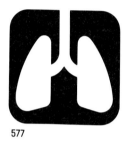

577

581

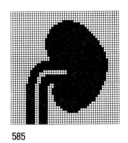

585

578

582

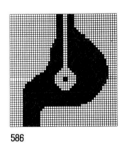

586

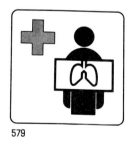

579

583

587

588

589

592

590

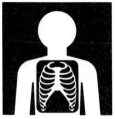

591

593

597

601

594

598

602

595

599

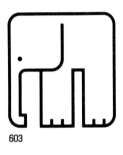

603

596

600

604

605

609

613

606

610

614

607

611

615

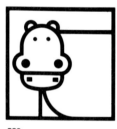

608

612

616

617

621

625

618

622

626

619

623

627

620

624

628

629

633

637

630

634

638

631

635

639

632

636

640

641

645

649

642

646

650

643

647

651

644

648

652

653

657

661

654

658

662

655

659

663

656

660

664

665

669

673

666

670

674

667

671

675

668

672

676

677

681

685

678

682

686

679

683

687

680

684

688

689

693

697

690

694

698

691

695

699

692

696

700

701

702

704

703

705

709

713

706

710

714

707

711

715

708

712

716

717

721

725

718

722

726

719

723

727

720

724

728

729

730

731

732

733

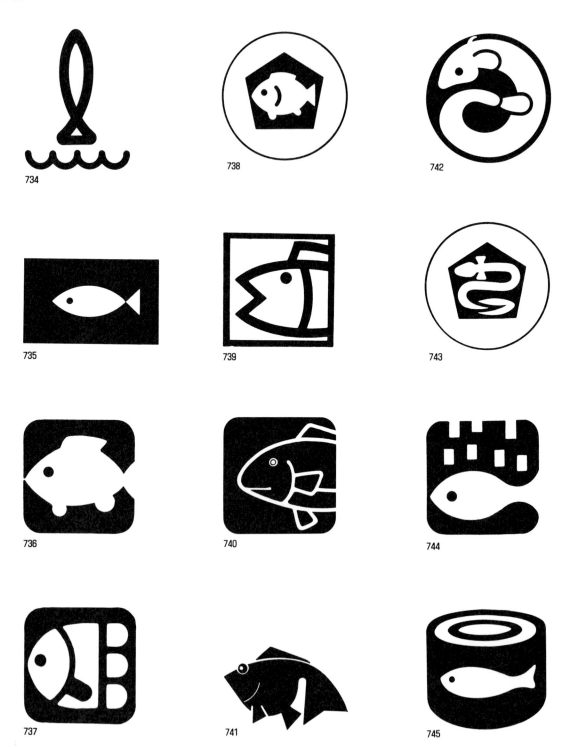

734

738

742

735

739

743

736

740

744

737

741

745

746

750

754

747

751

755

748

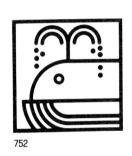

752

756

749

753

757

758

762

759

763

760

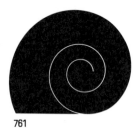

761

764

765

769

773

766

770

774

767

771

775

768

772

776

777

778

781

779

780

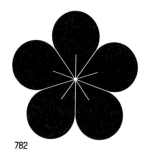

782

786

790

783

787

791

784

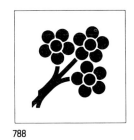

788

792

785

789

793

794

798

802

795

799

803

796

800

804

797

801

805

806

807

810

808

809

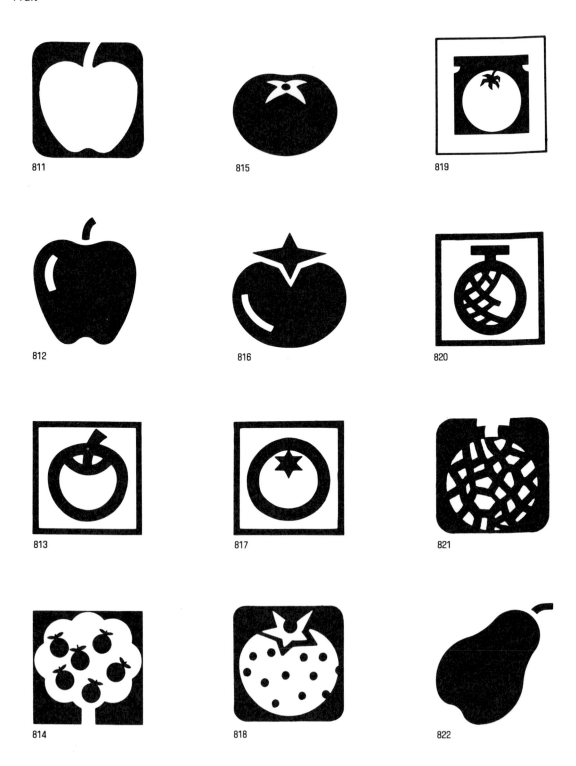

811

815

819

812

816

820

813

817

821

814

818

822

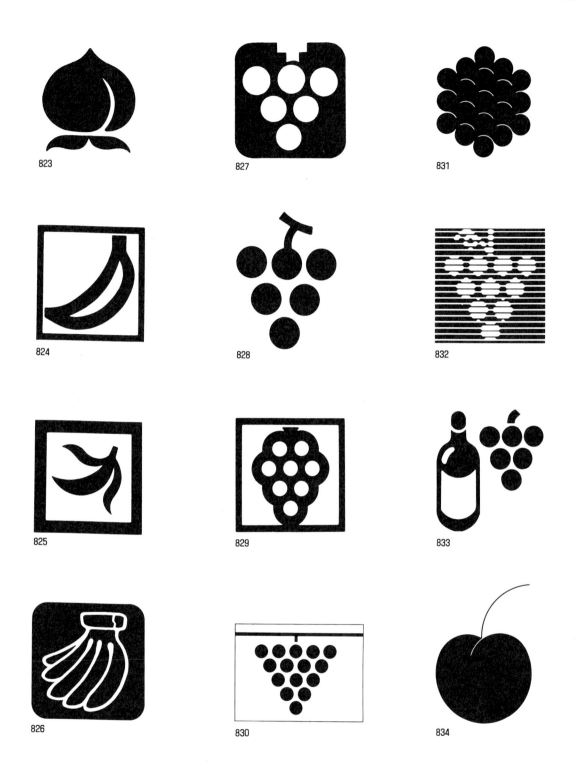

823

827

831

824

828

832

825

829

833

826

830

834

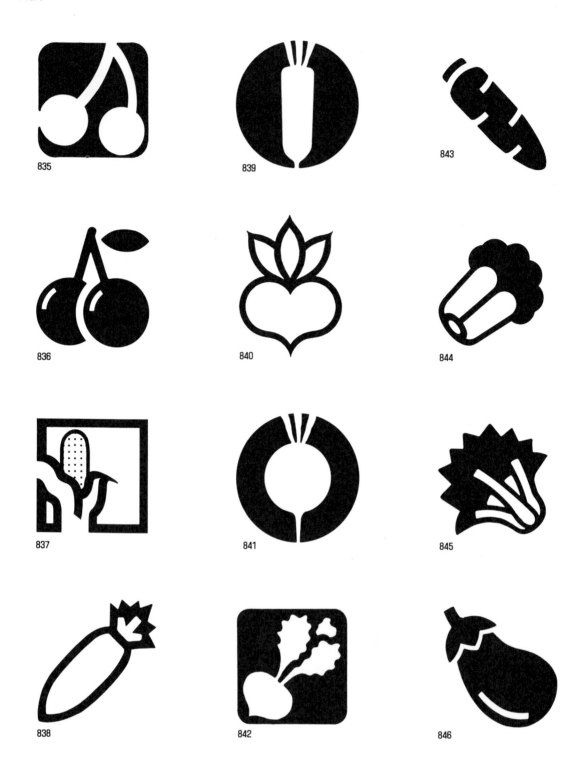

835

839

843

836

840

844

837

841

845

838

842

846

847

851

855

848

852

856

849

853

857

850

854

858

859

863

860

861

862

864

868

872

865

869

873

866

870

874

867

871

875

876

877

880

878

879

881

882

883

884

885

886

887

888

889

890

891

892

893

894

897

895

896

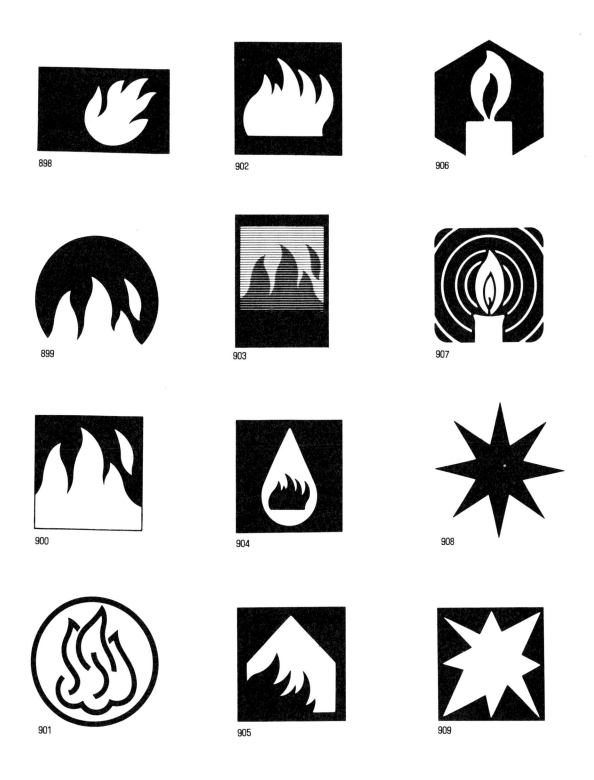

898

899

900

901

902

903

904

905

906

907

908

909

910

911

914

912

913

915

919

923

916

920

924

917

921

925

918

922

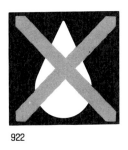

926

927

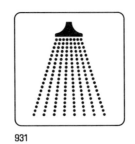

931

935

928

932

936

929

933

937

930

934

938

939

940

943

941

942

944

948

952

945

949

953

946

950

954

947

951

955

956

960

964

957

961

965

958

962

966

959

963

967

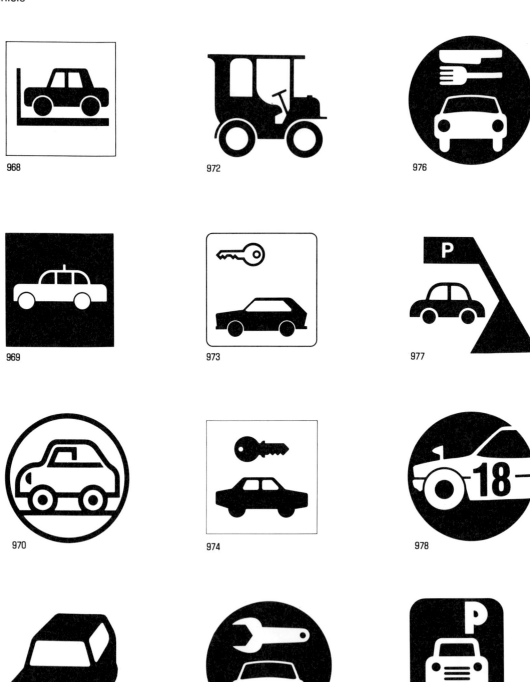

968

972

976

969

973

977

970

974

978

971

975

979

980

984

988

981

985

989

982

986

990

983

987

991

Vehicle

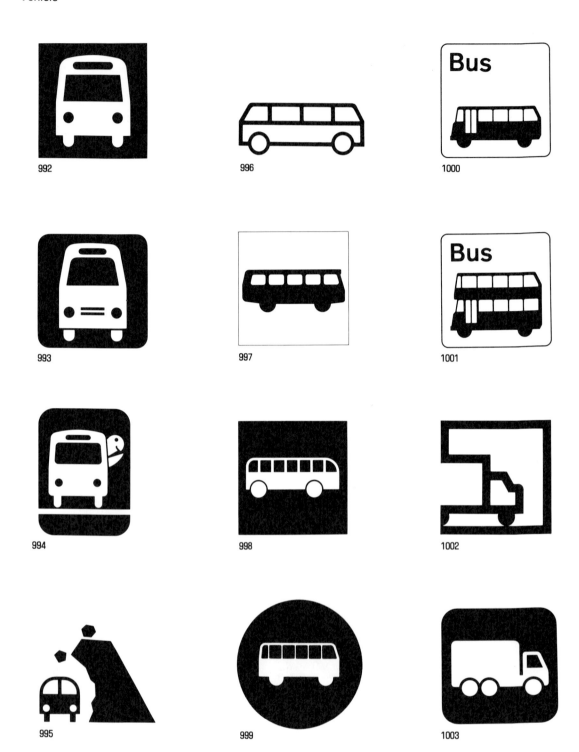

992

996

1000

993

997

1001

994

998

1002

995

999

1003

110

1004

1008

1012

1005

1009

1013

1006

1010

1014

1007

1011

1015

Vehicle

1016

1020

1024

1017

1021

1025

1018

1022

1026

1019

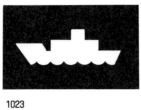

1023

1027

1028

1032

1036

1029

1033

1037

1030

1034

1038

1031

1035

1039

1040

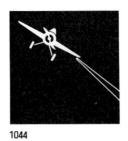

1044

1041

1042

1043

1045

1046

1050

1054

1047

1051

1055

1048

1052

1056

1049

1053

1057

1058

1062

1066

1059

1063

1067

1060

1064

1068

1061

1065

1069

1070

1074

1078

1071

1075

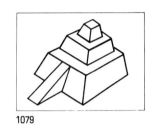

1079

1072

1076

1080

1073

1077

1081

Building

1082

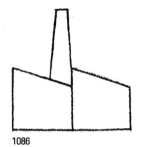

1086

1090

1083

1087

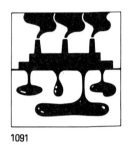

1091

1084

1088

1092

1085

1089

1093

1094

1095

1098

1096

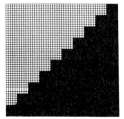

1097

1099

1103

1107

1100

1104

1108

1101

1105

1109

1102

1106

1110

1111

1115

1119

1112

1116

1120

1113

1117

1121

1114

1118

1122

1123

1127

1131

1124

1128

1132

1125

1129

1133

1126

1130

1134

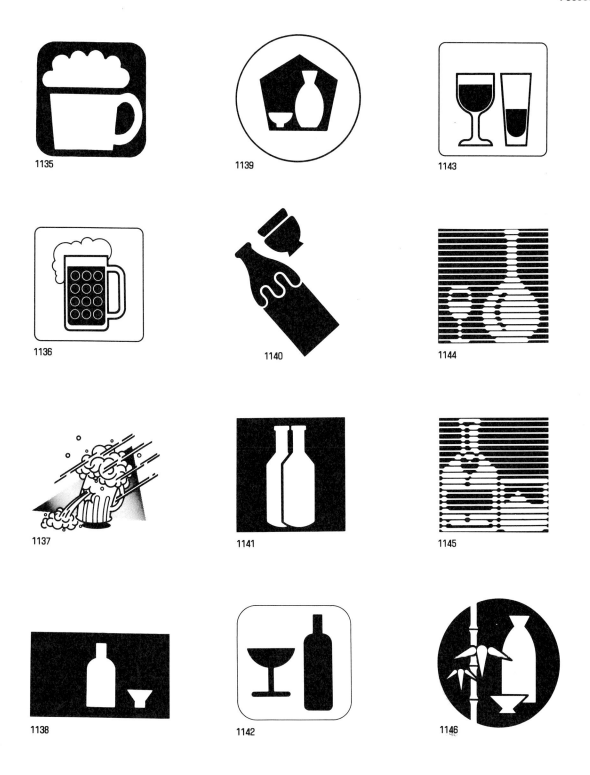

1135

1139

1143

1136

1140

1144

1137

1141

1145

1138

1142

1146

1147

1151

1155

1148

1152

1156

1149

1153

1157

1150

1154

1158

1159

1163

1167

1160

1164

1168

1161

1165

1169

1162

1166

1170

1171

1175

1179

1172

1176

1180

1173

1177

1181

1174

1178

1182

1183

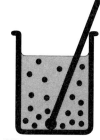

1187

1191

1184

1188

1192

1185

1189

1193

1186

1190

1194

1195

1199

1203

1196

1200

1204

1197

1201

1205

1198

1202

1206

1207

1211

1208

1209

1210

1212

1216

1220

1213

1217

1221

1214

1218

1222

1215

1219

1223

1224

1228

1232

1225

1229

1233

1226

1230

1234

1227

1231

1235

1236

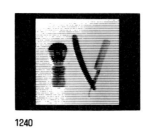

1240

1244

1237

1241

1245

1238

1242

1246

1239

1243

1247

1248

1252

1256

1249

1253

1257

1250

1254

1258

1251

1255

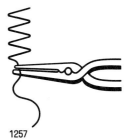

1259

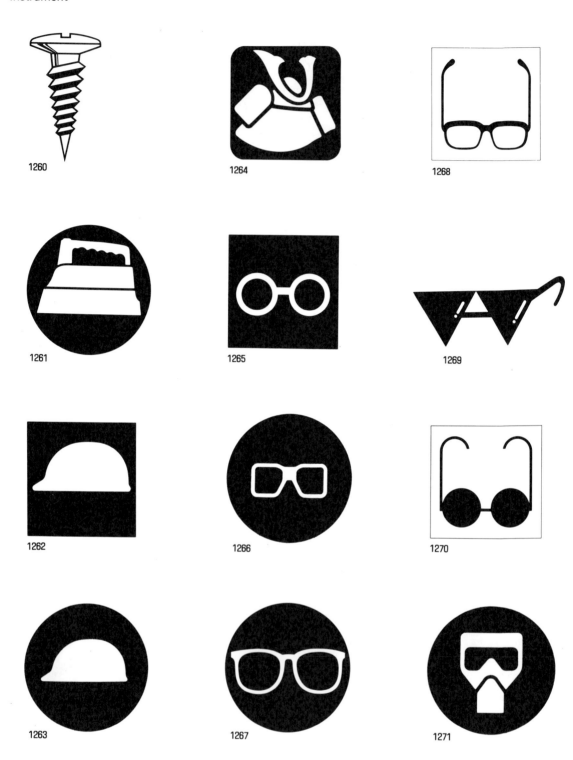

1260

1264

1268

1261

1265

1269

1262

1266

1270

1263

1267

1271

1272

1276

1280

1273

1277

1281

1274

1278

1282

1275

1279

1283

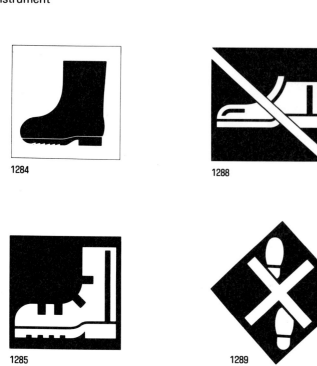

1284

1288

1292

1285

1289

1293

1286

1290

1294

1287

1291

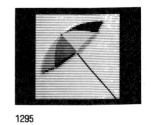

1295

1296

1300

1304

1297

1301

1305

1298

1302

1306

1299

1303

1307

1308

1312

1316

1309

1313

1317

1310

1314

1318

1311

1315

1319

1320

1324

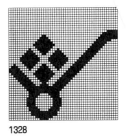

1328

1321

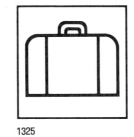

1325

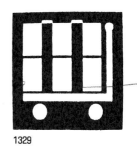

1329

1322

1326

1330

1323

1327

1331

1332

1336

1340

1333

1337

1341

1334

1338

1342

1335

1339

1343

1344

1348

1352

1345

1349

1353

1346

1350

1354

1347

1351

1355

Instrument

1356

1360

1364

1357

1361

1365

1358

1362

1366

1359

1363

1367

1368

1372

1376

1369

1373

1377

1370

1374

1378

1371

1375

1379

1380

1384

1388

1381

1385

1389

1382

1386

1390

1383

1387

1391

1392

1396

1400

1393

1397

1401

1394

1398

1402

1395

1399

1403

1404

1405

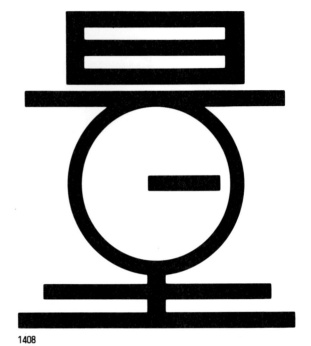

1408

1406

1407

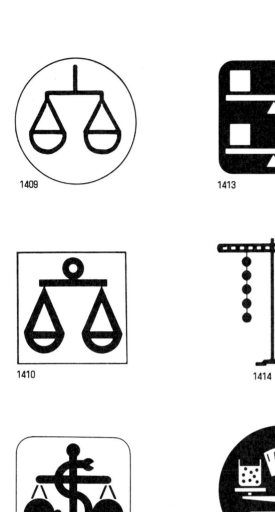

1409

1410

1411

1412

1413

1414

1415

1416

1417

1418

1419

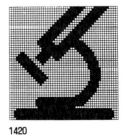

1420

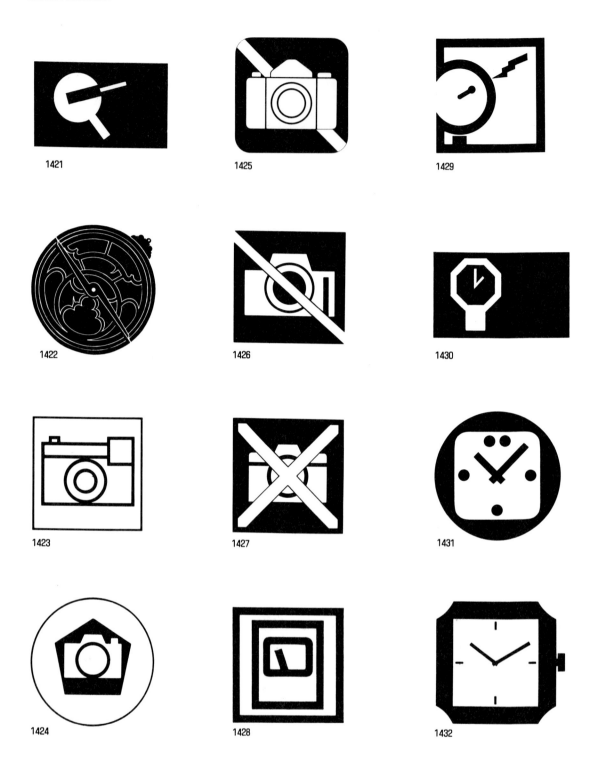

1421

1425

1429

1422

1426

1430

1423

1427

1431

1424

1428

1432

1433

1434

1437

1435

1436

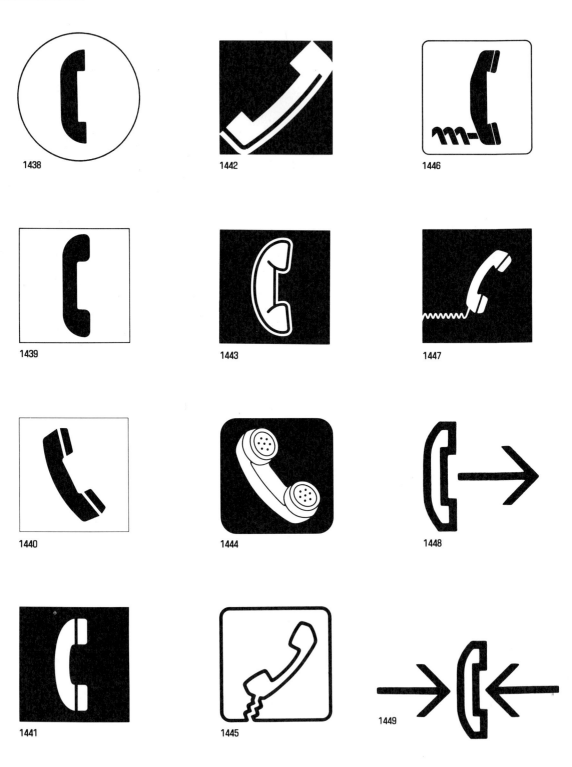

1438

1442

1446

1439

1443

1447

1440

1444

1448

1441

1445

1449

1450

1454

1458

1451

1455

1459

1452

1456

1460

1453

1457

1461

1462

1466

1470

1463

1467

1471

1464

1468

1472

1465

1469

1473

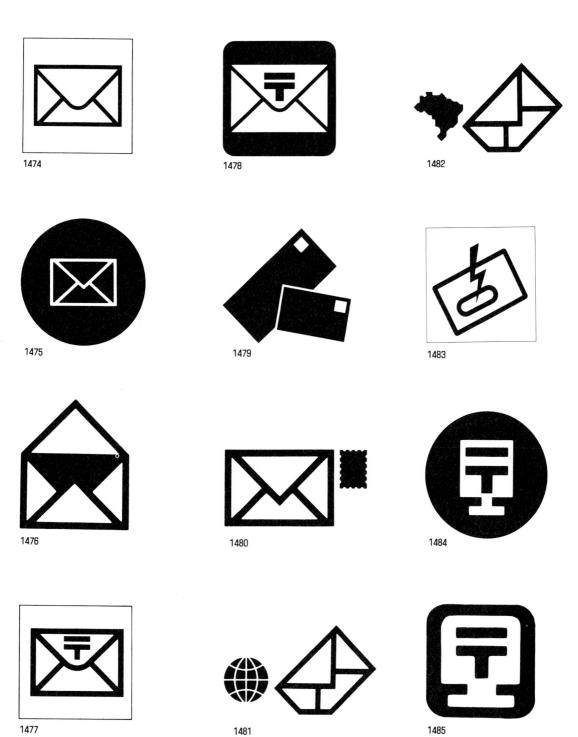

1474

1478

1482

1475

1479

1483

1476

1480

1484

1477

1481

1485

1486

1487

1490

1488

1489

1491

1495

1499

1492

1496

1500

1493

1497

1501

1494

1498

1502

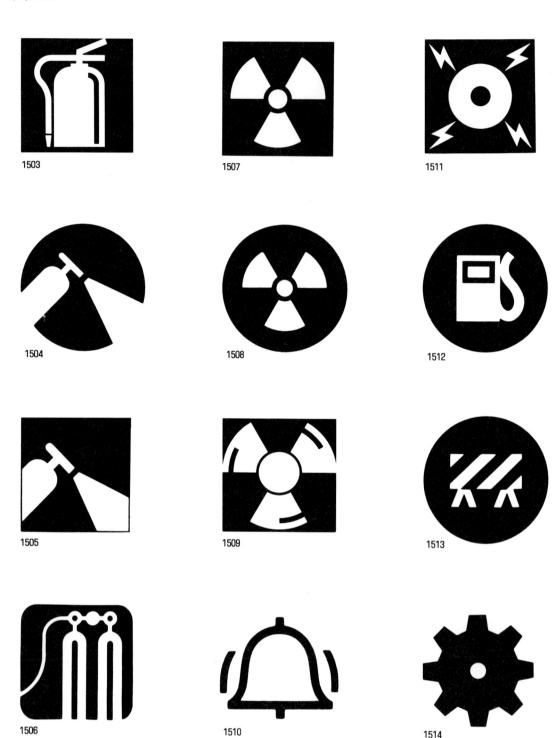

1503

1507

1511

1504

1508

1512

1505

1509

1513

1506

1510

1514

1515

1516

1517

1518

1519

1520

1524

1528

1521

1525

1529

1522

1526

1530

1523

1527

1531

1532

1536

1540

1533

1537

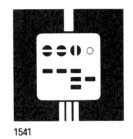

1541

1534

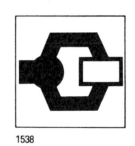

1538

1542

1535

1539

1543

1544

1545

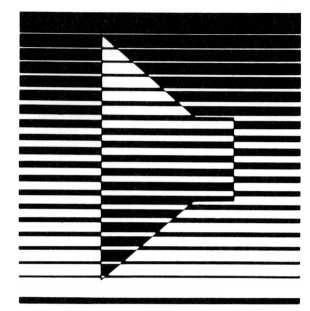

1548

1546

1547

1549

1553

1557

1550

1554

1558

1551

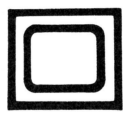

1555

1559

1552

1556

1560

Sound or Reflex/Medical care

1561

1565

1562

1563

1564

1566

1567

1571

1575

1568

1572

1576

1569

1573

1577

1570

1574

1578

1579

1580

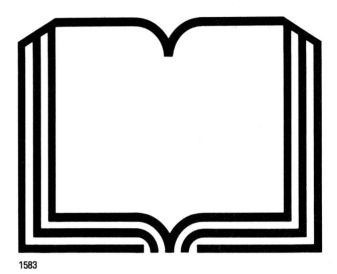

1583

1581

1582

1584

1588

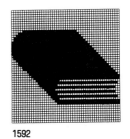

1592

1585

1589

1593

1586

1590

1594

1587

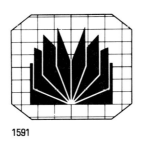

1591

1595

1596

1600

1604

1597

1601

1605

1598

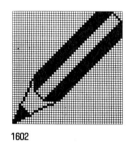

1602

1606

1599

1603

1607

1608

1612

1616

1609

1613

1617

1610

1614

1618

1611

1615

1619

1620

1621

1624

1622

1623

1625

1629

1633

1626

1630

1634

1627

1631

1635

1628

1632

1636

Cigarette or goods

1637

1641

1638

1642

1639

1643

1640

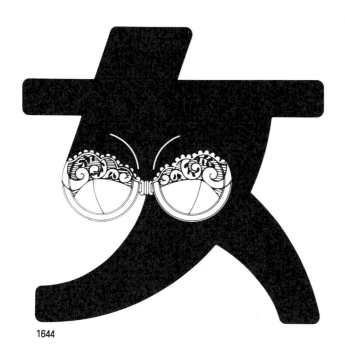

1644

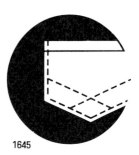

1645

1646

1647

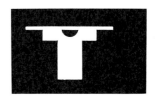

1648

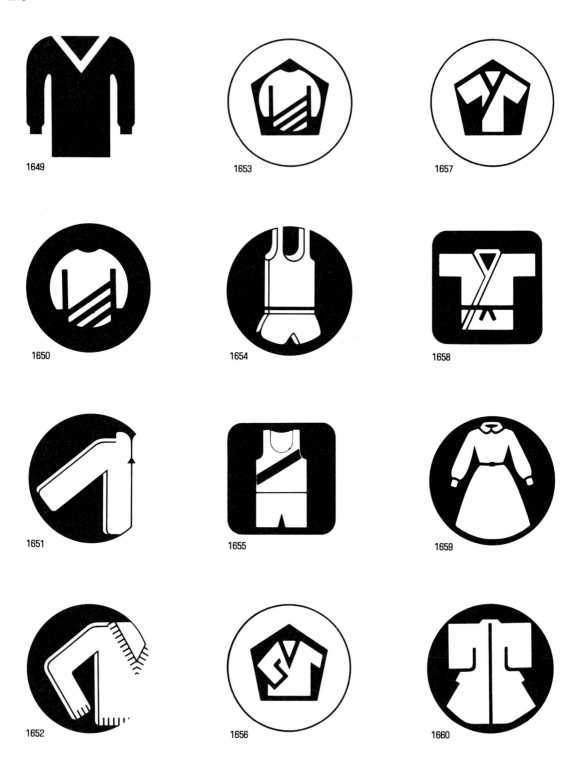

1649

1653

1657

1650

1654

1658

1651

1655

1659

1652

1656

1660

1661

1665

1669

1662

1666

1670

1663

1667

1671

1664

1668

1672

1673

1677

1681

1674

1678

1682

1675

1679

1683

1676

1680

1684

1685

1689

1693

1686

1690

1694

1687

1691

1695

1688

1692

1696

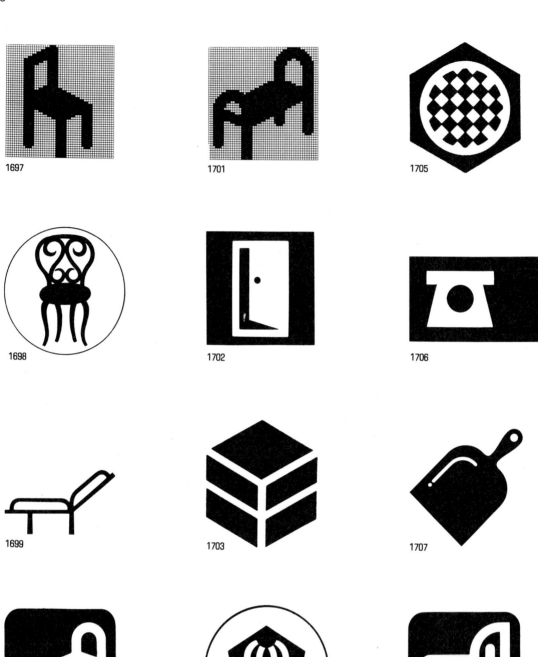

1697

1701

1705

1698

1702

1706

1699

1703

1707

1700

1704

1708

1709

1713

1717

1710

1714

1718

1711

1715

1719

1712

1716

1720

1721

1726

1727

1722

1724

1728

1723

1725

1729

1730

1734

1738

1731

1735

1739

1732

1736

1740

1733

1737

1741

1747

1742

1748

1743

1745

1749

1744

1746

1750

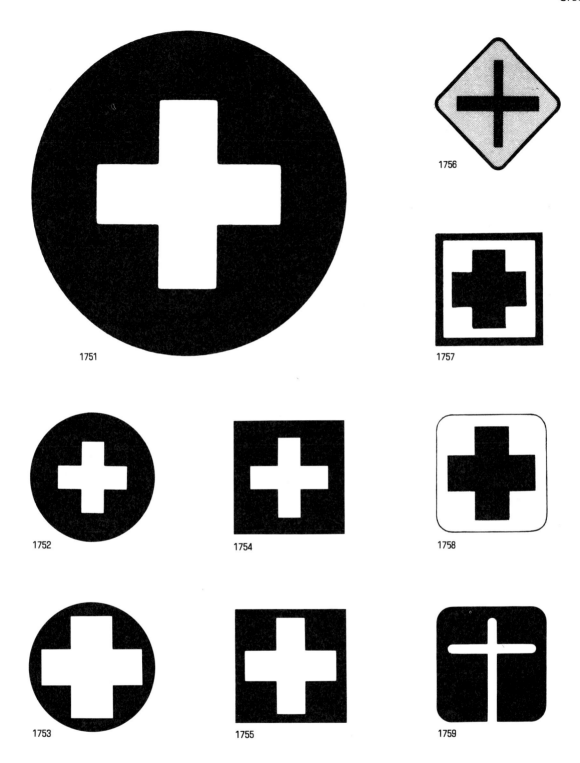

1751

1756

1752

1754

1758

1757

1753

1755

1759

1760

1765

1766

1761

1763

1767

1762

1764

1768

1769

1773

1777

1770

1774

1778

1771

1775

1779

1772

1776

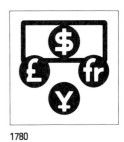

1780

1781

1786

1787

1782

1784

1788

1783

1785

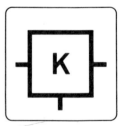

1789

1790

1794

1798

1791

1795

1799

1792

1796

1800

1793

1797

1801

		S2 -1	-9	-17
-41	-49			
-42	-50	-2	-10	Bus -18
-43	-51	-3	-11	Bus -19
-44	-52	-4	-12	-20
-45	-53	-5	-13	-21
-46	-54	-6	-14	Taxi -22
-47	-55	-7	-15	P -23
-48	-56	-8	-16	P -24

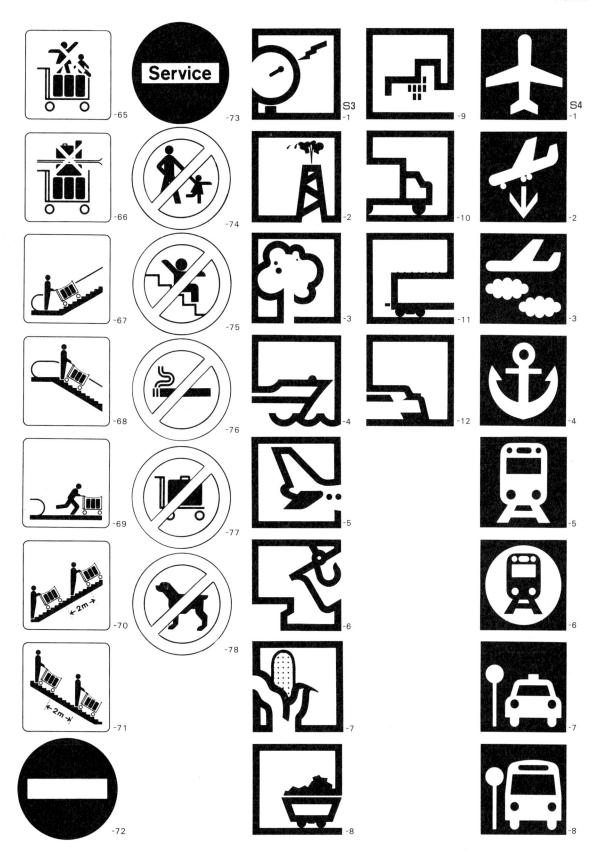

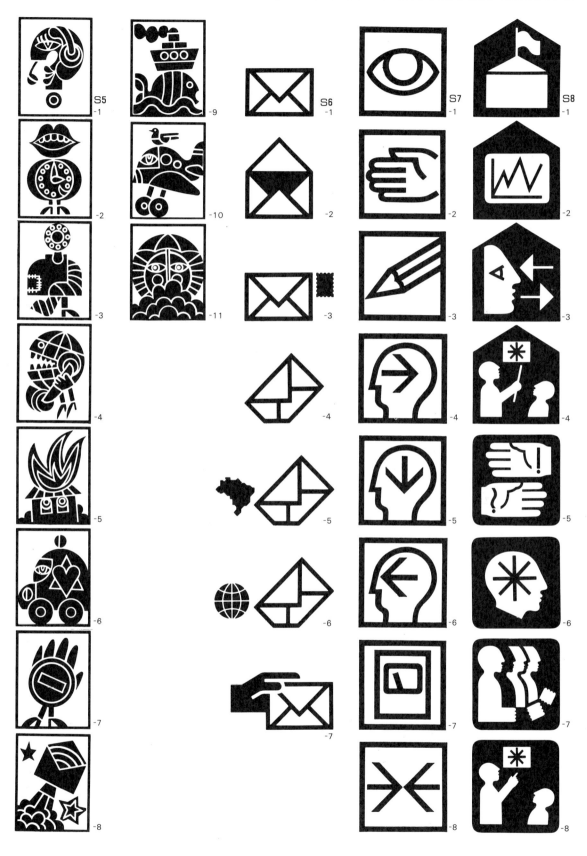

S9-1, S9-2, S9-3, S9-4, S9-5, S9-6, S9-7, S9-8, -9, -10, -11, -12, -13, -14, -15, -16

S10-1, -2, -3, -4, -5, -6

S11-1, -2, -3, -4, -5, -6, -7, -8

S12-1, -2, -3, -4, -5, -6, -7, -8

S13
-1 -2 -3 -4 -5 -6 -7 -8 -9 -10 -11 -12 -13 -14

S14
-1 -2 -3 -4 -5 -6 -7 -8 -9 -10 -11 -12 -13 -14 -15 -16 -17 -18 -19 -20 -21 -22 -23 -24

S15
-1

-9

-17

-25

-33

-2

-10

-18

-26

-34

-3

-11

-19

-27

-35

-4

-12

-20

-28

-5

-13

-21

-29

-6

-14

-22

-30

-7

-15

-23

-31

-8

-16

-24

-32

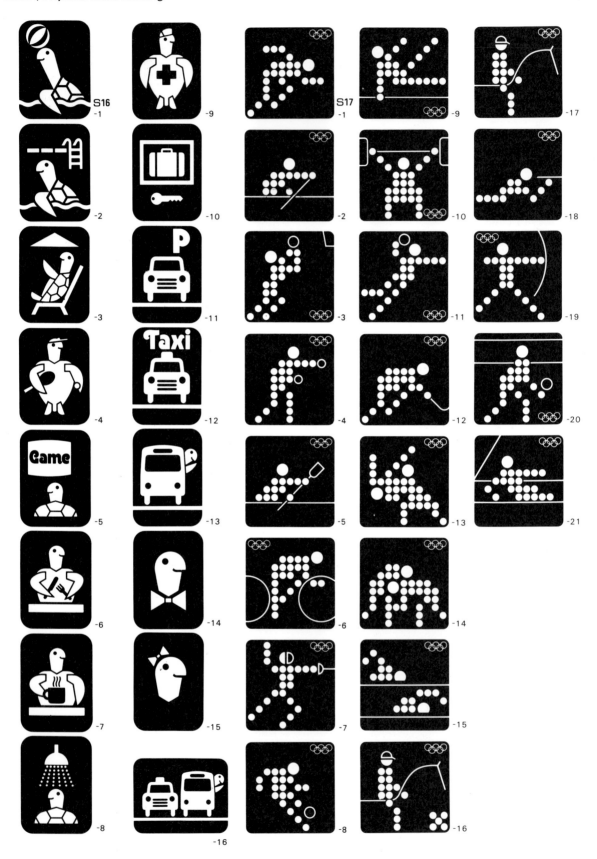

S16
-1
-2
-3
-4
-5
-6
-7
-8
-9
-10
-11
-12
-13
-14
-15
-16

S17
-1
-2
-3
-4
-5
-6
-7
-8
-9
-10
-11
-12
-13
-14
-15
-16
-17
-18
-19
-20
-21

S18

-1 -9 -17 -25
-2 -10 -18 -26
-3 -11 -19 -27
-4 -12 -20 -28
-5 -13 -21 -29
-6 -14 -22 -30
-7 -15 -23
-8 -16 -24

Index

1) Applicable Industries
2) Art Director
3) Designer
4) Client
5) Year Produced
(Place Produced)
6) Data on Color

1 1) mens lavatory
2),3) PVDI
4) São Paulo Gas Company
5) 1972(Brazil)
2 1) mens lavatory
2),3) PVDI
4) Fulnus Electric Center
5) 1972(Brazil)
3 1) library／mens lavatory
2) Takenobu Igarashi
3) Akiteru Nakajima／Kumi Shirahama
4) Keio Gijuku University
5) 1982(Japan)
4 1) department store／mens lavatory
3) Shigeo Fukuda
4) Seibu Department Store
5) 1976(Japan)
5 1) ocean exhibition／mens lavatory
2) Masaru Katsumi／Akiteru Nakajima
3) Teruyuki Kunito／Yukio Ota／Akira Kuroyone
4) Okinawa International Ocean Exhibition Association
5) 1975(Japan)
6) blue(4PB3, 5／12)／beige(3Y8, 5／1)
6 1) mens lavatory
2) Akiteru Nakajima
3) Akiteru Nakajima／Kumi Sirahama
4) The Iraqi Government
5) 1981／1982(Japan)
7 1) shopping center／mens lavatory
2),3) Shuji Torigoe
4) Tokyu Store Co., Ltd.
5) 1976(Japan)
8 1) "Shiritori Kanji"
2),3) Yasaburo Kuwayama
4) Typo-Eye Exhibition of "A Picture Book of Letter"
5) 1977(Japan)
6) black
9 1) company sign／mens lavatory
2) Shigeru Shimooka
3) Masanobu Watanabe
4) Mitsubishi Motors Co., Ltd. (MMC)
5) 1983(Japan)
6) dark blue(sub-color red)
10 1) sports／public hygienic service
2) Shakespear Design Studio
3) Ronald Shakespear／Raul Shakespear
4) Buenos Aires Sports Center
5) 1980(Argentina)
11 1) hospital／mens lavatory
2) Shakespear Design Studio

3) Raul Shakespear／Ronald Shakespear
4) Buenos Aires City Hospital
5) 1970／1980(Argentina)
6) red／blue
12 1) supermarket／mens lavatory
2),3) Takao Yoguchi
4) Chujitsuya
5) 1979(Japan)
13 1) airport／mens lavatory
2) Ernest Lehfeld
3) Ernest Lehfeld／Manuel Sanchez／Francisco Gallardo／Jorge Fernandez
4) Mexico Airport
5) 1977-78(Mexico)
6) black／yellow(ground)
14 1) lavatory
2),3) Yoshihiro Yoshida
4) New Yunohama Hotel
5) 1979(Japan)
15 1) mens lavatory
2),3) Shuji Torigoe
4) The Gunma Prefectual Office
5) 1981(Japan)
16 1) automobile(service station)／mens lavatory
2) Akiteru Nakajima
3) Akiteru Nakajima／Takeshi Ogawa／Kumi Shirahama
4) Toyota Motors
5) 1982(Japan)
17 1) safety & hygiene／Men
2),3) Tokyo Shibaura Denki Design Department
4) Tokyo Shibaura Denki
5) 1975(Japan)
6) yellow／black(partly white・red)
18 1) mens lavatory
3) Ruedi Rüegg
5) 1983(Switzerland)
19 1) mens lavatory(sign)
2) Ichiro Saito
3) Ichiro Saito／Miyuki Hoshi
4) Itoki
5) 1983(Japan)
20 1) mens lavatory
2),3) PVDI
4) Copek Oil Co., Ltd.
5) 1974(Brazil)
21 1) remedy／rest room
3) Asher Kalderon
4) Dead Sea Hot Spring Building
5) 1983(Israel)
22 1) package of injector-needles
2) Hajime Nakamura／Yasaburo Kuwayama
3) Yasaburo Kuwayama／Hajime Ikeda／Norio Ikeda
4) Hakko Shoji
5) 1980(Japan)
23 1) off limit
2) Hajime Nakamura／Yasaburo Kuwayama
3) Yasaburo Kuwayama／Hajime Ikeda／Norio Ikeda
4) The Regional Meeting of Jehovah's Witnesses
5) 1980(Japan)
24 1) physiotherapy
3) Asher Kalderon

4) Dead Sea Hot Spring Building
5) 1983(Israel)
25 1) mens lavatory
2) Hajime Nakamura／Yasaburo Kuwayama
3) Yasaburo Kuwayama／Hajime Ikeda／Norio Ikeda
4) The Regional Meeting of Jehovah's witnesses
5) 1980(Japan)
26 1) company signs／off limit
2) Shigeru Shimooka
3) Masanobu Watanabe
4) Mitsubishi Motors Co., Ltd. (MMC)
5) 1983(Japan)
6) dark blue(sub-color red)
27 1) supermarket／keep out
2),3) Takao Yoguchi
4) Chujitsuya
5) 1979(Japan)
28 1) off limit
2),3) Shuji Torigoe
4) The Gunma Prefectual Office
5) 1981(Japan)
29 1) Male patient
2),3) PVDI
4) Guanabara State University
5) 1974(Brazil)
30 1) hospital／combatant
3) Miloš Ćirić
4) Army Hospital
5) 1977(Yugoslavia)
6) red／blue／green
31 1) hospital／research worker
3) Miroš Ćirić
4) Army Hospital
5) 1977(Yugoslavia)
6) red／blue／green
32 1) the olympics／players(trial)
2) Tadashi Ikeda
3) Kenichi Miyata／Seiji Masuike
4) 1988 Seoul OLympiad
5) 1982(Japan)
6) black
33 1) "Shiritori Kanji"
2),3) Yasaburo Kuwayama
4) Typo-Eye Exhibition of "A Picture Book of Letter"
5) 1977(Japan)
6) black
34 1) company sign／mens dressing room
2) Shigeru Shimooka
3) Masanobu Watanabe
4) Mitsubishi Motors Co., Ltd. (MMC)
5) 1983(Japan)
6) dark blue(sub-color red)
35 1) mens dressing room
3) Ruedi Rüegg
5) 1983(Switzerland)
36 1) "Shiritori Kanji"
2),3) Yasaburo Kuwayama
4) Exhibition of "A Picture Book of Letter"
5) 1977(Japan)
6) black
37 1) graphic indication of detergent／for men
2) Akiteru Nakajima
3) Seiko Aoki／Hisako Kataoka／Yoko Kobayashi

4) Chuo Bijutsu Gakuin Pictorial Course
5) 1983(Japan)
38 1) "A Picture Book of A-I-U-E-O"
2),3) Yasaburo Kuwayama
4) Exhibition of "Kami No Mojikku"
5) 1979(Japan)
39 1) A City Budge
3) Eduard Prüssen
4) City of Bergish Gladbach
5) 1975(The Féderal Repúblic of Germany)
6) black
40 1) supermarket／rest room
2),3) Takao Yoguchi
4) Chujitsuya
5) 1979(Japan)
41 1) supermarket／rest room
2),3) Shuji Torigoe
4) Tokyu Store
5) 1976(Japan)
42 1) rest room
2),3) Shuji Torigoe
4) The Gunma Prefectual Office
5) 1981(Japan)
43 1) sit down
2) Hajime Nakamura／Yasaburo Kuwayama
3) Yasaburo Kuwayama／Hajime Ikeda／Norio Ikeda
4) the Regional Meeting of Jehovah's Witnesses
5) 1980(Japan)
44 1) lounge
2) Akiteru Nakajima
3) Akiteru Nakajima／Kumi Shirahama
4) The Iraqi Government
5) 1981／1982(Japan)
45 1) studying room
2),3) Akira Hirata
4) Kamei
5) 1975(Japan)
6) Pantone 299
46 1) Japanese traditional room
2),3) Akira Hirata
4) Kamei
5) 1975(Japan)
6) Pantone 174C
47 1) company signs
2) Shigeru Shimooka
3) Masanobu Watanabe
4) Mitsubishi Motors Co., Ltd. (MMC)
5) 1983(Japan)
6) dark blue(sub-color red)
48 1) ocean exhibition／a drawing room
2) Masaru Katsumi／Akiteru Nakajima
3) Teruyuki Kunito／Yukio Ota／Akira Kuroyone
4) Okinawa International Ocean Exhibition Association
5) 1975(Japan)
49 1) "Monomi-no-To" centenial／prisoner
2) Yasaburo Kuwayama
3) Yasaburo Kuwayama／Hajime Ikeda
4) Jehovah's Witnesses
5) 1979(Japan)

50 1) parlor
2),3) Akira Hirata
4) Kamei
5) 1975(Japan)
6) Pantone 410
51 1) dining room
2),3) Akira Hirata
4) Kamei
5) 1975(Japan)
6) Pantone 340
52 1) editorial e.t.c.
2) Kenzo Nakagawa
3) Hiroyasu Nobuyama∕Satoshi Morikami
4) Bolt & Nuts Studio
5) 1983(Japan)
53 1) depertment store∕rescue equipment
3) Shigeo Fukuda
4) Seibu Department Store
5) 1976(Japan)
54 1) rescue equipment∕stretcher
2) Akiteru Nakajima
3) Akiteru Nakajima∕Kumi Shirahama
4) The Iraqi Government
5) 1981∕1982(Japan)
55 1) bed room
2),3) Akira Hirata
4) Kamei
5) 1975(Japan)
6) PantoneE 265C
56 1) hotel(information)
2) Jan Rajlich
3) Jan Rajlich∕Jan Rajlich Jr.
4) Hotel Morava
5) 1978(Czechoslovakia)
57 1) ocean exhibition∕nap room
2) Masaru Katsumi∕Akiteru Nakajima
3) Teruyuki Kunito∕Yukio Ota∕Akira Kuroyone
4) Okinawa International ocean Exhibition Association
5) 1975(Japan)
58 1) "A Picture Book of A-I-U-E-O"∕to sleep
2),3) Yasaburo Kuwayama
4) Typo Eye Exhibition of "Kami no Mojikku"
5) 1979(Japan)
59 1) association(insurance)∕hospital(admission)
2),3) Bill Wood
4) The Association of Administrators(Insurance)
5) 1977(U.S.A.)
6) black
60 1) editorial e.t.c.
2) Kenzo Nakagawa
3) Hiroyasu Nobuyama∕Satoshi Morikami
4) Bolt & Nuts Studio
5) 1983(Japan)
61 1) mud-therapy medical treatment
3) Asher Kalderon
4) Dead Sea Hot Spring Building
5) 1983(Israel)
62 1) airport∕hotel information
2) Lehfeld Ernest
3) Lehfeld Ernest∕Manuel

Sanchez∕Gallardo Francisco∕Jorge Fernandez
4) Mexico Airport
5) 1977-78(Mexico)
6) black∕yellow(ground)
63 1) remedy for limbs
3) Asher Kalderon
4) Dead Sea Hot Spring Building
5) 1983(Israel)
64 1) bathing therapy
3) Asher Kalderon
4) Dead Sea Hot Spring Building
5) 1983(Israel)
65 1) massage by water
3) Asher Kalderon
4) Dead Sea Hot Spring Building
5) 1983(Israel)
66 1) massage below the water
3) Asher Kalderon
4) Dead Sea Hot Spring Building
5) 1983(Israel)
67 1) hospital∕dermatology
2) Ichiro Saito
3) Ichiro Saito∕Miyuki Hoshi
4) Itoki
5) 1983(Japan)
6) dark brown∕dark green
68 1) hospital∕orthopaedics
2) Ichiro Saito
3) Ichiro Saito∕Miyuki Hoshi
4) Itoki
5) 1983(Japan)
6) dark brown∕dark green
69 1) books∕domestic book of medicine
3) Yasumasa Oka
4) Shueisha
5) 1983(Japan)
70 1) books∕domestic book of medicine
3) Yasumasa Oka
4) Shueisha
5) 1983(Japan)
71 1) books∕domestic book of medicine
3) Yasumasa Oka
4) Shueisha
5) 1983(Japan)
72 1) books∕domestic book of medicine
3) Yasumasa Oka
4) Shueisha
5) 1983(Japan)
73 1) publication(magazine)
3) Yasumasa Oka
4) Heibon Shuppan
5) 1983(Japan)
74 1) medicines∕to plaster
3) Akiteru Nakajima
4) Mine Medicines
5) 1980(Japan)
75 1) company signs
2) Shigeru Shimooka
3) Masanobu Watanabe
4) Mitsubishi Motors Co., Ltd. (MMC)
5) 1983(Japan)
6) dark blue(sub-color red)
76 1) company sign
2) Shigeru Shimooka
3) Masanobu Watanabe

4) Mitsubishi Motors Co., Ltd. (MMC)
5) 1983(Japan)
6) dark blue(sub-color red)
77 1) ocean exhibition∕ladies lavatory
2) Masaru Katsumi∕Akiteru Nakajima
3) Teruyuki Kunito∕Yukio Ota∕Akira Kuroyone
4) Okinawa International Ocean Exhibition Associaoion
5) 1975(Japan)
6) blue(4PB3.5∕12)∕beige(3Y8.5∕1)
78 1) ladies lavatory
2) Akiteru Nakajima
3) Akiteru Nakajima∕Kumi Shirahama
4) The Iraqi Government
5) 1981∕1982(Japan)
79 1) department store∕ladies lavatory
3) Shigeo Fukuda
4) Seibu Department Store
5) 1976(Japan)
80 1) safety & hygiene∕women
2),3) Tokyo Shibaura Denki Design Department
4) Tokyo Shibaura Denki
5) 1975(Japan)
6) yellow∕black(partly white・red)
81 1) supermarket∕ladies lavatory
2),3) Shuji Torigoe
4) Tokyu Store
5) 1976(Japan)
82 1) supermarket∕ladies lavatory
2),3) Takao Yoguchi
4) Chujitsuya
5) 1979(Japan)
83 1) ladies lavatory
2),3) Shuji Torigoe
4) The Gunma Prefectual Office
5) 1981(Japan)
84 1) rest room
3) Asher Kalderon
4) Dead Sea Hot Spring Building
5) 1983(Israel)
85 1) hotel(information)
2) Jan Rajlich
3) Jan Rajlich∕Jan Railich Jr.
4) Hotel Molava
5) 1978(Czechoslovakia)
86 1) automobile(service station)∕ladies lavatory
2) Akiteru Nakajima
3) Akiteru Nakajima∕Takeshi Ogawa∕Kumi Shirahama
4) Toyota Motors
5) 1982(Japan)
87 1) ladies lavatory
3) Ruedi Rüegg
5) 1983(Switzerland)
88 1) ladies lavatory
2),3) PVDI
4) Furunasu Electric Center
5) 1972(Brazil)
89 1) library∕ladies lavatory
2) Takenobu Igarashi
3) Akiteru Nakajima∕Kumi

Shirahama
4) Keio Gijuku University
5) 1982(Japan)
90 1) ladies lavatory
2),3) PVDI
4) São Paulo Gas Co., Ltd.
5) 1972(Brazil)
91 1) ladies lavatory
2),3) PVDI
4) Copec Oil Co., Ltd.
5) 1974(Brazil)
92 1) airport∕ladies lavatory
2) Ernest Lehfeld
3) Ernest Lehfeld∕Manuel Sanchez∕Francisco Gallardo∕Jorge Fernandez
4) Mexico Airport
5) 1977-78(Mexico)
6) black∕yellow(ground)
93 1) ladies lavatory
2) Ichiro Saito
3) Ichiro Saito∕Miyuki Hoshi
4) Itoki
5) 1983(Japan)
94 1) company sign
2) Shigeru Shimooka
3) Masanobu Watanabe
4) Mitsubishi Motors Co., Ltd. (MMC)
5) 1983(Japan)
6) dark blue(sub-color red)
95 1) sports∕public hygienic service
2) Shakespeare Design Studio
3) Ronald Shakespear∕Raul Shakespear
4) Buenos Aires Sports Center
5) 1980(Argentina)
96 1) hospital∕ladies lavatory
2) Shakespear Design Studio
3) Ronald Shakespear∕Raul Shakespear
4) Buenos Aires City Hospital
5) 1970∕1980(Argentina)
6) red∕blue
97 1) ladies lavatory
2) Hajime Nakamura∕Yasaburo Kuwayama
3) Yasaburo Kuwayama∕Hajime Ikeda∕Norio Ikeda
4) The Regional Meeting of Jehovah's Witnesses
5) 1980(Japan)
98 1) hospital∕nurse
3) Miloš Ćirić
4) Army Hospital
5) 1977(Yugoslavia)
6) red∕blue∕green
99 1) University Hospital∕Female Patient
2),3) PVDI
4) Guanabara State University
5) 1974(Brazil)
100 1) business information∕reception
2) Yasaburo Kuwayama
3) Minoru Kamono
4) Maruko Birumen
5) 1977(Japan)
101 1) graphic indication of detergent∕for ladies
2) Akiteru Nakajima
3) Seiko Aoki∕Hisako Kataoka∕Yoko Kobayashi
4) Chuo Bijutsu Gakuen Pictorial

Course
5) 1983(Japan)
102 1) ladies lavatory
2),3) Yoshihiro Yoshida
4) New Yunohama Hotel
5) 1979(Japan)
103 1) company sign／ladies
dressing room
2) Shigeru Shimooka
3) Masanobu Watanabe
4) Mitsubishi Motors Co., Ltd.
(MMC)
5) 1983(Japan)
6) dark blue(sub-color red)
104 1) ladie's dressing room
3) Ruedi Rüegg
5) 1983(Switzerland)
105 3) Ruedi Rüegg
5) 1983(Switzerland)
106 1) ocean exhibition／lost
child
2) Masaru Katsumi／Akiteru
Nakajima
3) Teruyuki Kunito／Yukio Ota／
Akira Kuroyone
4) Okinawa International Ocean
Exhibition Association
5) 1975(Japan)
6) blue(4PB3, 5／12)／
beige(3Y8, 5／1)
107 1) event(space show)／lost
child center
2),3) Noriaki Tamura
4) Headquarters Japan
International Aerospace Show
1979
5) 1979(Japan)
6) sky blue
108 1) lost child center
2),3) Shuji Torigoe
4) The Gunma Prefectual Office
5) 1981(Japan)
109 1) lost child center
2) Hajime Nakamura／Yasaburo
Kuwayama
3) Yasaburo Kuwayama／Hajime
Ikeda／Norio Ikeda
4) The Regional Meeting of
Jehovah's Witnesses
5) 1980(Japan)
110 1) bill on the post／kinder
garden
2) Yonefusa Yamada
3) Shin Sasaki／Yuko Ishida
4) Toden Kokoku(Advertisement)
5) 1982(Japan)
111 1) hospital／lavatory
2),3) Guillermo Gonzales Ruiz
4) National Children's Hospital
5) 1975(Argentina)
112 1) child lavatory
2) Hajime Nakamura／Yasaburo
Kuwayama
3) Yasaburo Kuwayama／Hajime
Ikeda／Norio Ikeda
4) The Regional Meeting of
Johovah's Witnesses
5) 1980(Japan)
113 1) "A Picture Book of
A-I-U-E-O"／ghost
2),3) Yasaburo Kuwayama
4) Typo-Eye Exhibition of "Kami
no Mojikku"
5) 1979(Japan)
114 1) hospital

2),3) Joe Dieter
4) The John Hopkins Hospital
5) 1982(U.S.A.)
6) navy blue
115 1) editorial e.t.c.
2) Kenzo Nakagawa
3) Hiroyasu Nobuyama／Satoshi
Morikami
4) Bolt & Nuts Studio
5) 1983(Japan)
116 1) supermarket／nursery／
rest room for babies
2),3) Syuji Torigoe
4) Tokyu Store
5) 1976(Japan)
117 1) package of
injector-needles
2),3) Kunihiko Sugiyama
4) Hakko Shoji
5) (Japan)
118 1) package of
injector-needles
2),3) Kunihiko Sugiyama
4) Hakko Shoji
5) (Japan)
119 1) student
2),3) Kunihiko Hasegawa
4) Bunri
5) 1979(Japan)
120 1) hospital／cardiology
2),3) Guillermo Gonzales Ruiz
4) National Children's Hospital
5) 1975(Argentina)
121 1) hospital／lavatory
2),3) Guillermo Gonzales Ruiz
4) National Children's Hospital
5) 1975(Argentina)
122 1) hospital
2),3) Guillermo Gonzales Ruiz
4) National Children's Hospital
5) 1975(Argentina)
123 1) hospital
2),3) Guillermo Gonzales Ruiz
4) National Children's Hospital
5) 1975(Argentina)
124 1) hospital
2),3) Guillermo Gonzales Ruiz
4) National Children's Hospital
5) 1975(Argentina)
125 1) supermarket／parking
for baby carriage
2),3) Takao Yoguchi
4) Chujitsuya
5) 1979(Japan)
126 1) hospital
2),3) Guillermo Gonzales Ruiz
4) National Children's Hospital
5) 1975(Argentina)
127 1) hospital／x-rays
2),3) Guillermo Gonzales Ruiz
4) National Children's Hospital
5) 1975(Argentina)
128 1) hospital／washing room
2),3) Guillermo Gonzales Ruiz
4) National Children's Hospital
5) 1975(Argentina)
129 1) reference book
2),3) Kunihiko Sugiyama
4) Bunri
5) 1979(Japan)
130 1) hospital／reading room
2),3) Guillermo Gonzales Ruiz
4) National Children's Hospital
5) 1975(Argentina)
131 1) bill on the post／a

boarding school
2) Yonefusa Yamada
3) Shin Sasaki／Yuko Ishida
4) Toden Kokoku
5) 1982(Japan)
132 1) editorial e.t.c.
2) Kenzo Nakagawa
3) Hiroyasu Nobuyama／Satoshi
Morikami
4) Bolt & Nuts Studio
5) 1983(Japan)
133 1) graphic indication of
detergent／keep off children
2) Akiteru Nakajima
3) Seiko Aoki／Hisako
Kataoka／Yoko Kobayashi
4) Chuo Bijutsu Gakuen Pictorial
Course
5) 1983(Japan)
134 1) sign in a camera
company
2) Ken Nara／Akiteru Nakajima
3) Akiteru Nakajima／Ryoichi
Yamada／Kumi Shirahama
4) Canon
5) 1974(Japan)
135 1) transport
2),3) PVDI
4) Sinaliza
5) 1977(Brazil)
136 1) "Shiritori Kanji"
2),3) Yasaburo Kuwayama
4) Typo-Eye Exhibition of "A
Picture Book of Letter"
5) 1977(Japan)
6) black
137 1) don't run
2) Hajime Nakamura／Yasaburo
Kuwayama
3) Yasaburo Kuwayama／Hajime
Ikeda／Norio Ikeda
4) The Regional Meeting of
Jehovah's Witnesses
5) 1980(Japan)
138 1) a fire exit
2) Akiteru Nakajima
3) Akiteru Nakajima／Kumi
Shirahama
4) The Iraqi Government
5) 1981／1982(Japan)
139 1) ocean exhibition／a fire
exit
2) Masaru Katsumi／Akiteru
Nakajima
3) Teruyuki Kunito／Yukio Ota／
Akira Kuroyone
4) Okinawa International Ocean
Exhibition Association
5) 1975(Japan)
140 1) library／a fire exit
2) Takenobu Igarashi
3) Akiteru Nakajima／Kumi
Shirahama
4) Keio Gijuku University
5) 1982(Japan)
141 1) supermarket／a fire exit
2),3) Takao Yoguchi
4) Chujitsuya
5) 1979(Japan)
142 1) don't climb
2) Hajime Nakamura／Yasaburo
Kuwayama
3) Yasaburo Kuwayama／Hajime
Ikeda／Norio Ikeda
4) The Regional Meeting of

Jehovah's Witnesses
5) 1980(Japan)
143 1) keep out !
2) Hajime Nakamura／Yasaburo
Kuwayama
3) Yasaburo Kuwayama／Hajime
Ikeda／Norio Ikeda
4) The Regional Meeting of
Jehovah's Witnesses
5) 1980(Japan)
144 1) ocean exhibition／
lookout platform
2) Masaru Katsumi／Akiteru
Nakajima
3) Teruyuki Kunito／Yukio Ota／
Akira Kuroyone
4) Okinawa International Ocean
Exhibition Association
5) 1975(Japan)
145 1) hospital
2),3) Guillermo Gonzales Ruiz
4) National Children's Hospital
5) 1975(Argentina)
146 1) hospital
2),3) Joe Dieter
4) The John Hopkins Hospital
5) 1982(U.S.A.)
6) navy blue
147 1) library／no trespassing
2) Takenobu Igarashi
3) Akiteru Nakajima／Kumi
Shirahama
4) Keio Gijuku University
5) 1982(Japan)
148 1) airport／no transit
2) Ernest Lehfeld
3) Ernest Lehfeld／Manuel
Sanchez／Francisco Gallardo／
Jorge Fernandez
4) Mexico Airport
5) 1977-78(Mexico)
6) black(ground Yellow)
149 1) department store
3) Shigeo Fukuda
4) Seibu Department Store
5) 1976(Japan)
150 1) supermarket／stairs
2),3) Shuji Torigoe
4) Tokyu Store
5) 1976(Japan)
151 1) supermarket／stairs
2),3) Takao Yoguchi
4) Chujitsuya
5) 1979(Japan)
152 1) office／stairs
2) Ichiro Saito
3) Ichiro Saitô／Miyuki Hoshi
4) Itoki
5) 1983(Japan)
153 3) Ruedi Rüegg
5) 1983(Switzerland)
154 3) Ruedi Rüegg
5) 1983(Switzerland)
155 1) a fire escape
2) Akiteru Nakajima
3) Akiteru Nakajima／Kumi
Shirahama
4) The Iraqi Government
5) 1981／1982(Japan)
156 1) company sign
2) Shigeru Shimooka
3) Masanobu Watanabe
4) Mitsubishi Motors Co., Ltd.
(MMC)
5) 1983(Japan)

6) dark blue(sub-color red)
157 3) Ruedi Rüegg
5) 1983(Switzerland)
158 3) Ruedi Rüegg
5) 1983(Switzerland)
159 1) department store
2) Escalator
3) Shigeo Fukuda
4) Seibu Department Store
5) 1976(Japan)
160 1) supermarket／escalator
2),3) Takao Yoguchi
4) Chujitsuya
5) 1979(Japan)
161 1) supermarket／escalator
2),3) Shuji Torigoe
4) Tokyu Store
5) 1976(Japan)
162 1) airport／escalator
2) Ernest Lehfeld
3) Ernest Lehfeld／Manuel Sanchez／Francisco Gallardo／Jorge Fernandez
4) Mexico Airport
5) 1977-78(Mexico)
6) black／yellow(ground)
163 1) airport／escalator
2) Ernest Lehfeld
3) Ernest Lehfeld／Manuel Sanchez／Francisco Gallardo／Jorge Fernandez
4) Mexico Airport
5) 1977-78(Mexico)
6) black／yellow(ground)
164 1) department store／elevator
3) Shigeo Fukuda
4) Seibu Department Store
5) 1976(Japan)
165 1) sports／public hygienic service
2) Shakespeare Design Studio
3) Ronald Shakespear／Raul Shakespear
4) Buenos Aires Sports Center
5) 1980(Argentina)
6) red／blue
166 1) hospital／elevator
2) Shakespear Design Studio
3) Ronald Shakespear／Raul Shakespear
4) Buenos Aires City Hospital
5) 1970／1980(Argentina)
6) red／blue
167 3) Ruedi Rüegg
5) 1983(Switzerland)
168 1) Akagi Kokutai／conviviences for the physically handicapped
2),3) Shuji Torigoe
4) The Gunma Prefectual Office
5) 1981(Japan)
169 1) library／convinience for the physically handicapped
2) Takenobu Igarashi
3) Akiteru Nakajima／Kumi Shirahama
4) Keio Gijuku University
5) 1982(Japan)
170 1) conviviences for the physically handicapped
2) Akiteru Nakajima
3) Akiteru Nakajima／Kumi Shirahama
4) The Iraqi Government

5) 1981／1982(Japan)
171 1) hospital／don't disturb
3) Miloš Ćirić
4) Army Hospital
5) 1977(Yugoslavia)
6) red／blue／green
172 1) ocean exhibition／the physically handicapped
2) Masaru Katsumi／Akiteru Nakajima
3) Teruyuki Kumito／Yukio Ota／Akira Kuroyone
4) Okinawa International Ocean Exhibition Association
5) 1975(Japan)
6) blue(4PB3, 5／12)／beige(3Y8, 5／1)
173 1) department store／lavatory for the physically handicapped
3) Shigeo Fukuda
4) Seibu Department Store
5) 1976(Japan)
174 1) supermarket／lavatory For the physically handicapped
2),3) Takao Yoguchi
4) Chūjitsuya
5) 1979(Japan)
175 1) sports／public hygienic service
2) Shakespear Design Studio
3) Ronald Shakespear／Raul Shakespear
4) Buenos Aires Sports Center
5) 1980(Argentina)
176 3) Ruedi Rüegg
5) 1983(Switzerland)
177 1) assotiation(insurance)／hospital(the physically handicapped)
2),3) Bill Wood
4) the Association of Administrators(Insurance)
5) 1977(U.S.A.)
6) black
178 1) hospital／bath chair
2) Shakespear Design Studio
3) Ronald Shakespear／Raul Shakespear
4) Buenos Aires City Hospital
5) 1970／1980(Argentina)
6) red／blue
179 1) men's shower bath
2) Akiteru Nakajima
3) Akiteru Nakajima／Kumi Shirahama
4) The Iraqi Government
5) 1981／1982(Japan)
180 1) Ladie's shower bath
2) Akiteru Nakajima
3) Akiteru Nakajima／Kumi Shirahama
4) The Iraqi Government
5) 1981／1982(Japan)
181 1) ocean exhibition／men's shower bath
2) Masaru Katsumi／Akiteru Nakajima
3) Teruyuki Kunito／Yukio Ota／Akira Kuroyone
4) Okinawa International Ocean Exhibition Association
5) 1975(Japan)
182 1) shower bath
2) Ichiro Saito

3) Ichiro Saito／Miyuki Hoshi
4) Itoki
5) (Japan)
183 1) company sign
2) Shigeru Shimooka
3) Masanobu Watanabe
4) Mitsubishi Motors Co., Ltd. (MMC)
5) 1983(Japan)
6) dark blue(sub-color red)
184 1) weather report board／caution to gust
3) Akiteru Nakajima
4) Okinawa International Ocean Exhibition Association
5) 1975(Japan)
185 1) signs in a camera company／no transit
2) Ken Nara／Akiteru Nakajima
3) Akiteru Nakajima／Ryoichi Yamada／Kumi Shirahama
4) Canon
5) 1974(Japan)
186 1) airport／transit passenger
2) Ernest Lehfeld
3) Ernest Lehfeld／Manuel Sanchez／Gallardo Francisco／Jorge Fernandez
4) Mexico Airport
5) 1977-78(Mexico)
6) black／yellow(ground)
187 1) compaign clean up(trial)
2) Duane Wiens
3) Arvid Wallen
4) State of Colorado
5) 1978(U.S.A.)
6) blue
188 1) olympic／trash can
2) Tadashi Ikeda
3) Kenichi Miyata／Seiji Masuike
4) 1988 Seoul Oly'mpiad
5) 1982(Japan)
6) black
189 1) restaurant／
2),3) Hans Wyser
4) The Burger Land
5) 1980(Switzerland)
6) red
190 1) direct mail
2) Kenzo Nakagawa
3) Hiroyasu Nobuyama／Nobuyuki Suehiro
4) 5 TV Station in Tokyo
5) 1980(Japan)
191 1) direct mail
2) Kenzo Nakagawa
3) Hiroyasu Nobuyama／Nobuyuki Suehiro
4) 5 TV Station in Tokyo
5) 1980(Japan)
192 1) direct mail
2) Kenzo Nakagawa
3) Hiroyasu Nobuyama／Nobuyuki Suehiro
4) 5 TV Station in Tokyo
5) 1980(Japan)
193 1) dressing room
2),3) Akira Hirata
4) Kamei
5) 1975(Japan)
6) Pantone 219
194 1) drinking fountain
2) Akiteru Nakajima
3) Akiteru Nakajima／Kumi

Shirahama
4) The Iraqi Government
5) 1981／1982(Japan)
195 1) editorial e.t.c.
2) Kenzo Nakagawa
3) Hiroyasu Nobuyama／Satoshi Morikami
4) Bolt & Nuts Studio
5) 1983(Japan)
196 1) publication
2) Massimo Dradi
3) Aldo Travagliati
4) "Welcome"
5) 1983(Italy)
6) black／white
197 1) "A Picture Book of A-I-U-E-O"／to steal
2),3) Yasaburo Kuwayama
4) Typo-Eye Exhibition of "Kami no Mojikku"
5) 1979(Japan)
198 1) "Monomi-no-To" centennial／demonstration
2) Yasaburo Kuwayama
3) Yasaburo Kuwayama／Hajime Ikeda
4) Jehovah's Witnesses
5) 1979(Japan)
199 1) association(Insurance)／internal medicine
2),3) Bill Wood
4) The Association of Administrators(Insurauce)
5) 1977(U.S.A.)
6) black
200 1) hospital
2),3) Guillermo Gonzales Ruiz
4) National Children's Hospital
5) 1975(Argentina)
201 1) company sign
2) Shigeru Shimooka
3) Masanobu Watanabe
4) Mitsubishi Motors Co., Ltd. (MMC)
5) 1983(Japan)
6) dark blue
202 1) hospital
2),3) Guillermo Gonzales Ruiz
4) National Children's Hospital
5) 1975(Argentina)
203 1) ocean exhibiton／guard
2) Masaru Katumi／Akiteru Nakajima
3) Teruyuki Kunito／Yukio Ota／Akira Kuroyone
4) Okinawa International Ocean Exhibition Association
5) 1975(Japan)
204 1) guard
2) Yasaburo Kuwayama
3) Minoru Kamono
5) 1977(Japan)
205 1) guard office
2),3) Shuji Torigoe
4) Gunma Prefectual Office
5) 1981(Japan)
206 1) editorial e.t.c.
2) Kenzo Nakagawa
3) Hiroyasu Nobuyama／Satoshi Morikami
4) Bolt & Nuts Studio
5) 1983(Japan)
207 1) sports／officer(trial)
2) Tadashi Ikeda

3) Kenichi Miyata／Seiji Masuike
4) 1988 Seoul Olympiad
5) 1982(Japan)
6) Black
208 1) ocean exhibition／PTS booth
2) Masaru Katsumi／Akiteru Nakajima
3) Teruyuki Kunito／Yukio Ota／Akira Kuroyone
4) Okinawa International Ocean Exhibition Association
5) 1975(Japan)
209 1) sports／reporters(trial)
2) Tadashi Ikeda
3) Kenichi Miyata／Seiji Masuike
4) 1988 Seoul Olympiad
5) 1982(Japan)
6) Black
210 1) ocean exhibition／information
2) Masaru Katsumi／Akiteru Nakajima
3) Teruyuki Kunito／Yukio Ota／Akira Kuroyone
4) Okinawa International Ocean Exhibition Association
5) 1975(Japan)
211 1) information
2),3) Shuji Torigoe
4) The Gunma Prefectual Office
5) 1981(Japan)
212 1) university hospital／reception
2),3) PVDI
4) Guanabara State University
5) 1974(Brazil)
213 1) editorial e.t.c.
2) Kenzo Nakagawa
3) Hiroyasu Nobuyama／Satoshi Morikami
4) Bolt & Nuts Studio
5) 1983(Japan)
214 1) editorial e.t.c.
2) Kenzo Nakagawa
3) Hiroyasu Noburaya／Satoshi Morikami
4) Bolt & Nuts Studio
5) 1983(Japan)
215 1) hospital
2),3) Guillermo Gonzales Ruiz
4) National Children's Hospital
5) 1975(Argentina)
216 1) A Regional Meeting
2) Hajime Nakamura／Yasaburo Kuwayama
3) Yasaburo Kuwayama／Hajime Ikeda／Norio Ikeda
4) The Regional Meeting of Jehovah's Witnesses
5) 1980(Japan)
217 1) copying appliances
5) 1980(Japan)
218 1) editorial e.t.c.
2) Kenzo Nakagawa
3) Hiroyasu Nobuyama／Satoshi Morikami
4) Bolt & Nuts Studio
5) 1983(Japan)
219 1) "A Picture Book of A-I-U-E-O"／robot
2),3) Yasaburo Kuwayama
4) Typo-Eye Exhibition of "A Picture Book of Letter"
5) 1979(Japan)

220 1) automobile(service station)
2) Akiteru Nakajima
3) Akiteru Nakajima／Takeshi Ogawa／Kumi Shirahama
4) Toyota Motors
5) 1982(Japan)
221 1) automobile(service station)／maintenance
2) Akiteru Nakajima
3) Akiteru Nakajima／Takeshi Ogawa／Kumi Shirahama
4) Toyota Motors
5) 1982(Japan)
222 1) "Business Game"／preparation
3) Yoshitaka Shimizu
4) Sangyo Noritsu University
5) 1982(Japan)
223 1) safety & hygiene／life-line
2),3) Tokyo Shibaura Denki Design Department
4) Tokyo Shibaura Denki
5) 1975(Japan)
6) yellow／black(partly white／red)
224 1) hospital
2),3) Guillermo Gonzales Ruiz
4) National Children's Hospital
5) 1975(Argentina)
225 1) hospital
2),3) Guillermo Gonzales Ruiz
4) National Children's Hospital
5) 1975(Argentina)
226 1) steel-manufacturing industry
2),3) Kunihiko Sugiyama
4) Bunri
5) 1979(Japan)
227 1) agriculture
2),3) Kunihiko Sugiyama
4) Bunri
5) 1979(Japan)
228 1) editorial e.t.c.
2) Kenzo Nakagawa
3) Hiroyasu Nobuyama／Satoshi Morikami
4) Bolts & Nuts Studio
5) 1983(Japan)
229 1) olympics／athletics(trial)
2) Tadashi Ikeda
3) Kenichi Miyata／Seiji Masuike
4) 1988 Seoul Olympiad
5) 1982(Japan)
230 1) map of neighborhood
2) Akiteru Nakajima
3) Akiteru Nakajima／Kumi Shirahama／Tamio Takeuchi
4) Art & Graphic
5) 1981(Japan)
231 1) sports
2),3) Julien Van Der Wal
4) International Olympic Game Comittee
5) 1979(Switzerland)
232 1) editorial e.t.c.
2) Kenzo Nakagawa
3) Hiroyasu Nobuyama／Satoshi Morikami
4) Bolt & Nuts Studio
5) 1983(Japan)
233 1) sports(sponsors)
3) Carlo Malerba
4) Iveco

5) 1981／1983(Italy)
234 1) olympics／soccer(trial)
2) Tadashi Ikeda
3) Kenichi Miyata／Seiji Masuike
4) 1988 Seoul Olympiad
5) 1982(Japan)
235 1) sports
2),3) Julien Van Der Wal
4) International Olympic Game Committee
5) 1979(Switzerland)
236 1) textile products／sports-socks for each item
2),3) Michio Ogura
4) Nakamura Textile
5) 1978(Japan)
237 1) sports(supporting party)
3) Carlo Malerba
4) Iveco
5) 1981／1983(Italy)
238 1) olympics／gymnastics(trial)
2) Tadashi Ikeda
3) Kenichi Miyata／Seiji Masuike
4) 1988 Seoul Olympiad
5) 1982(Japan)
239 1) sports
2),3) Julien Van Der Wal
4) International Olympic Game Committee
5) 1979(Switzerland)
240 1) editorial e.t.c.
2) Kenzo Nakagawa
3) Hiroyasu Nobuyama／Satoshi Morikami
4) Bolt & Nuts Studio
5) 1983(Japan)
241 1) sports
2),3) Akira Hirata
4) Kamei
5) 1975(Japan)
6) antone 280
242 1) olympics／basketball(trial)
2) Tadashi Ikeda
3) Kenichi Miyata／Seiji Masuike
4) 1988 Seoul Olympad
5) 1982(Japan)
243 1) sport
2),3) Julien Van Der Wal
4) International Olympic Game Committee
5) 1979(Switzerland)
244 1) sport
2),3) Julien Van Der Wal
4) International Olympic Game Committee
5) 1979(Switzerland)
245 1) sporting goods
3) Yoshimitsu Kato
4) Usiver Sports
5) 1983(Japan)
246 1) sport
2),3) Julien Van Der Wal
4) International Olympic Game Committee
5) 1979(Switzerland)
247 1) sport
2) Kenzo Nakagawa
3) Hiroyasu Nobuyama／Satoshi Morikami
4) Bolt & Nuts Studio
5) 1983(Japan)
248 1) sport(sponsors)
3) Carlo Malerba

4) Iveco
5) 1981／1983(Italy)
249 1) sport(practical book)
3) Yutaka Hasegawa
4) Syufu to Seikatsusha
5) 1982(Japan)
250 1) textile products／sports-socks for each item
2),3) Michio Ogura
4) Nakamura Textile
5) 1978(Japan)
251 1) textile products／sports-socks for each item
2),3) Michio Ogura
4) Nakamura Textile
5) 1978(Japan)
252 1) company magazine／Game・recreation
2),3) Kunihiko Sugiuama
4) Bunri
5) 1980(Japan)
253 1) olympics／fencing(trial)
2) Tadashi Ikeda
3) Kenichi Miyata／Seiji Masuike
4) 1988 Seoul Olympad
5) 1982(Japan)
254 1) sport
2),3) Julien Sportan Der Wal
4) International Olympic Game Committee
5) 1979(Switzerland)
255 1) olympics／hockey(trial)
2) Tadashi Ikeda
3) Kenichi Miyata／Seiji Masuike
4) 1988 Seoul Olympiad
5) 1982(Japan)
256 1) sport
2),3) Julien Van Der Wal
4) International Olympic Game Committee
5) 1979(Switzerland)
257 1) map for a realty dealer／golf
2),3) Akiteru Nakajima
4) Anterope Valley Investment Company
5) 1976(Japan)
258 1) textile products／sports-socks for each item
2),3) Michio Ogura
4) Nakarura Textile
5) 1978(Japan)
259 1) golf
2) Kenzo Nakagawa
3) Hiroyasu Nobuyama／Satoshi Morikami
4) Bolt & Nuts Studio
5) 1983(Japan)
260 1) olyimpics／shooting(trial)
2) Tadashi Ikeda
3) Kenichi Miyata／Seiji Masuike
4) 1988 Seoul Olympiad
5) 1982(Japan)
261 1) sport
2),3) Julien Van Der Wal
4) International Olympic Game Committee
5) 1979(Switzerland)
262 1) sport
2),3) Julien Van Der Wal
4) International Olympic Game Committee
5) 1979(Switzerland)
263 1) sports(sponsors)
3) Carlo Malerba

4) Iveco
5) 1981／1983(Italy)
264 1) sport
2),3) Julien Van Der Wal
4) International Olympic Game Committee
5) 1979(Switzerland)
265 1) olympics／judo(trial)
2) Tadashi Ikeda
3) Kenichi Miyata／Seiji Masuike
4) 1988 Seoul Olympiad
5) 1982(Japan)
266 1) sport
2),3) Julien Van Der Wal
4) International Olympic Game Committee
5) 1979(Switzerland)
267 1) sports(sponsors)
3) Carlo Malerba
4) Iveco
5) 1981／1983(Italy)
268 1) sport
2),3) Julien Van Der Wal
4) International Olympic Game Committee
5) 1979(Switzerland)
269 1) leisure／cycle-track
2) Harry Murphy
3) Harry Murphy／Judy Kohn
4) Harbor Bay
5) 1978(U.S.A.)
270 1) olympics／cycle race(trial)
2) Tadashi Ikeda
3) Kenichi Miyata／Seiji Masuike
4) 1988 Seoul Olympiad
5) 1982(Japan)
271 1) sport
2),3) Julien Van Der Wal
4) International Olympic Game Committee
5) 1979(Switzerland)
272 1) cycling
2) Kenzo Nakagawa
3) Hiroyasu Nobuyama／Satoshi Morikami
4) Bolt & Nuts Studio
5) 1983(Japan)
273 1) sport／public hygienic service
2) Shakespear Design Studio
3) Ronald Shakespear／Raul Shakespear
4) Buenos Aires Sports Center
5) 1980(Argentina)
274 1) sport
2),3) Julien Van Der Wal
4) International Olympic Game Committee
5) 1979(Switzerland)
275 1) hospital／rehabilitation
2) Shakespear Design Studio
3) Ronald Shakespear／Raul Shakespear
4) Buenos Aires City Hospital
5) 1970／1980(Argentina)
6) red／blue
276 1) hospital
2),3) Guillermo Gonzales Ruiz
4) National Children's Hospital
5) 1975(Argentina)
277 1) weightlifting
2) Kenzo Nakagawa
3) Hiroyasu Nobuyama／Satoshi Morikami

4) Bolt & Nuts Studio
5) 1983(Japan)
278 1) sport
2),3) Julien Van Der Wal
4) International Olympic Game Committee
5) 1979(Switzerland)
279 1) sport
2),3) Julien Van Der Wal
4) International Obympic Game Committee
5) 1979(Switzerland)
280 1) publication
2) Massimo Dradi
3) Aldo Travagliati
4) "Welcome"
5) 1983(Italy)
6) black／white
281 1) sport
2),3) Julien Van Der Wal
4) International Olympic Game Committee
5) 1979(Switzerland)
282 1) main pool
3) Asher Kalderon
4) The Dead Sea Hot Spring Building
5) 1983(Israel)
283 1) hotel
2),3) PVDI
4) Rio Meridian Hotel
5) 1975(Brazil)
284 1) weather report board／no swimming
3) Akiteru Nakajima
4) Okinawa International Ocean Exhibition Association
5) 1975(Japan)
285 1) sport
2),3) Julien Van Der Wal
4) International Olympic Game Committee
5) 1979(Switzerland)
286 1) sport
2),3) Julien Van Der wal
4) International Olympic Game Committee
5) 1979(Switzerland)
287 1) sport
2),3) Julien Van Der Wal
4) International Olympic Game Committee
5) 1979(Switzerland)
288 1) map for a realty dealer／skiing
2),3) Akiteru Nakajima
4) Anterope Valley Investment Company
5) 1976(Japan)
289 1) map for a realty dealer／water skiing
2),3) Akiteru Nakajima
4) Anterope Vallay Investment Company
5) 1976(Japan)
290 1) textile products／sports-socks for each item
2),3) Michio Ogura
4) Nakamura Textile
5) 1978(Japan)
291 1) sports(sponsors)
3) Carlo Malerba
4) Iveco
5) 1981／1983(Italy)
292 1) sports(sponsors)

3) Carlo Malerba
4) Iveco
5) 1981／1983(Italy)
293 1) Sports(Sponsors)
3) Carlo Malerba
4) Iveco
5) 1981／1983(Italy)
294 1) "A Picture Book of A-I-U-E-O"／athletic meeting
2),3) Yasaburo Kuwayama
4) Typo-Eye Exhibition of "Kami no Mojikku"　＼
5) 1979(Japan)
295 1) encyclopedia／sound body
2) Katsuichi Ito
3) Katsuich Ito Design Studio
4) Tamagawa University Publishing Department
5) 1979(Japan)
296 1) leisure／walking
2) Harry Murphy
3) Harry Murphy／Judy Kohn
4) Harbor Bay Isle
5) 1978(U.S.A.)
297 1) map for a realty dealer／rock-climbing
2),3) Akiteru Nakajima
4) Anterope Valley Investment Company
5) 1976(Japan)
298 1) association(insurance)／unemployment
2),3) Bill Wood
4) The Assosiation of Administrators(Insurrance)
5) 1977(U.S.A.)
6) black
299 1) publication (encyclopedia)
2),3) Kunihiko Hasegawa
4) Kodansha
5) 1983(Japan)
300 1) dancing
2) Kenzo Nakagawa
3) Hiroyasu Nobuyama／Satoshi Morikami
4) Bolts & Nuts Studio
5) 1983(Japan)
301 1) direct Mail
2) Kenzo Nakagawa
3) Hiroyasu Nobuyama／Nobuyuki Suehiro
4) 5 TV Station in Tokyo
5) 1980(Japan)
302 1) automobile(service station)／lavatory
2) Akiteru Nakajima
3) Akiteru Nakajima／Takeshi Ogawa／Kumi Shirahama
4) Toyota Motors
5) 1982(Japan)
303 1) lavatory
2) Akiteru Nakajima
3) Akiteru Nakajira／Kumi Shirahama
4) The Iraqi Government
5) 1981／1982(Japan)
304 1) supermarket／lavatory
2),3) Takao Yoguchi
4) Chujitsuya
5) 1979(Japan)
305 1) lavatory
2) Ichiro Saito
3) Ichiro Saito／Miyuki Hoshi

4) Itoki
5) 1983(Japan)
306 1) airport／lavatory
2) Ernest Lehfeld
3) Erarest Lehfeld／Manuel Sanchez／Gallardo Francisco／Jorge Femandez
4) Mexico Airport
5) 1977-78(Mexico)
6) black／yellow(ground)
307 1) hospital／a civilian attached to the army
3) Miloš Ćirić
4) Army Hospital
5) 1977(Yugoslavia)
6) red／blue／green
308 1) hotel／information
2) Jan Rajlich
3) Jan Rajlich／Jan Rajlich Jr.
4) Hotel Molava
5) 1978(Czechoslovakia)
309 1) lavatory
2),3) Shuji Torigoe
4) The Gunma Prefectual Office
5) 1981(Japan)
310 3) Ruedi Rüegg
5) 1983(Switzerland)
311 1) safety & hygiene rest room
2),3) Tokyo Shibaura Denki Design Department
4) Tokyo Shibaura Denki
5) 1975(Japan)
6) yellow／black(partly white・red)
312 1) hospital
2),3) Guillermo Gonzales Ruiz
4) National Children's Hospital
5) 1975(Argentina)
313 1) reference book for studying
2),3) Kunihiko Sugiyama
4) Bunri
5) 1979(Japan)
314 1) reference book for studying
2),3) Kunihiko Sugiyama
4) Bunri
5) 1979(Japan)
315 1) marriage
2) Kenzo Nakagawa
3) Hiroyasu Nobuyama／Satoshi Morikami
4) Bolt & Nuts Studio
5) 1983(Japan)
316 1) association(Insurance)／child-birth
2),3) Bill Wood
4) The Association of Administrators(Insurance)
5) 1977(U.S.A.)
6) black
317 1) supermarket／elevator
2),3) Shuji Torigoe
4) Tokyu Store
5) 1976(Japan)
318 1) airport／observatory
2) Ernest Lehfeld
3) Ernest Lehfeld／Manuel Sanchez／Gallardo Francisco／Jorge Fernandez
4) Mexico Airport
5) 1977-78(Mexico)
6) black／yellow(ground)
319 1) hospital

2),3) Guillermo Gonzales Ruiz
4) National Children's Hospital
5) 1975(Argentina)
320 1) sports／public hygienic service
2) Shakespear Design Studio
3) Ronald Shakespear／Raul Shakespear
4) Buenos Aires Sports Center
5) 1980(Argentina)
321 1) hospital／obsterics & gynaecology
2) Shakespear Design Studio
3) Ronald Shakespear／Raul Shakespear
4) Buenos Aires City Hospital
5) 1970／1980(Argentina)
6) red／blue
322 1) hospital
2),3) Guilleromo Gonzales Ruiz
4) National Chindren's Hospital
5) 1975(Argentina)
323 1) university hospital／new born baby
2),3) PVDI
4) Guanabara State University
5) 1974(Brazil)
324 3) Ruedi Rüegg
5) 1983(Switzerland)
325 1) university hospital／pediatrics
2),3) PVDI
4) Guanabara State University
5) 1974(Brazil)
326 1) hospital
2),3) Guillermo Gonzales Ruiz
4) National Children's Hospital
5) 1975(Argentina)
327 1) parent & child
3) Ruedi Rüegg
5) 1983(Switzerland)
328 3) Ruedi Rüegg
5) 1983(Switzerland)
329 1) automobile service station／place for a business talk
2) Akiteru Nakajima
3) Akiteru Nakajima／Takeshi Ogawa／Kumi Shirahama
4) Toyota Mortors
5) 1982(Japan)
330 1) office appliance
3) A.G. Chiremanse
4) International Register
5) 1982(Netherlands)
331 1) children
2),3) PVDI
4) Copek Oil Co., Ltd.
5) 1974(Brazil)
332 1) entrance
2),3) Akira Hirata
4) Kamei
5) 1975(Japan)
6) Pantone 280
333 2),3) Ludvik Feller
4) Cedefop
5) 1979(West Germany)
334 1) airport／waiting room
2) Ernest Lehfeld
3) Ernest Lehfeld／Manuel Samchez／Gallardo Francisco／Jorge Fernandez
4) Mexico Airport
5) 1977-78(Mexico)
6) black／yellow(ground)
335 1) welfare

2),3) Kunihiko Sugiyama
4) Bunri
5) 1979(Japan)
336 1) supermarket／serving counter
2),3) Takao Yoguchi
4) Chujitsuya
5) 1979(Japan)
337 1) library／inspection
2) Takenobu Igarashi
3) Akiteru Nakajima／Kumi Shirahama
4) Keio Gijuku University
5) 1982(Japan)
338 1) symbol of "my wine"
2),3) Yasaburo Kuwayama
4) Riichi Ushiki
5) 1975(Japan)
339 1) map for a realty dealer／park
2),3) Akiteru Nakajima
4) Anterope Valley Investment Company
5) 1976(Japan)
340 1) wrapping paper
2),3) Yasaburo Kuwayama
4) Meibundo Book Shop
5) 1973(Japan)
341 3) Ruedi Rüegg
5) 1983(Switzerland)
342 1) association(insurance)／dentistry
2),3) Bill Wood
4) The Association of Administrators(Insurance)
5) 1977(U.S.A.)
6) black
343 1) health center
2),3) Jan Rajlich
5) 1979(Czechoslovakia)
6) blue/red
344 1) health center
2),3) Jan Rajlich
5) 1979(Czechoslovakia)
6) blue/red
345 1) massage
3) Asher Kalderon
4) Dead Sea Hot Spring Building
5) 1983(Israel)
346 health center
2),3) Jan Rajlich
5) 1979(Czechoslovakia)
6) blue/red
347 1) hospital
2),3) Guillermo Gonzales Ruiz
4) National Children's Hospital
5) 1976(Japan)
348 1) hospital
2),3) Guillermo Gonzales Ruiz
4) National Children's Hospital
5) 1975(Argentina)
349 1) hospital
2),3) Guillermo Gonzales Ruiz
4) National Children's Hospital
5) 1975(Argentina)
350 1) hospital
2),3) Guillermo Gonzales Ruiz
4) National Children's Hospital
5) 1975(Argentina)
351 1) hospital
2),3) Guillermo Gonzales Ruiz

4) National Children's Hospital
5) 1975(Argentina)
352 1) hospital
2),3) Guillermo Gonzales Ruiz
4) National Children's Hospital
5) 1975(Argentina)
353 1) olympics／interview room(trial)
2) Tadashi Ikeda
3) Kenichi Miyata／Seiji Masuike
4) 1988 Seoul Olympiad
5) 1982(Japan)
6) black
354 2) J. Forman
3) Mike Quon
5) 1982(U.S.A.)
6) black／white
355 1) library／lounge
2) Takenobu Igarashi
3) Akiteru Nakajima／Kumi Shirahama
4) Keio Gijuku University
5) 1982(Japan)
356 1) ocean exhibition／lounge
2) Masaru Katsumi／Akiteru Nakajima
3) Teruyuki Kunito／Yukio Ota／Akira Kuroyone
4) Okinawa International Ocean Exhibition Association
5) 1975(Japan)
357 1) Company signs
2) Shigeru Shimooka
3) Masanobu Watanabe
4) Mitsubishi Motors Co., Ltd. (MMC)
5) 1983(Japan)
6) dark blue(sub-color red)
358 1) living room
2),3) Akira Hirata
4) Kamei
5) 1975(Japan)
6) Pantone 186
359 1) publication(colum in an international magazine)
3) Tsuyokatsu Kudo
4) Saitama Prefecture
5) 1980(Japan)
360 1) publication
2) Massimo Dradi
3) Aldo Travagliati
4) "Welcome"
5) 1983(Italy)
6) black／white
361 1) department store／rest room
3) Shigeo Fukuda
4) Seibu Department Store
5) 1976(Japan)
362 1) cinema
2) Akiteru Nakajima
3) Akiteru Nakajima／Kumi Shirahama
4) The Iraqi Government
5) 1981／1982(Japan)
363 1) map of neighborhood／cinema
2) Akiteru Nakajima
3) Akiteru Nakajima／Yumi Shirahama／Tamio Takeuchi
4) Art & Graphic
5) 1981(Japan)
364 1) putting the attendee in order
2) Hajime Nakamura／Yasaburo

Kuwayama
3) Yasaburo Kuwayama／Hajime Ikeda／Norio Ikeda
4) The Regional Meeting of Jenovah's Witnesses
5) 1980(Japan)
365 1) hospital／group
3) Miloš Ćirić
4) Army Hospital
5) 1977(Yugoslavia)
6) red／blue／green
366 1) hospital／group practice
3) Miloš Ćirić
4) Army Hospital
5) 1977(Yugoslavia)
6) red／blue／green
367 1) "Business Game"／orientation
3) Yoshitaka Shimizu
4) Sangyo Noritsu University
5) 1982(Japan)
368 1) company magazine／editorial・producing business
2),3) Kunihiko Sugiyama
4) Bunri
5) 1980(Japan)
369 1) family
2) Kenzo Nakagawa
3) Hiroyasu Nobuyama／Satoshi Morikami
4) Bolt & Nuts Studio
5) 1983(Japan)
370 1) editorial e.t.c.
2) Kenzo Nakagawa
3) Hiroyasu Nobuyama／Satoshi Morikami
4) Bolts & Nuts Studio
5) 1983(Japan)
371 1) democratics and lives in the modern society
2),3) Kunihiko Hasegawa
4) Bunri
5) 1979(Japan)
372 1) automobile(service station)／reseption
2) Akiteru Nakajima
3) Akiteru Nakajima／Takeshi Ogawa／Kumi Shirahama
4) Toyota Motors
5) 1982(Japan)
373 1) supermarket／elevator
2),3) Takao Yoguchi
4) Chujitsuya
5) 1979(Japan)
374 1) elevator
2),3) Ichiro Saito
4) Itoki
5) 1983(Japan)
375 1) sports／public hygienic service
2) Shakespear Design Studio
3) Ronald Shakespear／Raul Shakespear
4) Buenos Aires Sports Center
5) 1980(Argentina)
376 1) "business game／meeting
3) Yoshitaka Shimizu
4) Sangyo Noritsu University
5) 1982(Japan)
377 1) theater
2) Akiteru Nakajima
3) Akiteru Nakajima／Kumi Shirahama

4) The Iraqi Government
5) 1981／1982(Japan)
378 1) biblical association game／Shadrach, Meshach and Abedenego
2) Norio Ikeda
3) Norio Ikeda／Shigeo Ikeda／So Nakamura
4) Ikedamura Aseduction
5) 1980(Japan)
379 2),3) Ludvik Feller
4) Cedefop
5) 1979(West Germany)
380 1) print
3) Akiteru Nakajima
4) Iwaki
5) (Japan)
381 1) sign in a camera company／observer
2) Ken Nara／Akiteru Nakajima
3) Akiteru Nakajima／Ryoichi Yamada／Kumi Shirahama
4) Canon
5) 1974(Japan)
372 1) office appliance
3) A.G.Chiremanse
4) International Register
5) 1982(Netherlands)
383 1) educational system
2),3) Harry Murphy
4) Guide to Self-Analysis
5) 1973(U.S.A.)
6) black／white
384 1) "A Picture Book of A-I-U-E-O"／to put on a cap
2),3) Yasaburo Kuwayama
4) Typo-Eye Exhibition of "Kami no Mojikku"
5) 1979(Japan)
385 1) map of neighborhood／a kind neighbor
2) Akiteru Nakajima
3) Akiteru Nakajima／Yumi Shirahama／Tamio Takeuchi
4) Art & Graphic
5) 1981(Japan)
386 1) weather report board／pleasant
3) Akiteru Nakajima
4) Okinawa International Ocean Exhibition Association
5) 1975(Japan)
387 1) map of neighborhood／a nice restaurant
2) Akiteru Nakajima
3) Akiteru Nakajima／Yumi Shirahama
4) Art & Graphic
5) 1981(Japan)
388 1) company magazine／human relation
2),3) Kunihiko Sugiyama
4) Bunri
5) 1980(Japan)
389 1) map of neighborhood／a terrible neighbor
2) Akiteru Nakajima
3) Akiteru Nakajima／Yumi Shirahama／Tamio Takeuchi
4) Art & Graphic
5) 1981(Japan)
390 1) "Shiritori Kanji"
2),3) Yasaburo Kuwayama
4) Typo-Eye Exhibition of "A Picture Book of Letter"

5) 1977(Japan)
6) black
391 1) map of neighborhood／a house of a boy friend
2) Akiteru Nakajima
3) Akiteru Nakajima／Yumi Shirahama／Tamio Takeuchi
4) Art & Graphic
5) 1981(Japan)
392 1) hospital
2),3) Guillermo Gonzales Ruiz
4) National Children's Hospital
5) 1975(Argentina)
393 1) hospital
2),3) Guillermo Gonzales Ruiz
4) National Children's Hospital
5) 1975(Argentina)
394 1) weather report board／little discomfort
3) Akiteru Nakajima
4) Okinawa International Ocean Exhibition Association
5) 1975(Japan)
395 1) exhibition／take good care of works
2) Kenzo Nakagawa
3) Kenzo Nakagawa／Hiroyasu Nobuyama
4) Tokyo Designer's Space
5) 1980(Japan)
396 1) medicine／rash
3) Akiteru Nakajima
4) Mine Yakuhin
5) 1980(Japan)
397 1) hospital
2),3) Guillermo Gonzales Ruiz
4) National Children's Hospital
5) 1975(Argentina)
398 1) hospital
2),3) Guillermo Gonzales Ruiz
4) National Children's Hospital
5) 1975(Argentina)
399 1) hospital
2),3) Guillermo Gonzales Ruiz
4) National Children's Hospital
5) 1975(Argentina)
400 1) hospital
2),3) Guillermo Gonzales Ruiz
4) National Children's Hospital
5) 1975(Argentina)
401 1) "Shiritori Kanji"
2),3) Yasaburo Kuwayama
4) Typo-Eye Exhibition of "A Picture Book of Letter"
5) 1977(Japan)
6) black
402 1) army's medical academy／citizen・man
3) Miloš Ćirić
5) 1977(Yugoslauia)
6) red／blue／green
403 1) army's medical academy／citizen・woman
3) Miloš Ćirić
5) 1977(Yugoslava)
6) red／blue／green
404 1) army's medical academy／officer
3) Miloš Ćirić
5) 1977(Yugoslavia)
6) red／blue／green
405 1) publication(magazine)
3) Yasumasa Oka
4) Heibon Shuppan

5) 1983(Japan)
406 1) publication(magazine)
3) Yasumasa Oka
4) Heibon Shuppan
5) 1983(Japan)
407 1) medicine／for infants
3) Akiteru Nakajima
4) Mine Yakuhin
5) 1980(Japan)
408 1) sports／public hygienic service
2) Shakespear Design Studio
3) Ronald Shakespear／Paul Shakespear
4) Buenos Aires Sports Center
5) 1980(Argentina)
409 1)
2),3) Guillermo Gonzales Ruiz
4) National Children's Hospital
5) 1975(Argentina)
410 1) hospital
2),3) Guillermo Gonzales Ruiz
4) National Children's Hospital
5) 1975(Argentina)
411 1) hospital
2),3) Guillermo Gonzales Ruiz
4) National Children's Hospital
5) 1975(Argentina)
412 1) hospital
2),3) Guillermo Gonzales Ruiz
4) National Children's Hospital
5) 1975(Argentina)
413 1) hospital
2),3) Guillermo Gonzales Ruiz
4) National Children's Hospital
5) 1975(Argentina)
414 1) hospital
2),3) Guillermo Gonzales Ruiz
4) National Children's Hospital
5) 1975(Argentin)
415 1) hospital
2),3) Guillermo Gonzales Ruiz
4) National Children's Hospital
5) 1975(Argentina)
416 1) hospital
2),3) Guillermo Gonzales Ruiz
4) National Children's Hospital
5) 1975(Argentina)
417 1) company sign
3) Masanobu Watanabe
4) Mitsubishi Motors Co., Ltd. (MMC)
5) 1983(Japan)
6) dark blue(sub-color red)
418 1) put on a mask
2) Akiteru Nakajima
3) Seiko Aoki／Hisako Kataoka／Yoko Kobayashi
4) Chuo Bijutsu Gakuen Pictorial Course
5) 1983(Japan)
419 1) company sign
2) Shigeru Shimooka
3) Masanobu Watanabe
4) Mitsubishi Motors Co., Ltd. (MMC)
5) 1983(Japan)
6) dark blue(sub-color red)
420 1) hospital
2),3) Guillermo Gonzales Ruiz
4) National Children's Hospital
5) 1975(Argentina)
421 1) sports／public hygienic service
2) Shakespear Design Studio

3) Ronald Shakespear／Raul Shakespear
4) Buenos Aires Sports Center
5) 1980(Argentina)
422 1) hospital
2),3) Guillermo Gonzales Ruiz
4) National Children's Hospital
5) 1975(Argentina)
423 1) army's medical Acadamy／Doctor
3) Miloš Ćirić
5) 1977(Yugoslavia)
6) red／blue／green
424 1) army's medical academy／nurse
3) Miloš Ćirić
5) 1977(Yugoslavia)
6) red／blue／green
425 1) nurse
3) Asher Kalderon
4) Dead Sea Hot Spring Building
5) 1983(Israel)
426 1) university hospital／be quiet
2),3) PVDI
4) Guanabara State University
5) 1974(Brazil)
427 1) hospital／nurse station
2) Ichiro Saito
3) Ichiro Saito／Miyuki Hoshi
4) Itoki
5) 1983(Japan)
6) dark brown／dark green
428 1) doctor
3) Asher Kalderon
4) Dead Sea Hot Spring Building
5) 1983(Israel)
429 1) army's medical academy／fighter
3) Miloš Ćirić
5) 1977(Yugoslavia)
6) red／blue／green
430 1) book shop／movies・novels
3) Miloš Ćirić
5) 1974(Yugoslavia)
6) red
431 1) weather report board／take precautions against sunstroke
3) Akiteru Nakajima
4) Okinawa International Ocean Exhibition Association
5) 1975(Japan)
432 1) hospltal／surgery
2) Shakespear Design Studio
3) Raul Shakespear／Ronald Shakesper
4) Buenos Aires City Hospital
5) 1970／1980(Argentina)
6) red／blue
433 1) hospital／vocal remedy
2) Shakespear Design Studio
3) Raul Shakespear／Ronald Shakespear
4) Buenos Aires City Hospital
5) 1970／1980(Argentina)
6) red／blue
434 1) hospital／surgery
2) Shakespear Design Studio
3) Raul Shakespear／Ronald Shakespear
4) Buenos Aires City Hospital

5) 1970／1980(Argentina)
6) red／blue
435 1) hotel
2),3) PVDI
4) Rio Meridian Hotel
5) 1975(Brazil)
436 1) hotel
2),3) PVDI
4) Rio Meridian Hotel
5) 1975(Brazil)
437 1) signs in a camera
company／watch above your
head
2) Ken Nara／Akiteru Nakajima
3) Akiteru Nakajima／Ryoichi
Yamada／Kumi Shirahama
4) Canon
5) 1974(Japan)
438 1) Electoronic program
2),3) Ludvik Feller
5) 1974(West germany)
439 1) sports／public hygienic
service
2) Shakespear Design Studio
3) Ronald Shakespear／Raul
Shakespear
4) Buenos Aires Sports Center
5) 1980(Argentina)
440 1) sports／public hygienic
service
2) Shakespear Design Studio
3) Ronald Shakespear／Raul
Shakespear
4) Buenos Aires Sports Center
5) 1980(Argentina)
441 2),3) Ludvik Feller
4) CEDEFOP
5) 1979(West Germany)
442 1) map of neighborhood／
an elementary school
2) Akiteru Nakajima
3) Akiteru Nakajima／Yumi
Shirahama／Tamio Takeuchi
4) Art & Graphic
5) 1981(Japan)
443 1) map of neighborhood／
police box
2) Akiteru Nakajira
3) Akiteru Nakajima／Yumi
Shirahama／Tamio Takeuchi
4) Art & Graphic
5) 1981(Japan)
444 1) sign in a camera
company／the other fire
equipment
2) Ken Nara／Akiteru Nakajima
3) Akiteru Nakajima／Ryoichi
Yamada／Kumi Shirahama
4) Canon
5) 1974(Japan)
445 1) safety & hygiene／safety
cap
2),3) Tokyo Shibaura Denki
Design Department
4) Tokyo Shibaura Denki
5) 1975(Japan)
6) yellow／black(partly white ·
red)
446 1) graphic indication of a
detergent／for nomal hair
2) Akiteru Nakajima
3) Seiko Aoki／Hisako
Kataoka／Yoko Kobayashi
4) Chuo Bijutsu Gakuen Pictorial
Course

5) 1983(Japan)
447 1) graphic indication of a
detergent／for dandruffy hair
2) Akiteru Nakajima
3) Seiko Aoki／Hisako
Kataoka／Yoko Kobayashi
4) Chuo Bijutsu Gakuen Pictorial
Course
5) 1983(Japan)
448 1) graphic indication of a
detergent／for permed hair
2) Akiteru Nakajima
3) Seiko Aoki／Hisako
Kataoka／Yoko Kobayashi
4) Chuo Bijutsu Gakuen Pictorial
Course
5) 1983(Japan)
449 2),3) Ludvik Feller
4) Cedefop
5) 1979(West germany)
450 3) Asher Kalderon
4) Dead Sea Hot Spring
Building
5) 1983(Israel)
451 1) hospital
2),3) Guillermo Gonzales Ruiz
4) National Children's Hospital
5) 1975(Argentina)
452 1) advertisement in the
paper
2) Takashi Onoe
3) Takao Yoguchi
4) KDD
5) 1980(Japan)
453 1) advertisement in the
paper
2) Takashi Onoe
3) Takao Yoguchi
4) KDD
5) 1980(Japan)
454 1) advertisement in the
paper
2) Takashi Onoe
3) Takao Yoguchi
4) KDD
5) 1980(Japan)
455 1) poison
2),3) PVDI
4) Copek Oil Co., Ltd.
5) 1974(Brazil)
456 1) signs in a camera
company／poison
2) Ken Nara／Akiteru Nakajima
3) Akiteru Nakajima／Ryoichi
Yamada／Kumi Shirahama
4) Canon
5) 1974(Japan)
457 1) medicine／violent poison
3) Akiteru Nakajima
4) Mine Yakuhin
5) 1980(Japan)
458 1) hospital
2),3) Joe Dieter
4) The John Hopkins Hospital
5) 1982(U.S.A.)
6) navy blue
459 1) company sign
2) Shigeru Shimooka
3) Masanobu Watanabe
4) Mitsubishi Motors Co., Ltd.
(MMC)
5) 1983(Japan)
6) dark blue(sub-color red)
460 1) seats for spectators
2),3) Syuji Torigoe

4) The Gunma Prefectual Office
5) 1981(Japan)
461 1) sports／public hygienic
service
2) Shakespear Design Studio
3) Ronald Shakespear／Raul
Shakespear
4) Buenos Aires Sports Center
5) 1980(Argentina)
462 2),3) Ludvik Feller
5) 1974(West Germany)
463 1) "Shiritori Kanji"
2),3) Yasaburo Kuwayama
4) Typo-Eye Exhibition of "A
Picture Book of Letter"
5) 1977(Japan)
6) black
464 1) the iris
2),3) Kunihiko Sugiyama
4) Kensu Shoin
5) 1978(Japan)
465 1) hospital／ophthalmology
2) Shakespear Design Studio
3) Raul Shakespear／Ronald
Shakespear
4) Buenos Aires City Hospital
5) 1970／1980(Argentina)
6) red／blue
466 1) medicine／for eyes
3) Akiteru Nakajima
4) Mine Yakuhin
5) 1980(Japan)
467 1) hospital／ophthalmology
2) Ichiro Saito
3) Ichiro Saito／Miyuki Hoshi
4) Itoki
5) 1983(Japan)
6) dark brown／dark green
468 1) book store／detective
novels
3) Miloš Ćirić
5) 1974(Yugoslavia)
6) red
469 1) airport／customhouse
2) Ernest Lehfeld
3) Emest Lehfeld／Manuel
Sanchez／Francisco Gallardo／
Jorge Ferunandez
4) Mexico Airport
5) 1977-78(Mexico)
6) black yellow(ground)
470 1) the lachrymal gland
2),3) Kunihiko Sugiyama
4) Kensu Shyoin
5) 1978(Japan)
471 1) graphic indication of a
detergent
2) Akiteru Nakajima
3) Seiko Aoki／Hisako
Kataoka／Yoko Kobayashi
4) Chuo Bijutsu Gakuen Pictorial
Course
5) 1983(Japan)
472 1) proverb cards
2),3) Yuji Baba
4) Uni Design Co., Ltd.
5) 1976(Japan)
473 1) map of neighborhood
2) Akiteru Nakajima
3) Akiteru Nakajima／Yumi
Shirahama／Tamio Takeuchi
4) Art & Graphic
5) 1981(Japan)
474 1) sign in a camera
company／look on both sides

2) Ken Nara／Akiteru Nakajima
3) Akiteru Nakajima／Ryoichi
Yamada／Kumi Shirahama
4) Canon
5) 1974(Japan)
475 1) the electronic
(television, video-tape,
audio-tape)／ear-phone
476 1) safety & hygiene／
ear-plug
2),3) Tokyo Shibaura Denki
Design Depertment
4) Tokyo Shibaura Denki
5) 1975(Japan)
6) yellow／black(partly white ·
red)
477 1) encyclopedic yearbook／
column "language"
2) Kenzo Nakagawa
3) Satoshi Morikami
4) Heibonsha
5) 1980(Japan)
468 1) encyclopedic yearbook／
colum "language"
2) Kenzo Nakagawa
3) Satoshi Morikami
4) Heibonsha
5) 1980(Japan)
479 2),3) Ludvik Feller
5) 1974(West Germany)
480 1) "Shiritori Kanji"
2),3) Yasaburo Kuwayama
4) Typo-Eye Exhibition of "A
Picture Book of Letter"
5) 1977(Japan)
6) black
481 1) text of the preparatory
school(English)
2),3) Kunihiko Sugiyama
4) Yoyogi Seminar
5) 1982(Japan)
482 1) food／don't eat
2) Akiteru Nakajima
3) Akira Yagi／Takeshi Ogawa／
Toru Konno／Hideko Kurihara／
Keiko Komazawa
4) Chuo Bijutsu Gakuen Pictorial
Corse
5) 1983(Japan)
483 1) "Shiritori Kanji"
2),3) Yasaburo Kuwayama
4) Typo-Eye Exhihition of "A
Picture Book of Letter"
5) 1977(Japan)
6) black
484 1) no talking
2) Hajime Nakamura／Yasaburo
Kuwayama
3) Yasaburo Kuwayama／Hajime
Ikeda／Norio Ikeda
4) The Regional Meeting of
Jehovah's Witnesses
5) 1980(Japan)
485 1) library／no chatting
2) Takenobu Igarashi
3) Akiteru Nakajima／Kumi
Shirahama
4) Keio Gijuku University
5) 1982(Japan)
486 1) medicine
3) Akiteru Nakajima
4) Mine Yakuhin
5) 1980(Japan)
487 1) proverb cards／

double-tongue
2),3) Yuji Baba
4) Uni Design Co., Ltd.
5) 1976(Japan)
488 1) hospital／
otorhinolaryngology
2) Ichiro Saito
3) Ichiro Saito／Miyuki Hoshi
4) Itoki
5) 1983(Japan)
6) dark Brown／Dark Green
489 1) sports／public hygienic
service
2) Shakespear Design Studio
3) Ronald Shakespear／Raul
Shakespear
4) Buenos Aires Sports Center
5) 1980(Argentina)
490 1) hospital／dentistry
2) Shakespear Design Studio
3) Raul Shakespear／Ronald
Shakespear
4) Buenos Aires City Hospital
5) 1970／1980(Argentina)
6) red／blue
491 1) medicine／for teeth
3) Akiteru Nakajima
4) Mine Yakuhin
5) 1980(Japan)
492 1) hospital／dentistry
2) Ichiro Saito
3) Ichiro Saito／Miyuki Hoshi
4) Itoki
5) 1983(Japan)
6) dark brown／dark green
493 1) talking clock
2),3) Asher Kalderon
5) 1983(Israel)
494 1) medicine
／for nose
3) Akiteru Nakajima
4) Mine Yakuhin
5) 1980(Japan)
495 2) Jan Railich
3) Jan Rajlich Jr.
4) CSVD
5) 1973(Czechoslovakia)
496 2),3) Ludvik Feller
5) 1974(West Germany)
497 3) Adrian Frutiger
4) Air France
5) France
498 1) publication(magazine)
3) Yasumasa Oka
4) Heibon Shuppan
5) 1983(Japan)
499 1) management
2) Helmut M. Schmitt-Siegel
4) European Management
Center
5) 1970(West Germany)
500 1) books
3) Yasumasa Oka
4) Shueisha
5) 1983(Japan)
501 1) sign in a camera
company／a course guide for
observers
2) Ken Nara／Akiteru Nakajima
3) Akiteru Nakajima／Ryoichi
Yamada／Kumi Shirahama
4) Canon
5) 1974(Japan)
502 1) university hospital／no
entrance

2),3) PVDI
4) Guanabara State University
5) 1974(Brazil)
503 1) "Shiritori Kanji"
2),3) Yasaburo Kuwayama
4) Typo-Eye Exhibition of "A
Picture Book of Letter"
5) 1977(Japan)
6) black
504 1) sign in a company
2) Shigeru Shimooka
3) Masanobu Watanabe
4) Mitsubishi Motors Co., Ltd.
(MMC)
5) 1983(Japan)
6) dark blue(sub-color red)
505 1) publication(practical
book)／cover and title page
3) Yutaka Hasegawa
4) Syufu to Seikatusha
5) 1982(Japan)
506 1) hospital
2) Shakespear Design Studio
3) Raul Shakespear／Ronald
Shakespear
4) Buenos Aires City Hospital
5) 1970／1980(Argentina)
6) red／blue
507 1) text of the preparatory
school(English)
2),3) Kunihiko Sugiyama
4) Yoyogi Seminar
5) 1982(Japan)
508 1) thin-type
2) Koichi Nishimura
3) Yoshimi Segawa
4) Matsushita Tsushin Kogyo
5) 1980(Japan)
509 1) ocean exhibition／ticket
booth
2) Masaru Katsumi／Akiteru
Nakajima
3) Teruyuki Kunito／Yukio Ota／
Akira Kuroyone
4) Okinawa International Ocean
Exhibition Association
5) 1975(Japan)
510 1) event(space show)／
ticket office
2),3) Noriaki Tamura
4) Headquarters Japan
International Aerospace Show
1979
5) 1979(Japan)
6) sky blue
511 1) airport／passenger
documents・passport
2) Ernest Lehfeld
3) Ernest Lehfeld／Manuel
Sanchez／Francisco Gallardo／
Jorge Fernandez
4) Mexico
5) 1977-78(Mexico)
6) black／yellow(ground)
512 1) delivery service
2),3) PVDI
4) Empresa Brasileira de
Correiose Telégrafos
5) 1971(Brazil)
513 1) management
2) Helmut M. Schmitt-Siegel
4) European Management
Center
5) 1970(West Germany)
514 1) management

2) Helmut M. Schmitt-Siegel
4) European Management
Center
5) 1970(West Germany)
515 1) democratics & the
japanese administration／ballot
box
2),3) Kunihiko Sugiyama
4) Bunri
5) 1979(Japan)
516 2),3) Ludvik Feller
5) 1974(West Germany)
517 1) pen
2),3) Kunihiko Sugiyama
4) Bunri
5) 1979(Japan)
518 1) publication(practical
book)／cover and title page
3) Yutaka Hasegawa
4) Syufu to Seikatsusha
5) 1982(Japan)
519 1) management
2) Helmut M. Schmitt-Siegel
4) European Management
Center
5) 1970(West Germany)
520 1) airport
2) Ernest Lehfeld
3) Ernest Lehfeld／Manuel
Sanchez／Francisco Gallardo／
Jorge Fernandez
4) Mexico Airport
5) 1977-78(Mexico)
6) black／yellow(ground)
521 1) food／shake
2) Akiteru Nakajima
3) Akira Yagi／Takeshi Ogawa／
Toru Konno／Hideko Kurihara／
Keiko Komazawa
4) Chuo Bijutsu Gakuen Pictorial
Course
5) 1980(Japan)
522 1) graphic indication of a
detergent／shake
2) Akiteru Nakajima
3) Seiko Aoki／Hisako
Kataoka／Yoko Kobayashi
4) Chuo Bijutsu Gakuen Pictorial
Course
5) 1983(Japan)
523 1) company sign
2) Shigeru Shimooka
3) Masanobu Watanabe
4) Mitsubishi Motors Co., Ltd.
(MMC)
5) 1983(Japan)
6) dark blue(sub-color red)
524 1) office articles
2),3) Yoshihiro Kishimoto
4) Karu Jimuki
5) 1977(Japan)
525 1) shopping center／
Service
2),3) Syuji Torigoe
4) Tokyu Store
5) 1976(Japan)
526 1) books
2),3) Kunihiko Sugiyama
4) Bunri
5) 1979(Japan)
527 1) books
2),3) Kunihiko Sugiyama
4) Bunri
5) 1979(Japan)

528 1) management
2) Helmut M. Schmitt-Siegel
4) European Management
Center
5) 1970(West Germany)
529 1) sign in a camera
company／washing hands・
drinking water
2) Ken Nara／Akiteru Nakajima
3) Akiteru Nakajima／Ryoichi
Yamada／Kumi Shirahama
4) Canon
5) 1974(Japan)
530 1) supermarket／wash your
hands
2),3) Takao Yoguchi
4) Chujitsuya
5) 1979(Japan)
531 1) airport／hygiene
(washing hands)
2) Ernest Lehfeld
3) Ernest Lehfeld／Manuel
Sanchez／Francisco Gallardo／
Jorge Fernandez
4) Mexico Airport
5) 1977-78(Mexico)
6) black／yellow(ground)
532 1) safety & hygiene／wash
your hands
2),3) Tokyo Shibaura Denki
Design Department
4) Tokyo Shibaura Denki
5) 1975(Japan)
6) yellow／black(partly white・
red)
533 1) sign in a camera
company／switch
2) Ken Nara／Akiteru Nakajima
3) Akiteru Nakajima／Ryoichi
Yamada／Kumi Shirahama
4) Canon
5) 1974(Japan)
534 1) office articles(products
and package)
2),3) Yoshihiro Kishimoto
4) Karu Jimuki
5) 1977(Japan)
535 1) Ruedi Rüegg
5) 1983(Switzerland)
536 1) wired・remote control
2) Koichi Nishimura
3) Yoshimi Segawa
4) Matsushita Tsushin Kogyo
5) 1981(Japan)
537 1) wireless・remote control
2) Koichi Nishimura
3) Yoshimi Segawa
4) Matsushita Tsushin Kogyo
5) 1981(Japan)
538 1) publication(thesaurus)／
bag
2),3) Kunihiko Sugiyama
4) Kodansha
5) 1983(Japan)
539 1) publication(thesaurus)／
ruler
2),3) Kunihiko Sugiyama
4) Kodansha
5) 1983(Japan)
540 1) department store／
smoking room
3) Shigeo Fukuda
4) Seibu Department Store
5) 1976(Japan)
541 1) supermarket／smoking

room
2),3) Syuji Torigoe
4) Tokyu Store
5) 1976(Japan)
542 1) safety & hygiene⁄smoking room
2),3) Tokyo Shibaura Denki Design Department
4) Tokyo Shibaura Denki
5) 1975(Japan)
6) yellow⁄black(partly white・red)
543 1) medicine⁄hurt
3) Akiteru Nakajima
4) Mine Yakuhin
5) 1980(Japan)
544 1) sports⁄public hygienic service
2) Shakespear Design Studio
3) Ronald Shakespear⁄Raul Shakespear
4) Buenos Aires Sports Center
5) 1980(Argentina)
545 1) first-aid treatment(trial)
2) Tadashi Ikeda
3) Kenichi Ikeda⁄Seiji Masuike
4) 1988 Seoul Olympiad
5) 1982(Japan)
6) black
546 3) Ruedi Rüegg
5) 1983(Switzerland)
547 1) department store
3) Shigeo Fukuda
4) Seibu Department Store
5) 1976(Japan)
548 1) airport⁄first-aid
2) Ernest Lehfeld
3) Ernest Lehfeld⁄Manuel Sanchez⁄Francisco Gallardo⁄Jorge Fernandez
4) Mexico Airport
5) 1977-78(Mexico)
6) black⁄yellow(ground)
549 1) first-aid station
2),3) Syuji Torigoe
4) The Gunma Prefectual Office
5) 1981(Japan)
550 1) University Hospital⁄first-aid
2),3) PVDI
4) Guanabara State University
5) 1974(Brazil)
551 1) ocean exhibition⁄electric shock
2) Masaru Katsumi⁄Akiteru Nakajima
3) Teruyuki Kunito⁄Yukio Ota⁄Akira Kuroyone
4) Okinawa International Ocean Exhibition Association
5) 1975(Japan)
552 1) company sign
2) Shigeru Shimooka
3) Masanobu Watanabe
4) Mitsubishi Motors Co., Ltd. (MMC)
5) 1983(Japan)
6) dark blue(sub-color red)
553 1) safety & hygiene⁄don't touch
2),3) Tokyo Shibaura Denki Design Department
4) Tokyo Shibaura Denki
5) 1975(Japan)
6) yellow⁄black(partly white・red)
554 1) food⁄don't push with fingers
2) Akiteru Nakajima
3) Akira Yagi⁄Takeshi Ogawa⁄Toru Konno⁄Hideko Kurihara⁄Keiko Komazawa
4) Chuo Bijutsu Gakuen Pictorial Course
5) 1980(Japan)
555 1) copying machine⁄don't touch
5) 1980(Japan)
556 1) don't touch
2) Akiteru Nakajima
3) Akiteru Nakajima⁄Kumi Shirahama
4) The Iraqi Government
5) 1981⁄1982(Japan)
557 1) medicine⁄for fatigue
3) Akiteru Nakajima
4) Mine Yakuhin
5) 1980(Japan)
558 1) racket
2),3) Kunihiko Sugiyama
4) Bunri
5) 1979(Japan)
559 1) guitar
2),3) Kunihiko Sugiyama
4) Bunri
5) 1979(Japan)
560 1) company magazine an outward force
2),3) Kunihiko Sugiyama
4) Bunri
5) 1980(Japan)
561 1) "A Picture Book of A-I-U-E-O"⁄handshake
2),3) Yasaburo Kuwayama
4) Typo-Eye Exhibition of "Kami no Mojikku"
5) 1979(Japan)
562 1) text of the preparatory school⁄handshake
3) Kunihiko Sugiyama
4) Yoyogi Seminar
5) 1982(Japan)
563 1) airport⁄handshake
2),3) Yasaburo Kuwayama
4) Shin Tokyo Kokusai Kuko
5) 1973(Japan)
564 1) a guide book of teaching⁄handshake
2),3) Kunihiko Sugiyama
4) Tokyo Shoseki
5) 1978(Japan)
565 1) encyclopedia⁄friend
2) Katsuichi Ito
3) Katsuich Ito Design Studio
4) Tamagawa University Pablishing Part
5) 1979(Japan)
566 2) Ludvik Feller
4) Cedefop
5) 1979(West Germany)
567 1) japan in the world
2),3) Kunihiko Sugiyama
4) Bunri
5) 1979(Japan)
568 1) signs in a camera company⁄handle with care
2) Ken Nara⁄Akiteru Nakajima
3) Akiteru Nakajima⁄Ryoichi Yamada⁄Kumi Shirahama
4) Canon
5) 1974(Japan)
569 1) publication(magazine)
3) Yasumasa Oka
4) Heibon Shuppan
5) 1983(Japan)
570 1) copying machine⁄water
5) 1980(Japan)
571 1) watch your step
2),3) PVDI
4) Copek Oil Co., Ltd.
5) 1974(Brazil)
572 1) sign in a camera company
2) Ken Nara⁄Akiteru Nakajima
3) Akiteru Nakajima⁄Ryoich Yamada⁄Kunihiko Sugiyama
4) Canon
5) 1974(Japan)
573 1) foot-switch
2) Koichi Nishimura
3) Yoshimi Segawa
4) Matsushita Tsushin Kogyo
5) 1980(Japan)
574 1) "shiritori kanji"
3) Yasaburo Kuwayama
4) Typo-Eye Exhibition of "A Picture Book of Letter"
5) 1977(Japan)
6) black
575 1) text of the preparatory school⁄the world history
3) Akiteru Nakajima
4) Yoyogi Seminar
5) 1982(Japan)
576 1) sports⁄public hygienic service
2) Shakespear Design Studio
3) Ronald Shakespear⁄Raul Shakespear
4) Buenos Aires Sports Center
5) 1980(Argentina)
577 1) lung
2),3) Kunihiko Sugiyama
4) Kensu Shoin
5) 1978(Japan)
578 1) the organization of poly-cellular
2),3) Kunihiko Sugiyama
4) Bunri
5) 1979(Japan)
579 3) Ruedi Rüegg
5) 1983(Switzerland)
580 1) medicine⁄bowels
3) Akiteru Nakajima
4) Mine Yakuhin
5) 1980(Japan)
581 1) publication(thesaurus)⁄man
2),3) Kunihiko Sugiyama
4) Kodansha
5) 1983(Japan)
582 1) sports⁄public hygienic service
2) Shakespear Design Studio
3) Ronald Shakespear⁄Raul Shakespear
4) Buenos Aires Sports Center
5) 1980(Argentina)
583 1) stomach・small intestine・pancrea
2),3) Kunihiko Sugiyama
4) Kensu Shoin
5) 1978(Japan)
584 1) rectum
2),3) Kunihiko Sugiyama
5) 1974(Japan)
585 1) hospital⁄urology
2) Shakespear Design Studio
3) Raul Shakespear⁄Ronald Shakespear
4) Bunenos Aires City Hospital
5) 1970⁄1980(Argentina)
6) red⁄blue
586 1) hospital
2) Shakespear Design Studio
3) Raul Shakespear⁄Ronald Shakespear
4) Buenos Aires City Hospital
5) 1970⁄1980(Argentina)
6) red⁄blue
587 1) sports⁄public hygienic service
2) Shakespear Design Studio
3) Ronald Shakespear⁄Raul Shakespear
4) Buenos Aires Sports Center
5) 1980(Argentina)
588 1) medicine⁄stomach
3) Akiteru Nakajima
4) Mine Yakuhin
5) 1980(Japan)
589 1) heart
2),3) Kunihiko Sugiyama
4) Kensu Shoin
5) 1978(Japan)
590 1) medicine⁄ladies
3) Akiteru Nakajima
4) Mine Yakuhin
5) 1980(Japan)
591 1) university hospital x-ray
2),3) PVDI
4) Guanabara State University
5) 1974(Brazil)
592 1) encyclopedia⁄beast
2) Katsuichi Ito
3) Katsuichi Ito Design Studio
4) Tamagawa University Publishing Part
5) 1979(Japan)
593 1) zoo⁄lion
2),3) PVDI
5) 1976(Brazil)
594 1) map of neighborhood⁄a domain of fierce animals
2) Akiteru Nakajima
3) Akiteru Nakajima⁄Yumi Shirahama⁄Tamio Takeuchi
4) Art & Graphic
5) 1981(Japan)
595 1) products⁄the lion
2),3) Shigeji Kobayashi
4) The Lion Sekken Co., Ltd.
5) 1981(Japan)
596 1) lion
2) Fumio Inoue
3) Chikako Inoue
4) The Design House Carrot
5) 1980(Japan)
6) pink(DIC 28)
597 1) game
2),3) Yoshihiro Yoshida
4) Typo Eye
5) 1976(Japan)
598 1) zoo⁄lion
2) Joao Carlos Cauduro⁄Ludovico Antono Martino
5) 1972⁄1973(Brazil)
599 1) print goods⁄lion
2) Yasaburo Kuwayama

3) Minoru Kamono
4) Sutamu Print(Kyodo Insatsu)
5) 1978(Japan)
600 1) "wonderful animals"/ tiger
2),3) Yasaburo Kuwayama
4) Typo-Eye Exhibition of "A Picture Book of Letter"
5) 1977(Japan)
6) black
601 1) zoo/leopard
2),3) PVDI
5) 1976(Brazil)
602 1) "wonderful animals"/ snow leopard
2),3) Yasaburo Kuwayama
4) Typo-Eye Exhibition of "A Picture Book of Letter"
5) 1977(Japan)
6) black
603 1) zoo/elephant
2) Joao Carlos Cauduro/ Ludovico Antonio Martino
5) 1972/1973(Brazil)
604 1) elephant
2) Fumio Inoue
3) Chikako Inoue
4) The Design House Carrot
5) 1980(Japan)
6) pink(DIC 28)
605 1) "wonderful animals"/ elephant
2),3) Yasaburo Kuwayama
4) Typo-Eye Exhibition of "A Picture Book of Letter"
5) 1977(Japan)
6) black
606 1) zoo/elephant
2),3) PVDI
5) 1976(Brazil)
607 1) game/elephant
2),3) Yoshihiro Yoshida
4) Typo Eye
5) 1976(Japan)
608 1) hippopotamus
2) Fumio Inoue
3) Chikako Inoue
4) The Design House Carrot
5) 1980(Japan)
6) pink(DIC 28)
609 1) zoo/hippopotamus
2),3) PVDI
5) 1976(Brazil)
610 1) rhinoceros
2) Fumio Inoue
3) Chikako Inoue
4) The Design House Carrot
5) 1980(Japan)
6) pink(DIC 28)
611 1) "wonderful animals"/ rhinoceros
2),3) Yasaburo Kuwayama
4) Typo-Eye Exhibition of "A Picture Book of Letter"
5) 1977(Japan)
6) black
612 1) game/rhinoceros
2),3) Yoshihiro Yoshida
4) Typo Eye
5) 1976(Japan)
613 1) bear
2) Fumio Inoue
3) Chikako Inoue
4) The Design House Carrot
5) 1980(Japan)

6) pink(DIC 28)
614 1) zoo/bear
2),3) PVDI
5) 1976(Brazil)
615 1) "wonderful animals"/ koala
2),3) Yasaburo Kuwayama
4) Typo-Eye Exhibition of "A Picture Book of Letter"
5) 1977(Japan)
6) black
616 1) koala
2) Fumio Inoue
3) Chikako Ionue
4) The Design House Carrot
5) 1980(Japan)
6) pink(DIC 28)
617 1) giraffe
2) Fumio Inoue
3) Chikako Inoue
4) The Desion House Carrot
5) 1980(Japan)
6) pink(DIC 28)
618 1) "wonderful animals"/ giraffe
2),3) Yasaburo Kuwayama
4) Typo-Eye Exhibition of "A Picture Book of Letter"
5) 1977(Japan)
6) black
619 1) "wonderful animals"/ Kangaroo
2),3) Yasaburo Kuwayama
4) Typo-Eye Exhibition of "A Picture Book of Letter"
5) 1977(Japan)
6) black
620 1) exhibition/kangaroo
2) Kenzo Nakagawa
3) Kenzo Nakagawa/Satoshi Morikami
4) Tokyo Designers Space
5) 1980(Japan)
621 3) Istvan Szekeres
4) Service House
5) 1970(Hungary)
6) black
622 1) zoo/zebra
2),3) PVDI
5) 1976(Brazil)
623 1) prints/new year's card
3) Toshio Sonohara
4) Sonohara Toshio Design Studio
5) 1980(Japan)
624 1) "Monomino To" Centanial
2) Yasaburo Kuwayama
3) Yasaburo Kuwayama/Hajime Ikeda
4) Jehovah's Witnesses
5) 1979(Japan)
625 1) "wonderful animals"/ gibbon
2),3) Yasaburo Kuwayama
4) Typo-Eye Exhibition of "A Picture Book of Letter"
5) 1977(Japan)
6) black
626 1) zoo/chimpanzee
2),3) PVDI
5) 1976(Brazil)
627 1) zoo/monkey
2),3) PVDI
5) 1976(Brazil)

628 1) zoo/monkey
2) Joao Carlos Cauduro/ Ludovico Antonio Martino
5) 1972/1973(Brazil)
629 1) game/alligator
2),3) Yoshihiro Yoshida
4) Typo Eye
5) 1976(Japan)
630 1) zoo/anteater
2),3) PVDI
5) 1976(Brazil)
631 1) greeting cards/boar
3) Takao Yoguchi
4) Holbein Gazai
5) 1982(Japan)
632 1) greeting cards/boar
3) Takao Yoguchi
4) Holbein Gazai
5) 1982(Japan)
633 1) game/fox
2),3) Yoshihiro Yoshida
4) Typo Eye
5) 1976(Japan)
634 1) hcdgchog
2) Fumio Inoue
3) Chikako Inoue
4) The Design House Carrot
5) 1980(Japan)
6) pink(DIC 28)
635 1) game/skunk
2),3) Yoshihiro Yoshida
4) Typo Eye
5) 1976(Japan)
636 1) pet equipment(produce)/how to keep a pet
2) Motoki Hiramatsu
3) Isato Nakamura
4) Midori Shobo
5) 1982(Japan)
637 1) a fur seal
2) Fumio Inoue
3) Chikako Inoue
4) The Design House Carrot
5) 1980(Japan)
6) pink(DIC 28)
638 1) food/keep in cold storage
3) Akiteru Nakajima
4) Chuo Bijutsu Gakuen Pictorial Course
5) (Japan)
639 1) ocean exhibition/ beware of habus
2) Masaru Katsumi/Akiteru Nakajima
3) Teruyuki Kunito/Yukio Ota/ Akira Kuroyone
4) Okinawa International Ocean Exhibition Association
5) 1975(Japan)
6) fluorescent yellow/ red(5R4/14)
640 1) zoo/snake
2),3) PVDI
5) 1976(Brazil)
641 1) "wonderful animals"/ snake
2),3) Yasaburo Kuwayama
4) Typo-Eye Exhibition of "A Picture Book of Letter"
5) 1977(Japan)
6) black
642 1) "A Picture Book of A-I-U-E-O"/striped snake

2),3) Yasaburo Kuwayama
4) Typo-Eye Exhibition of "Kami no Mojikku"
5) 1979(Japan)
643 1) "A Picture Book of A-I-U-E-O"/cobra
2),3) Yasaburo Kuwayama
4) Typo-Eye Exhibition of "Kami no Mojikku"
5) 1979(Japan)
644 1) snake
2) Fumio Inoue
3) Chikako Inoue
4) The Design House Carrot
5) 1980(Japan)
6) pink(DIC 28)
645 1) sign in camera company/slow down
2) Ken Nara/Akiteru Nakajima
3) Akiteru Nakajima/Ryoich Yamada/Kumi Shirahama
4) Canon
5) 1974(Japan)
646 1) pet equipment(produce)/how to keep a pet
2) Motoki Hiramatsu
3) Isato Nakamura
4) Midori Shobo
5) 1982(Japan)
647 1) turtle
2) Fumio Inoue
3) Chikako Inoue
4) The Design House Carrot
5) 1980(Japan)
6) pink(DIC 28)
648 1) facilities in a resort/ pool
2) Wataru Tsuchiya/Kenzo Nakagawa
3) Kenzo Nakagawa/Hiroyasu Nobuyama/Satoshi Morikami
4) Manza Beach Resort
5) 1982(Japan)
649 1) facilities in a resort/ pavilion
2) Wataru Tsuchiya/Kenzo Nakagawa
3) Kenzo Nakagawa/Hiroyasu Nobuyama/Satoshi Morikami
4) Manza Beach Resort
5) 1982(Japan)
650 1) facilities in a resort/ tennis court
2) Wataru Tsuchiya/Kenzo Nakagawa
3) Kenzo Nakagawa/Hiroyasu Nobuyama/Satoshi Morikami
4) Manza Beach Resort
5) 1982(Japan)
651 1) facilities in a resort/ restaurant
2) Wataru Tsuchiya/Kenzo Nakagawa
3) Kenzo Nakagawa/Hiroyasu Nobuyama/Satoshi Morikami
4) Manza Beach Resort
5) 1982(Japan)
652 1) facilities in a resort/ shower bath
2) Wataru Tsuchiya/Kenzo Nakagawa
3) Kenzo Nakagawa/Hiroyasu Nobuyama/Satoshi Morikami
4) Manza Beach Resort

5) 1982(Japan)
653 1) facilities in a resort／a first-aid station
2) Wataru Tsuchiya／Kenzo Nakagawa
3) Kenzo Nakagawa／Hiroyasu Nobuyama／Satoshi Morikami
4) Manza Beach Resort
5) 1982(Japan)
654 1) facilities in a resort
2) Wataru Tsuchiya／Kenzo Nakagawa
3) Kenzo Nakagawa／Hiroyasu Nobuyama／Satoshi Morikami
4) Manza Beach Resort
5) 1982(Japan)
655 1) facilities in a resort／ladie's room
2) Wataru Tsuchiya／Kenzo Nakagawa
3) Kenzo Nakagawa／Hiroyasu Nobuyama／Satoshi Morikami
4) Manza Beach Resort
5) 1982(Japan)
656 1) facilities in a resort／mens room
2) Wataru Tsuchiya／Kenzo Nakagawa
3) Kenzo Nakagawa／Hiroyasu Nobuyama／Satoshi Morikami
4) Manza Beach Resort
5) 1982(Japan)
657 1) "wonderful animals"／frog
2),3) Yasaburo Kuwayama
4) Typo-Eye Exhibition of "A Picture Book of Letter"
5) 1977(Japan)
6) black
658 1) playing facilities／golf
2),3) Yasuhiko Shibukawa
4) Komatsubara-Kenshu-Jigyodan
5) 1978(Japan)
659 1) playing facilities／vollybdl
2),3) Yasuhiko Shibukawa
4) Komatsubara-Kenshu-Jigyodan
5) 1978(Japan)
660 1) playing facilities／tennis
2),3) Yasuhiko Shibukawa
4) Komatsubara-Kenshu-Jigyodan
5) 1978(Japan)
661 1) playing facilities／golf
2),3) Yasuhiko Shibukawa
4) Komatsubara-Kenshu-Jigyodan
5) 1978(Japan)
662 1) playing facilities
2),3) Yasuhiko Shibukawa
4) Komatsubara-Kenshu-Jigyodan
5) 1978(Japan)
663 1) prints(calendar)
2) Teruo Fujishige
3) Teruo Fujishige／Tomoko Fujimoto
4) Group PARO 407
5) 1981(Japan)
664 1) map of a realty dealer／farm
2),3) Akiteru Nakajima
4) Anterope Valley Investment

Company
5) 1976(Japan)
665 1) cow
2),3) Kunihiko Sugiyama
4) Burni
5) 1979(Japan)
666 1) milch cow
2),3) Kunihiko Sugiyama
4) Bunri
5) 1979(Japan)
667 1) cow
2) Akiteru Nakajima
3) Akiteru Nakajima／Yoichi Moroishi／Kumi Shirahama
4) Hakugen
5) 1978／1980(Japan)
668 1) food／beef
3) Akiteru Nakajima
4) Chuo Bijutsu Gakuen Pictorial Course
5) (Japan)
669 1) tools／the bull
3) Istvan Szekeres
5) 1975(Hungary)
670 1) supermarket／cow
2),3) Takao Yoguchi
4) Chujitsuya
5) 1979(Japan)
671 1) cow
3) Istvan Szekeres
5) 1980(Hungary)
6) blue
672 1) encyclopedia／cattle
2) Kastuichi Ito
3) Kastuichi Ito Design Studio
4) Tamagawa University Publishing Part
5) 1979(Japan)
673 1) supermarket／cow
2) Shakespear Design Studio
3) Ronald Shapespear／Raul Shakespear
4) Disco Supermarket
5) 1982／1983(Argentina)
674 1) cow
2) Akiteru Nakajima
3) Akiteru Nakajima／Yoich Moroishi／Kumi Shirahama
4) Hakugen
5) 1978／1980(Japan)
675 1) "Shiritori Kanji"
2),3) Yasaburo Kuwayama
4) Typo-Eye Exhibition of "A Picture Book of Letter"
5) 1977(Japan)
6) black
676 1) "wonderful animals"／donkey
2),3) Yasaburo Kuwayama
4) Typo-Eye Exhibition of "A Picture Book of Letter"
5) 1977(Japan)
6) black
677 1) publication(practical book)／cover and title page
3) Yutaka Hasegawa
4) Shufu to Seikatusha
5) 1982(Japan)
678 1) horse
3) Istvan Szekeres
5) 1980(Hungary)
6) blue
679 1) playing facilities
2),3) Yasuhiko Shibukawa
4) Komatsubara-Kenshu-

Jigyodan
5) 1978(Japan)
680 1) print ariticle／two horses
2) Yasaburo Kuwayama
3) Minoru Kamono
4) Sutamu Print(Kyodo Insatsu)
5) 1978(Japan)
681 1) "wonderful animals"
2),3) Yasaburo Kuwayama
4) Typo-Eye Exhibition of "A Picture Book of Letter"
5) 1977(Japan)
6) black
682 1) zoo／camel
2),3) PVDI
5) 1976(Brazil)
683 1) sheep
2),3) Kunihiko Sugiyama
4) Bunri
5) 1979(Japan)
684 1) "wonderful animals"／sheep
2),3) Yasaburo Kuwayama
4) Typo-Eye Exhibition of "A Picture Book of Letter"
5) 1977(Japan)
6) black
685 1) sheep
2) Fumio Inoue
3) Chikako Inoue
4) The Design House Carrot
5) 1980(Japan)
6) pink(DIC 28)
686 1) sheep
3) Istvan Szekeres
5) 1980(Hungary)
6) blue
687 1) products／the goat
2),3) Shigeji Kobayashi
4) The Lion Sekken Co., LtD.
5) 1981(Japan)
688 1) pig
2),3) Kunihiko Sugiyama
4) Bunri
5) 1979(Japan)
689 1) pig
3) Istvan Szekeres
5) 1980(Hungary)
6) blue
690 1) pig
2) Akiteru Nakajima
3) Akitere Nakajima／Yoichi Moroishi／Kumi Shimahama
4) Hakugen
5) 1978／1980(Japan)
691 1) "wonderful animals"／dog
2),3) Yasaburo Kuwayama
4) Typo-Eye Exhibition of "A Picture Book of Letter"
5) 1977(Japan)
6) black
692 1) greeting cards
3) Takao Yoguchi
4) Holbein Gazai
5) 1981(Japan)
693 1) greeting cards
3) Takao Yoguchi
4) Holbein Gazai
5) 1981(Japan)
694 1) bill on the post／veterinarian
2) Yonefusa Yamada
3) Shin Sasaki／Yuko Ishida
4) Toden Kokoku

5) 1982(Japan)
695 1) supermarket／no pets
2),3) Takao Yoguchi
4) Chujitsuya
5) 1979(Japan)
696 3) Ruedi Rüegg
5) 1983(Switzerland)
697 1) airport
2) Ernest Lehfeld
3) Ernest Lehfeld／Manuel Sanchez／Francisco Gallardo／Jorge Fernandez
4) Mexico Airport
5) 1977-78(Mexico)
6) black／yellow(ground)
698 1) Strict Guard
3) Ruedi Rüegg
5) 1983(Switzerland)
699 1) rabbit
2) Fumio Inoue
3) Chikako Inoue
4) The Design House Carrot
5) 1980(Japan)
6) pink(DIC 28)
700 1) rabbit
3) Istvan Szekeres
5) 1980(Hungary)
6) blue
701 1) game／rabbit
2),3) Yoshihiro Yoshida
4) Typo Eye
5) 1976(Japan)
702 1) "wonderful animals"／squirrel
2),3) Yasaburo Kuwayama
4) Typo-Eye Exhibition of "A Picture Book of Letter"
5) 1977(Japan)
6) black
703 1) bank
3) Eduardo A. Canovas
5) 1980(Argentina)
6) dark green／green
704 1) t-shirt／cock
2),3) Tadashi Mizui
4) Typo Eye
5) 1975(Japan)
705 1) cock
3) Istvan Szekeres
5) 1980(Hungary)
6) blue
706 1) biblical association game／St. Peter
2) Norio Ikeda
3) Norio Ikeda／Shigeo Ikeda／So Nakamura
4) Ikedamura Aseduction
5) 1980(Japan)
707 1) publication(practical book)cover and title page／cock
3) Yutaka Hasegawa
4) Shufu to Seikatsusha
5) 1982(Japan)
708 1) food／chiken
2) Akiteru Nakajima
3) Akira Yagi／Takeshi Ogawa／Toru Konno／Hideko Kurihara／Keiko Komazawa
4) Chuo Bijutsu Gakuen Pictorial Course
5) 1980(Japan)
709 1) company magazine／birth・foundation／chick
2),3) Kunihiko Sugiyama
4) Bunri

5) 1980(Japan)
710 1) prints(new year's card)
3) Toshio Sonohara
4) Yoshiro Sonohara
5) 1981(Japan)
711 1) prints(new year's card)/
cock
2) Kenzo Nakagawa
3) Hiroyasu Nobuyama/Sumiko
Tsutani
4) Nomura Kogei
5) 1980(Japan)
712 1) "wonderful animals"/
dove
2),3) Yasaburo Kuwayama
4) Typo-Eye E hibition of "A
Picture Book of Letter"
5) 1977(Japan)
6) black
713 1) zoo/dove
2),3) PVDI
5) 1976(Brazil)
714 1) encyclopedia/bird
2) Katsuichi Ito
3) Katsuichi Ito Design Studio
4) Tamagawa University
Publishing Department
5) 1979(Japan)
715 1) cock
2),3) Kunihiko Sugiyama
4) Bunri
5) 1979(Japan)
716 1) "Shiritori Kanji"
2),3) Yasaburo Kuwayama
4) Typo-Eye Exhibition of "A
Picture Book of Letter"
5) 1977(Japan)
6) black
717 1) a chain of the biological
world/dove
2),3) Kunihiko Sugiyama
4) Bunri
5) 1979(Japan)
718 1) t-shirt/dove
2),3) Tadashi Mizui
4) Typo Eye
5) 1975(Japan)
719 1) urgency
2),3) Masami Ichikawa
4) Tanabe Rotary Club
5) 1975(Japan)
720 1) zoo/eagle
2),3) PVDI
5) 1976(Brazil)
721 1) "wonderful animals"/
golden eagle
2),3) Yasaburo Kuwayama
4) Typo-Eye Exhibition of "A
Picture Book of Letter"
5) 1977(Japan)
6) black
722 1) t-shirt/eagle
2),3) Tadashi Mizui
4) Typo Eye
5) 1975(Japan)
723 1) department store's ad in
a paper/events
2) Kenzo Nakagawa
3) Hiroyasu Nobuyama
4) Isetan Department Store
5) 1978(Japan)
724 1) "wonderful animals"/
sparrow
2),3) Yasaburo Kuwayama
4) Typo-Eye Exhibition of "A

Picture Book of Letter"
5) 1977(Japan)
6) black
725 1) zoo/owl
2),3) PVDI
5) 1976(Brazil)
726 1) zoo/toucan
2),3) PVDI
5) 1976(Brazil)
727 1) "wonderful animals"/
toucan
2),3) Yasaburo Kuwayama
4) Typo-Eye Exhibition of "A
Picture Book of Letter"
5) 1977(Japan)
6) black
728 1) zoo/toucans
2) Joao Carlos Cauduro/
Ludovico Antonio Martino
5) 1972/1973(Brazil)
729 1) zoo/peacock
2),3) PVDI
5) 1976(Brazil)
730 1) zoo/parrot
2),3) PVDI
5) 1976(Brazil)
731 1) hospital/obsterics/
stork
2) Shakespear Design Studio
3) Raul Shakespear/Ronald
Shakespear
4) Buenos Aires City Hospital
5) 1970/1980(Argentina)
6) Red/Blue
732 1) t-shirt/crane
2),3) Tadashi Mizui
4) Typo Eye
5) 1975(Japan)
733 1) "A Picture Book of
A-I-U-E-O"/octopus
2),3) Yasaburo Kuwayama
4) Typo-Eye Exhibition of "Kami
no Mojikku"
5) 1979(Japan)
734 1) map of a realty dealer/
fish
2),3) Akiteru Nakajima
4) Anterope Valley Investment
Company
5) 1976(Japan)
735 1) "Shiritori Kanji"/fish
2),3) Yasaburo Kuwayama
4) Typo-Eye Exhibition "A
Picture Book of Letter"
5) 1977(Japan)
6) black
736 1) fish
2) Akiteru Nakajima
3) Akiteru Nakajima/Yoichi
Moroishi/Kumi Shirahama
4) Hakugen
5) 1978/1980(Japan)
737 1) map/pond
2) Teruo Ishikawa
3) Teruo Ishikawa/Yoshiko
Wada
4) Shufu to Seikatsusha
5) 1982(Japan)
738 1) map of neighborhood/
fishmonger
2) Akiteru Nakajima
3) Akiteru Nakajima/Yumi
Shirahama/Tamio Takeuchi
4) Art & Graphic
5) 1981(Japan)

739 1) food/fish
2) Akiteru Nakajima
3) Akira Yagi/Takeshi Ogawa/
Toru Ogawa/Hideko Kurihara/
Keiko Komazawa
4) Chuo Bijutsu Gakuen Pictorial
Course
5) 1980(Japan)
740 1) supermarket/fish
2),3) Takao Yoguchi
4) Chujitsuya
5) 1977(Japan)
741 1) Pet equipment/how to
keep a pet
2) Motoki Hiramatsu
3) Isao Nakamura
4) Midori Shobo
5) 1982(Japan)
742 1) bill on the post/eel
2) Yonefusa Yamada
3) Shin Sasaki/Yuko Ishida
4) Toden Kokoku
5) 1982(Japan)
743 1) map of neighborhood/
unagiya
2) Akiteru Nakajima
3) Akiteru Nakajima/Kumi
Shirahama/Tamio Takeuchi
4) Art & Graphic
5) 1981(Japan)
744 1) fish
2) Akiteru Nakajima
3) Akiteru Nakajima/Yoichi
Moroishi/Kumi Shirahama
4) Hakugen
5) 1978/1980(Japan)
745 1) processed food
2),3) Kunihiko Sugiyama
4) Bunri
5) 1979(Japan)
746 1) food/cut off fish head
2) Akiteru Nakajima
3) Akira Yagi/Takeshi Ogawa/
Toru Konno/Hideko Kurihara/
Keiko Komazawa
4) Chuo Bijutsu Gakuen Pictorial
Course
5) 1980(Japan)
747 1) fish
2) Akiteru Nakajima
3) Akiteru Nakajima/Yoichi
Moroishi/Kumi Shirahama
4) Hakugen
5) 1978/1980(Japan)
748 1) dried fish
2) Akiteru Nakajima
3) Akiteru Nakajima/Yoichi
Moroishi/Kumi Shirahama
4) Hakugen
5) 1978/1980(Japan)
749 1) facilities in a resort/fish
2),3) Yasuhiko Shibukawa
4) Komatsubara-Kenshu-
Jigyodan
5) 1978(Japan)
750 1) "A Picture Book of
A-I-U-E-O"/fresh fish
2),3) Yasaburo Kuwayama
4) Typo-Eye Exhibition "Kami no
Mojikku"
5) 1979(Japan)
751 1) whale
2) Akiteru Nakajima
3) Akiteru Nakajima/Yoichi
Moroishi/Kumi Shirahama

4) Hakugen
5) 1978/1980(Japan)
752 2) whale
3) Chikako Inoue
4) The Design House Carrot
5) 1980(Japan)
6) pink(DIC 28)
753 1) prints(calendar)/fish
2),3) Shinichi Takahara
4) Shinichi Takahara
5) 1980(Sapporo)
754 1) telephone service/call
up a ship at sea
3) Asher Kabderon
4) Asher Kalderon
5) 1983(Israel)
755 1) growth of fish
2),3) Kunihiko Sugiyama
4) Tokyo Shoseki
5) 1978(Japan)
756 1) encyclopedia/fish
2) Katsuichi Ito
3) Katsuichi Ito Design Studio
4) Tamagawa University
Publishing Part
5) 1979(Japan)
757 1) "wonderful animals"/
octopus
2),3) Yasaburo Kuwayama
4) Typo-Eye Exhibition of "A
Picture Book of Letter"
5) 1977(Japan)
6) black
758 1) products/the crab
2),3) Shigeji Kobayashi
4) The Lion Sekken Co., Ltd.
5) 1981(Japan)
759 1) supermarket/shrimp
2),3) Takao Yoguchi
4) Chujituya
5) 1977(Japan)
760 1) pet supplies/how to
keep a pet
2) Motoki Hiramatsu
3) Isato Nakamura
4) Midori Shobo
5) 1982(Japan)
761 1) gift shop/snail
2) Harry Murphy
3) Harry Murphy/Stanton Klose
4) The Small Things Co., Ltd.
5) 1980(U.S.A.)
762 3) Eduard Prüssen
4) Bergish Gladbach City
5) 1980(West Germany)
6) black
763 1) gift shop/shell
2) Harry Murphy
3) Harry Murphy/Stanton Klose
4) The Small Things Co., Ltd.
5) 1980(U.S.A.)
764 1) publication/guidance of
teaching/grasshopper
2),3) Hiroshi Fukushima
4) Tokyo Shoseki
5) 1979(Japan)
765 1) gift shop/butterfly
2) Harry Murphy
3) Harry Murphy/Stanton Klose
4) The Small Things Co., Ltd.
5) 1980(U.S.A.)
766 1) encyclopedia/insect/
butterfly
2) Katsuichi Ito
3) Katsuichi Ito Design Studio

4) Tamagawa University
Publishing Part
5) 1979(Japan)
767 1) publication(practical
book)／cover and title page／
butterfly
3) Yutaka Hasegawa
4) Shufu to Seikatsusha
5) 1982(Japan)
768 1) t-shirt／butterfly
2),3) Tadashi Mizui
4) Typo Eye
5) 1975(Japan)
769 1) publication／guidance of
teaching／lady-bug
2),3) Hiroshi Fukushima
4) Tokyo Shoseki
5) 1979(Japan)
770 1) pet supplies／how to
keep a pet／insect
2) Motoki Hiramatsu
3) Isato Nakamura
4) Midori Shobo
5) 1982(Japan)
771 1) "A Picture Book of
A-I-U-E-O"／insect
2),3) Yasaburo Kuwayama
4) Typo-Eye Exhibition of "Kami
no Mojikku"
5) 1979(Japan)
772 1) pet supplies／how to
keep a pet／grasshoppr
2) Motoki Hiramatsu
3) Isato Nakamura
4) Midori Shobo
5) 1982(Japan)
773 1) pet's／how to keep a pet
2) Motoki Hiramatsu
3) Isato Nakamura
4) Midori Shobo
5) 1982(Japan)
774 1) publication／guidance of
teaching／ant
2),3) Hiroshi Fukushima
4) Tokyo Shoseki
5) 1979(Japan)
775 1) "A Picture Book of
A-I-U-E-O"／ant
2),3) Yasaburo Kuwayama
4) Typo-Eye Exhibition of "Kami
no Mojikku"
5) 1979(Japan)
776 1) medicine／vermin
3) Akiteru Nakajima
4) Mine Yakuhin
5) 1980(Japan)
777 1) t-shirt／bee
2),3) Tadashi Mizui
4) Typo Eye
5) 1975(Japan)
778 1) publication／guidance of
teaching／snail
2),3) Hiroshi Fukushima
4) Tokyo Shoseki
5) 1979(Japan)
779 1) exhibition／snail
2) Kenzo Nakagawa
3) Kenzo Nakagawa／Hiroyasu
Nobuyama
4) Tokyo Designers Space
5) 1980(Japan)
780 1) desolvers in the
biological world
2),3) Kunihiko Sugiyama
4) Bunri

5) 1979(Japan)
781 1) gift shop／rose bud
2) Harry Murphy
3) Harry Murphy／Stanton Klose
4) The Small Things Co., Ltd.
5) 1980(U.S.A.)
782 1) gift shop／flower
2) Harry Murphy
3) Harry Murphy／Stanton Klose
4) The Small Things Co., Ltd.
5) 1980(U.S.A.)
783 1) flower
2) Akiteru Nakajima
3) Akiteru Nakajima／Yoichi
Moroishi／Kumi Shirahama
4) Hakugen
5) 1978／1980(Japan)
784 1) Bookshop／Fiction／
flower
3) Miloš Ćirić
5) 1974(Yugoslavia)
6) red
785 1) Bookshop／General／
flower
3) Miloš Ćirić
5) 1974(Yugoslavia)
6) red
786 1) bill on the post／
gardening／flower
2) Yonefusa Yamada
3) Shin Sasaki／Yuko Ishida
4) Toden Kokoku
5) 1982(Japan)
787 1) tea
2),3) Kunihiko Sugiyama
4) Bunri
5) 1979(Japan)
788 1) airport／flower shop
2) Ernest Lehfeld
3) Ernest Lefeld／Manuel
Sanchez／Francisco Gallardo／
Jorge Fernandez
4) Mexico Airport
5) 1977-78(Mexico)
6) black／yellow(ground)
789 1) cotton
2),3) Kunihiko Sugiyama
4) Bunri
5) 1979(Japan)
790 1) encyclopedia／flowers
and trees
2) Katsuichi Ito
3) Katsuichi Ito Design Studio
4) Tamagawa University
5) 1979(Japan)
791 1) calendar／flower
2),3) Tadashi Mizui
4) Tadashi Mizui
5) 1973(Japan)
792 1) calendar
2),3) Tadashi Mizui
4) Tadashi Mizui
5) 1973(Japan)
793 1) floor-number indicating
seal in elevator
2) Osamu Ogawa
3) Masanari Himi
4) Kagaya
5) 1981(Japan)
794 1) floor-number indicating
seal in elevator
2) Osamu Ogawa
3) Masanari Himi
4) Kagaya
5) 1981(Japan)

795 1) gift shop／leaf
2) Harry Murphy
3) Harry Murphy／Stanton Klose
4) The Small Things Co., Ltd.
5) 1980(U.S.A.)
796 1) gift shop／clover leaf
2) Harry Murphy
3) Harry Murphy／Stanton Klose
4) The Small Things Co., Ltd.
5) 1980(U.S.A.)
797 1) farm produce
2) István Szekeres
5) 1971(Hungary)
6) black／white
798 1) leaf
2) Akiteru Nakajima
3) Akiteru Nakajima／Yoichi
Moroishi／Kumi Shirahama
4) Hakugen
5) 1978／1980(Japan)
799 1) olive
2),3) Kunihiko Sugiyama
4) Bunri
5) 1979(Japan)
800 1) encyclopedia／soil
2) Katsuichi Ito
3) Katsuichi Ito Design Studio
4) Tamagawa University
Publishing Part
5) 1979(Japan)
801 1) producing and
consuming in the biological
world
2),3) Kunihiko Sugiyama
4) Bunri
5) 1979(Japan)
802 1) "A Picture Book of
A-I-U-E-O"／thin
2),3) Yasaburo Kuwayama
4) Typo-Eye Exhibition of "Kami
no Mojikku"
5) 1979(Japan)
803 1) encyclopedia／gardening
2) Katsuichi Ito
3) Katsuichi Ito Design Studio
4) Tamagawa University
Publishing Part
5) 1979(Japan)
804 1) bank
3) Eduardo A. Canovas
5) 1980(Argentina)
6) dark green／green
805 1) paper／material supply
2),3) Rey R. Dacosta
4) Mendoza Enterprize
5) 1972／1973(Venezuela)
6) green
806 1) "Shiritori Kanij"
2),3) Yasaburo Kuwayama
4) Typo-Eye Exhibition of "A
Picture Book of Letter"
5) 1977(Japan)
6) black
807 2) Peter Steiner
3) Michael Friedland
4) Canadian Pacific
5) 1983(canada)
6) blue
808 1) campaign
2) Kuniharu Masubuchi
3) Emiko Tachiyama／Hiroshi
Iseya
4) Mikimoto
5) 1983(Japan)
809 1) exhibition

2) Kenzo Nakagawa
3) Kenzo Nakagawa／Hiroyasu
Nobuyama
4) Tokyo Disigners Spece
5) 1980(Japan)
810 1) supermarket
2) Shakespear Design Studio
3) Ronald Shakespear／Raul
Shakespear
4) Disco Supermarket
5) 1982-83(Argentina)
811 1) apple
2) Akiteru Nakajima
3) Akiteru Nakajima／Yoichi
Moroishi／Kumi Shirahama
4) Hakugen
5) 1978／1980(Japan)
812 1) apple
2),3) Kunihiko Sugiyama
4) Bunri
5) 1979(Japan)
813 1) food／apple
2) Akiteru Nakajima
3) Akiteru Nakajima／Takeshi
Ogawa／Toru Konno／Hideko
Kurihara／Keiko Komazawa
4) Chuo Bijutsu Gakuen Pictorial
Course
5) 1980(Japan)
814 1) playing facilities
2),3) Yasuhiko Shibukawa
4) Komatsubara-Kenshu-
Jigyodan
5) 1978(Japan)
815 1) orange
2),3) Kunihiko Sugiyama
4) Bunri
5) 1979(Japan)
816 1) tomato
2),3) Kunihiko Sugiyama
4) Bunri
5) 1979(Japan)
817 1) orange
2) Akiteru Nakajima
3) Akira Yagi／Takeshi Ogawa／
Toru Konno／Hideko Kurihara／
Keiko Komazawa
4) Chuo Bijutsu Gakuen Pictorial
Course
5) 1980(Japan)
818 2) Akiteru Nakajima
3) Akiteru Nakajima／Yoichi
Moroishi／Kumi Shirahama
4) Hakugen
5) 1978／1980(Japan)
819 3) István Szekeres
4) Service House
5) 1970(Hungary)
6) black
820 1) food／melon
2) Akiteru Nakajima
3) Akira Yagi／Takeshi Ogawa／
Toru Konno／Hideko Kurihara／
Keiko Komazawa
4) Chuo Bijutsu Gakuen Pictorial
Course
5) 1980(Japan)
821 2) Akiteru Nakajima
3) Akiteru Nakajima／Yoichi
Moroishi／Kumi Shirahama
4) Hakugen
5) 1978／1980(Japan)
822 1) pear
2),3) Kunihiko Sugiyama
4) Bunri

5) 1979(Japan)
823 1) peach
2),3) Kunihiko Sugiyama
4) Bunri
5) 1979(Japan)
824 1) food/banana
2) Akiteru Nakajima
3) Akira Yagi/Takeshi Ogawa/Toru Konno/Hideko Kurihara/Keiko Komazawa
4) Chuo Bijutsu Gakuen Pictorial Course
5) 1980(Japan)
825 1) Regional Meeting
2) Hajime Nakamura/Yasaburo Kuwayama
3) Yasaburo Kuwayama/Hajime Ikeda/Norio Ikeda
4) The Regional Meeting of Jehovah's Witnesses
5) 1980(Japan)
826 1) supermarket/bananas
2),3) Yoguchi Takao
4) Chujitsuya
5) 1977(Japan)
827 1) grapes
2) Akiteru Nakajima
3) Akiteru Nakajima/Yoichi Moroishi/Kumi Shirahama
4) Hakugen
5) 1978/1980(Japan)
828 1) grapes
2),3) Kunihiko Sugiyama
4) Bunri
5) 1979(Japan)
829 1) food/grapes
2) Akiteru Nakajima
3) Akira Yagi/Takeshi Ogawa/Toru Konno/Hideko Kurihara/Keiko Komazawa
4) Chuo Bijutsu Gakuen Pictorial Course
5) 1980(Japan)
830 1) biblical association game/spy
2) Norio Ikeda
3) Norio Ikeda/Shigeo Ikeda/So Nakamura
4) Ikedamura Aseduction
5) 1980(Japan)
831 1) gift shop/grapes
2) Harry Murphy
3) Harry Murphy/Stanton Klose
4) The Small Things Co., Ltd.
5) 1980(U.S.A.)
832 1) supermarket/grapes
2) Shakespear Design Studio
3) Ronald Shakespear/Raul Shakespear
4) Disco Supermarket
5) 1982-83(Argentina)
833 1) wine
2),3) Kunihiko Sugiyama
4) Bunri
5) 1979(Japan)
834 1) gift shop
2) Harry Murphy
3) Harry Murphy/Stanton Klose
4) The Small Things Co., Ltd.
5) 1980(U.S.A.)
835 1) cherries
2) Akiteru Nakajima
3) Akiteru Nakajima/Yoichi Moroishi/Kumi Shirahama
4) Hakugen

5) 1978/1980(Japan)
836 1) cherries
2),3) Kunihiko Sugiyama
4) Bunri
5) 1979(Japan)
837 2) Peter Steiner
3) Micheal Friedland
4) Canadian Pacific
5) 1983(Canada)
6) blue
838 1) radish
2),3) Kunihiko Sugiyama
4) Bunri
5) 1979(Japan)
839 1) farm produce
3) Istvan Szekeres
5) 1971(Hungary)
6) black/white
840 1) publication/radish
2),3) Ludvic Feller
4) Ulistein Verlag
5) 1972(West Germany)
841 1) farm produce/radish
3) Istvan Szekeres
5) 1971(Hungary)
6) black/white
842 1) radish
2) Akiteru Nakajima
3) Akiteru Nakajima/Yoichi Moroishi/Kumi Shirahama
4) Hakugen
5) 1978/1980(Japan)
843 1) carrot
2),3) Kunihiko Sugiyama
4) Bunri
5) 1979(Japan)
844 1) chinese cabbage
2),3) Kunihiko Sugiyama
4) Bunri
5) 1979(Japan)
845 1) lettuce
2),3) Kunihiko Sugiyama
4) Bunri
5) 1979(Japan)
846 1) egg plant
2),3) Kunihiko Sugiyama
4) Bunri
5) 1979(Japan)
847 1) egg plant
2) Akiteru Nakajima
3) Akiteru Nakajima/Yoichi Moroishi/Kumi Shirahama
4) Hakugen
5) 1978/1980(Japan)
848 1) green pepper
2),3) Kunihiko Sugiyama
4) Bunri
5) 1979(Japan)
849 1) supermarket/green pepper
2),3) Takao Yoguchi
4) Chujitsuya
5) 1977(Japan)
850 1) cucumber
2),3) Kunihiko Sugiyama
4) Bunri
5) 1979(Japan)
851 1) cucumber
2) Akiteru Nakajima
3) Akiteru Nakajima/Yoichi Moroishi/Kumi Shirahama
4) Hakugen
5) 1978/1980(Japan)
852 1) mushroom
2) Akiteru Nakajima

3) Akiteru Nakajima/Yoichi Moroishi/Kumi Shirahama
4) Hakugen
5) 1978/1980(Japan)
853 2) Akiteru Nakajima
3) Akiteru Nakajima/Yoichi Moroishi/Kumi Shirahama
4) Hakugen
5) 1978/1980(Japan)
854 1) sub textbook/onion
2),3) Kunihiko Sugiyama
4) Bunri
5) 1979(Japan)
855 2) Akiteru Nakajima
3) Akiteru Nakajima/Yoichi Moroishi/Kumi Shirahama
4) Hakugen
5) 1978/1980(Japan)
856 2) Akiteru Nakajima
3) Akiteru Nakajima/Yoichi Moroishi/Kumi Shirahama
4) Hakugen
5) 1978/1980(Japan)
857 1) farm produce
2),3) Kunihiko Sugiyama
4) Bunri
5) 1979(Japan)
858 1) peanuts
2),3) Kunihiko Sugiyama
4) Bunri
5) 1979(Japan)
859 1) gift shop/acorn
2) Harry Murphy
3) Harry Murphy/Stanton Klose
4) The Small Things Co., Ltd.
5) 1980(U.S.A.)
860 1) farm produce/poppy
2) Istvan Szekeres
5) 1971(Hungary)
6) Black/White
861 1) wheat
2),3) Kunihiko Sugiyama
4) Bunri
5) 1979(Japan)
862 1) farm produce
3) Istvan Szekeres
5) 1971(Hungary)
6) Black/White
863 1) new year's card
2),3) Ludvik Feller
4) Refrex/Ludvik Feller
5) 1974(West Germany)
864 1) school
2),3) Ludvik Feller
4) Berlin
5) 1974(West Germany)
865 1) weather report boads/fine
3) Akiteru Nakajima
4) Okinawa International Ocean Exhibition Association
5) 1975(Japan)
866 1) sun
2) Akiteru Nakajima
3) Akiteru Nakajima/Yoichi Moroishi/Kumi Shirahama
4) Hakugen
5) 1978/1980(Japan)
867 1) biblical association game/josiah
2) Norio Ikeda
3) Norio Ikeda/Shigeo Ikeda/So Nakamura
4) Ikedamura Aseduction
5) 1980(Japan)

868 1) new year's card
2),3) Ludvik Feller
4) Refrex/Ludvik Feller
5) 1974(West Germany)
869 1) "Shiritori Kanji"
2),3) Yasaburo Kuwayama
4) Typo-Eye Exhibition of "A Picture Book of Letter"
5) 1977(Japan)
6) black
870 1) encyclopedia/space
2) Katsuichi Ito
3) Katsuichi Ito Design Studio
4) Tamagawa University Publishing Department
5) 1979(Japan)
871 1) "A Picture Book of A-I-U-E-O"/sky
2),3) Yasaburo Kuwayama
4) Typo-Eye Exhibition of "Kami no Mojikku"
5) 1979(Japan)
872 1) telephone service/weather forecast
3) Asher Kalderon
5) 1983(Israel)
873 1) map of neighborhood/all-night service
2) Akiteru Nakajima
3) Akiteru Nakajima/Yumi Shirahama/Tamio Takeuchi
4) Art & Graphic
5) 1981(Japan)
874 3) star
4) Air France
5) (France)
875 1) guidance of teaching/motion of stars
2),3) Hiroshi Fukushima
4) Tokyo Shoseki
5) 1978(Japan)
876 1) airport/international
2) Ernest Lehfeld
3) Ernest Lehfeld/Manuel Sanchez/Francisco Gallardo/Jorge Fernandez
4) Mexico Airport
5) 1977-78(Mexico)
6) black/yellow(ground)
877 1) encyclopedia/the earth
2) Katsuichi Ito
3) Katsuichi Ito Design Studio
4) Tamagawa University Publishing Department
5) 1979(Japan)
878 1) encyclopedia/round trip of the world
2) Katsuichi Ito
3) Katsuichi Ito Design Studio
4) Tamagawa University Publishing Department
5) 1979(Japan)
879 1) the world
2),3) Kunihiko Sugiyama
4) Bunri
5) 1979(Japan)
880 1) encyclopedia/round trip of Japan
2) Katsuichi Ito
3) Katsuichi Ito Design Studio
4) Tamagawa University Publishing Department
5) 1979(Japan)
881 1) map of a realty dealer/mountain

2),3) Akiteru Nakajima
4) Anterope Valley Investment Company
5) 1976(Japan)
882 1) indication of branch
2) Syunji Niinomi
3) Tetsuharu Mabuchi
4) Tokai Sports
5) 1980(Japan)
883 1) "Shiritori Kanji"
2),3) Yasaburo Kuwayama
4) Typo-Eye Exhibition of "A Picture Book of Letter"
5) 1977(Japan)
6) black
884 1) text of preparatory school(chemistry)
2),3) Kunihiko Sugiyama
4) Yoyogi Seminar
5) 1982(Japan)
885 1) Insurance
2),3) Donald Patiwael
5) 1983(Netherland)
886 1) "A Picture Book of A I U E O"/ridge
2),3) Yasaburo Kuwayama
4) Typo-Eye Exhibition of "Kami no Mojikku"
5) 1979(Japan)
887 1) Diastrophism
2),3) Kunihiko Sugiyama
4) Bunri
5) 1979(Japan)
888 1) publication(guidance of teaching)
2),3) Hiroshi Fukushima
4) Tokyo Shoseki
5) 1979(Japan)
889 1) "Shiritori Kanji"
2),3) Yasaburo Kuwayama
4) Typo-Eye Exhibition of "A Picture Book of Letter"
5) 1977(Japan)
6) black
890 1) "Shiritori Kanji"
2),3) Yasaburo Kuwayama
4) Typo-Eye Exhibition of "A Picture Book of Letter"
5) 1977(Japan)
6) black
891 1) steel
2),3) Kunihiko Sugiyama
4) Bunri
5) 1979(Japan)
892 1) gold
2),3) Kunihiko Sugiyama
4) Bunri
5) 1979(Japan)
893 1) coal
2),3) Kunihiko Sugiyama
4) Bunri
5) 1979(Japan)
894 1) under-ground resouces
2),3) Kunihiko Sugiyama
4) Bunri
5) 1979(Japan)
895 1) diamond
2),3) Kunihiko Sugiyama
4) Bunri
5) 1979(Japan)
896 1) bill on the post/precious metals
2) Yonefusa Yamada
3) Shin Sasaki/Yuko Ishida

4) Toden Kokoku
5) 1982(Japan)
897 1) sign in a camera company/no overheat
2) Ken Nara/Akiteru Nakajima
3) Akiteru Nakajima/Ryoichi Yamada/Kumi Shirahama
4) Canon
5) 1974(Japan)
898 1) "Shiritori Kanji"
2),3) Yasaburo Kuwayama
4) Typo-Eye Exhibition of "A Picture Book of Letter"
5) 1977(Japan)
6) black
899 1) no fire
2),3) PVDI
4) Copeq Oil Co., Ltd.
5) 1974(Brazil)
900 2),3) PVDI
4) Furnas Electric Center
5) 1972(Brazil)
901 1) encyclopedia/fire
2) Katsuichi Ito
3) Katsuich Ito Design Studio
4) Tamagawa University Publishing Department
5) 1979(Japan)
902 1) sign in a camera company/no fire
2) Ken Nara/Akiteru Nakajima
3) Akiteru Nakajima/Ryoichi Yamada/Kumi Shirahama
4) Canon
5) 1974(Japan)
903 1) hotel
2),3) PVDI
4) Lio Meridian Hotel
5) 1975(Brazil)
904 1) sign in a camera company/inflammable fluid
2) Ken Nara/Akiteru Nakajima
3) Akiteru Nakajima/Ryoichi Yamada/Kumi Shirahama
4) Canon
5) 1974(Japan)
905 1) sign in a camera company
2) Ken Nara/Akiteru Nakajima
3) Akiteru Nakajima/Ryoichi Yamada/Kumi Shirahama
4) Canon
5) 1974(Japan)
906 1) candle
2),3) Kunihiko Sugiyama
4) Bunri
5) 1979(Japan)
907 1) chemical reaction and heat
2),3) Kunihiko Sugiyama
4) Bunri
5) 1979(Japan)
908 1) energy
2),3) Kunihiko Sugiyama
4) Bunri
5) 1979(Japan)
909 1) sign in a camera company/explosive
2) Ken Nara/Akiteru Nakajima
3) Akiteru Nakajima/Ryoichi Yamada/Kumi Shirahama
4) Canon
5) 1974(Japan)
910 1) no making a fire
2),3) PVDI

4) Copek Oil Co., Ltd.
5) 1974(Brazil)
911 1) graphic indication of a detergent/caution : inflammable
2) Akiteru Nakajima
3) Seiko Aoki/Hisako Kataoka/Yoko Kobayashi
4) Chuo Bijutsu Gakuen Pictorial Course
5) 1983(Japan)
912 1) a volcano and igneous stones
2),3) Kunihiko Sugiyama
4) Bunri
5) 1979(Japan)
913 1) oil field
2),3) Kunihiko Sugiyama
4) Bunri
5) 1979(Japan)
914 1) chemistry(branch of the environmental pollution)counter measure
2),3) Kunihiko Sugiyama
4) Sanso Kagaku
5) (Japan)
915 1) sports/public hygienic service
2) Shakespear Design Studio
3) Ronald Shakespear/Raul Shakespear
4) Buenos Aires Sports Center
5) 1980(Argentina)
916 1) hospital/analysis
2) Shakespear Design Studio
3) Raul Shakespear/Ronald Shakespear
4) Buenos Aires City Hospital
5) 1970/1980(Argentina)
6) red/blue
917 1) encyclopedia/water
2) Katsuichi Ito
3) Katsuichi Ito Design Studio
4) Tamagawa University Publishing Department
5) 1979(Japan)
918 1) solution
2),3) Kunihiko Sugiyama
4) Bunri
5) 1979(Japan)
919 1) oil
2),3) Kunihiko Sugiyama
4) Bunri
5) 1979(Japan)
920 1) food/get water
2) Akiteru Nakajima
3) Akira Yagi/Takeshi Ogawa/Toru Konno/Hideko Kurihara/Keiko Komazawa
4) Chuo Bijutsu Gakuen Pictorial Course
5) 1980(Japan)
921 1) food/keep dry
2) Akiteru Nakajima
3) Akira Yagi/Takeshi Ogawa/Toru Konno/Hideko Kurihara/Keiko Komazawa
4) Chuo Bijutsu Gakuen Pictorial Course
5) 1980(Japan)
922 1) sign in a camera company/no pouring water
2) Ken Nara/Akiteru Nakajima
3) Akiteru Nakajima/Ryoichi Yamada/Kumi Shirahama
4) Canon

5) 1974(Japan)
923 1) sign in a camera company
2) Ken Nara/Akiteru Nakajima
3) Akiteru Nakajima/Ryoichi Yamada/Kumi Shirahama
4) Canon
5) 1974(Japan)
924 1) "Shiritori Kanji"
2),3) Yasaburo Kuwayama
4) Typo-Eye Exhibition of "A Picture Book of Letter"
5) 1977(Japan)
6) black
925 1) the olympics/bath(trial)
2) Tadashi Ikeda
3) Kenichi Miyata/Seiji Masuike
4) 1988 Seoul Olympiad
5) 1982(Japan)
6) black
926 1) food/to wash in water
2) Akiteru Nakajima
3) Akira Yagi/Takeshi Ogawa/Toru Konno/Hideko Kurihara/Keiko Komazawa
4) Chuo Bijutsu Gakuen Pictorial Course
5) 1980(Japan)
927 1) food
2) Akiteru Nakajima
3) Akira Yagi/Takeshi Ogawa/Toru Konno/Hideko Kurihara/Keiko Komazawa
4) Chuo Bijutsu Gakuen Pictorial Course
5) 1980(Japan)
928 1) graphic indication of detergent/to water down
2) Akiteru Nakajima
3) Seiko Aoki/Hisako Kataoka/Yoko Kobayashi
4) Chuo Bijutsu Gakuen Pictorial Course
5) 1983(Japan)
929 1) playing facilities
2),3) Yasuhiko Shibukawa Komatsubara-Kenshu-Jigyodan
5) 1978(Japan)
930 2) Peter Steiner
3) Michael Friedland
4) Canadian Pacific
5) 1983(Canada)
6) blue
931 1) shower
3) Ruedi Rüegg
5) 1983(Switzerland)
932 1) weather report board/caution to big waves
3) Akiteru Nakajima
4) Okinawa International Ocean Exhibition Association
5) 1975(Japan)
933 1) sports/public hygienic service
2) Shakespear Design Studio
3) Ronald Shakespear/Raul Shakespear
4) Buenos Aires Sports Center
5) 1980(Argentina)
934 1) beach
2),3) PVDI
5) 1973(Brazil)
935 1) "A Picture Book of A-I-U-E-O"/wave
2),3) Yasaburo Kuwayama

4) Typo-Eye Exhibition of "Kami no Mojikku"
5) 1979(Japan)
936 1) new year's card
2),3) Ludvik Feller
4) Refrex／Ludvik Feller
5) 1974(West Germany)
937 1) map／public bathhouse
2) Teruo Ishikawa
3) Teruo Ishikawa／Yoshiko Wada
4) Syufu to Seikatsusha
5) 1982(Japan)
938 1) weather report board／cloudy
3) Akiteru Nakajima
4) Okinawa International Ocean Exhibition Association
5) 1975(Japan)
939 1) text of the preparatory school／science and mathematics
2),3) Kunihiko Sugiyama
4) Yoyogi Seminar
5) 1982(Japan)
940 1) weather report board／caution to a strong-wind
3) Akiteru Nakajima
4) Okinawa International Ocean Exhibition Association
5) 1975(Japan)
941 1) weather report board／caution to a thunderstorm
3) Akiteru Nakajima
4) Okinawa International Ocean Exhibition Association
5) 1975(Japan)
942 1) water in the air
2),3) Kunihiko Sugiyama
4) Bunri
5) 1979(Japan)
943 1) sports・public hygienic service／parking lot
2) Shakespear Design Studio
3) Ronald Shakespear／Raul Shakespear
4) Buenos Aires Sports Center
5) 1980(Argentina)
944 1) sports・public hygienic service／nursery
2) Shakespear Design Studio
3) Ronald Shakespear／Raul Shakespear
4) Buenos Aires Sports Center
5) 1980(Argentina)
945 1) parking lot for bicycles
2) Teruo Ishikawa
3) Teruo Ishikawa／Yoshiko Wada
4) Shufu to Seikatsusya
5) 1982(Japan)
946 1) exhibition(space show)／parking lot for bicycles and moter cycles
2),3) Noriaki Tamura
4) Headquarters／Japan International Aerospace Show 1979
5) 1979(Japan)
6) sky blue
947 1) sports／public hygienic service
2) Shakespear Design Studio
3) Ronald Shakespear／Raul Shakespear

4) Buenos Aires Sports Center
5) 1980(Argentina)
948 1) map of neighborhood／cycleway
2) Akiteru Nakajima
3) Akiteru Nakajima／Yumi Shirahama／Tamio Takeuchi
4) Art & Graphic
5) 1981(Japan)
949 1) parking lot for bicycles
2),3) Syuji Torigoe
4) The Gunma Prefectual Office
5) 1981(Japan)
950 1) bicycle
2) Masaaki Fukuda
3) Masaaki Fukuda／Tadashi Mizui／Narumi Fukuda
4) The Saitama Prefectual Office
5) 1983(Japan)
6) blue(Pantone 285)
951 1) bicycle
2),3) PVDI
4) Copek Oil Co., Ltd.
5) 1974(Brazil)
952 1) supermarket／parking lot for bicycles
2),3) Takao Yoguchi
4) Chujitsuya
5) 1979(Japan)
953 1) company sign／bicycle
2) Shigeru Shimooka
3) Masanobu Watanabe
4) Mitsubishi Motors Co., Ltd. (MMC)
5) 1983(Japan)
6) dark blue(sub-color red)
954 1) bicycle
2) Hajime Nakamura／Yasaburo Kuwayama
3) Yasaburo Kuwayama／Hajime Ikeda／Norio Ikeda
4) The Regional Meeting of Jehovah's Witnesses
5) 1980(Japan)
955 1) leisure／a little tour
2),3) Greg Siple
4) The Motor Cycle Centennial／Cycling Association
5) 1983(U.S.A.)
6) green
956 1) leisure
2),3) Greg Siple
4) The Motor Cycle Centennial／Cycling Association
5) 1983(U.S.A.)
6) green
957 1) leisure
2),3) Greg Siple
4) The Motor Cycle Centennial／Cycling Association
5) 1983(U.S.A.)
6) green
958 1) no bicycling
2),3) Kunihiko Sugiyama
4) Bunri
5) 1979(Japan)
959 2) Masaaki Fukuda
3) Masaaki Fukuda／Tadashi Mizui／Narumi Fukuda
4) The Saitama Prefectual Office
5) 1983(Japan)
6) red(Pantone 206)／blue(Pantone 285)
960

2) Masaaki Fukuda
3) Masaaki Fukuda／Tadashi Mizui／Narumi Fukuda
4) The Saitama Prefectual Office
5) 1983(Japan)
6) red(Pantone 206)／blue(Pantone 285)
961 1) leisure
2),3) Greg Siple
4) The Motor Cycle Centennial
5) 1983(U.S.A.)
6) green
962 1) prints(machine's catalog)／catalog of machire
2),3) Stefan Rzepecki
5) 1979(Poland)
6) black
963 1) map of neighborhood
2) Akiteru Nakajima
3) Akiteru Nakajima／Yumi Shirahama／Tamio Takeuchi
4) Art & Graphic
5) 1981(Japan)
964 1) map of neighborhood
2) Akiteru Nakajima
3) Akiteru Nakajima／Yumi Shirahama／Tamio Takeuchi
4) Art & Graphic
5) 1981(Japan)
965 1) sign in a camera company
2) Ken Nara／Akiteru Nakajima
3) Akiteru Nakajima／Ryoichi Yamada／Kumi Shirahama
4) Canon
5) 1974(Japan)
966 1) airport／ground transport
2) Ernest Lehfeld
3) Ernest Leheld／Manuel Sanchez／Francisco Gallardo／Jorge Fernandez
4) Mexico Airport
5) 1977-78(Mexico)
6) black／yellow(ground)
967 3) Ruedi Rüegg
5) 1983(Switzerland)
968 1) the olympics／parking lot(trial)
2) Tadashi Ikeda
3) Kenichi Miyata／Seiji Masuike
4) 1988 Seoul Olympiad
5) 1982(Japan)
6) black
969 1) ocean・exhibition／taxi stand
2) Masaru Katsumi／Akiteru Nakajima
3) Teruyuki Kunito／Yukio Ota／Akira Kuroyone
4) Okinawa International Ocean Exhibition Association
5) 1975(Japan)
6) blue(4PB3, 5／12)beige(3Y8, 5／1)
970 1) encyclopedia／automobile
2) Katsuichi Ito
3) Katsuichi Ito Design Studio
4) Tamagawa University Publishing Department
5) 1979(Japan)
971 1) automobile
2),3) Kunihiko Sugiyama
4) Bunri

5) 1979(Japan)
972 1) "Monomi no To" Centennial
2) Yasaburo Kuwayama
3) Yasaburo Kuwayama／Hajime Ikeda
4) Jehovah's Witnesses
5) 1979(Japan)
973 3) Ruedi Rüegg
5) 1983(Switzerland)
974 1) airport／rent-a-car
2) Ernest Lehfeld
3) Ernest Lehfeld／Manuel Sanchez／Francisco Gallardo／Jorge Fernandez
4) Mexico Airport
5) 1977-78(Mexico)
6) black／yellow(ground)
975 1) bill on the post／auto-repair
2) Yonefusa Yamada
3) Shin Sasaki／Yuko Ishida
4) Toden Kokoku
5) 1982(Japan)
976 1) bill on the post／drive-in
2) Yonefusa Yamada
3) Shin Sasaki／Yuko Ishida
4) Toden Kekoku
5) 1982(Japan)
977 1) "A Picture Book of A-I-U-E-O"／parking lot
2),3) Yasaburo Kuwayama
4) Typo-Eye Exhibition of "Kami no Mojikku"
5) 1979(Japan)
978 1) bill on the post／driver's school
2) Yonefusa Yamada
3) Shin Sasaki／Yuko Ishida
4) Toden Kokoku
5) 1982(Japan)
979 1) facilities in a resort／parking lot
2) Wataru Tsuchiya／Kenzo Nakagawa
3) Kenzo Nakagawa／Hiroyasu Nobuyama／Satoshi Morikami
4) Manza Beach Resort
5) 1982(Japan)
980 1) facilities in a resort／taxi
2) Wataru Tsuchiya／Kenzo Nakagawa
3) Kenzo Nakagawa／Hiroyasu Nobuyama／Satoshi Morikami
4) Manza Beach Resort
5) 1982(Japan)
981 1) automobile
2) Akiteru Nakajima
3) Akiteru Nakajima／Kumi Shirahama
4) The Iraqi Government
5) 1981／1982(Japan)
982 1) taxi stand
2),3) Syuji Torigoe
4) The Gunma Prefectual Office
5) 1981(Japan)
983 1) sports／public hygienic service／ambulance
2) Shakespear Design Studio
3) Ronald Shakespear／Raul Shakespear
4) Buenos Aires Sports Center
5) 1980(Argentina)
984 1) telephone service／ambulance

3) Asher Kalderon
5) 1983(Israel)
985 1) map of neighborhood／
heavy traffic
2) Akiteru Nakajima
3) Akiteru Nakajima／Yumi
Shirahama／Tamio Takeuchi
4) Art & Graphic
5) 1981(Japan)
986 1) airport／parking lot
2) Ernest Lehfeld
3) Ernest Lehfeld／Manuel
Sanchez／Francisco Gallardo／
Jorge Fernandez
4) Mexico Airport
5) 1977-78(Mexico)
6) black／yellow(ground)
987 1) map of neighorhood
2) Akiteru Nakajima
3) Akiteru Nakajima／Yumi
Shirahama／Tamio Takeuchi
4) Art & Graphic
5) 1981(Japan)
988 1) transport
2),3) PVDI
5) 1977(Brazil)
989 1) transport
2),3) PVDI
5) 1977(Brazil)
990 1) airport／ground
transport
2) Ernest Lehfeld
3) Ernest Lehfeld／Manuel
Sanchez／Francisco Gallardo／
Jorge Fernandez
4) Mexico Airport
5) 1977-88(Mexico)
6) black／yellow(ground)
991 1) facilities in a resort
2) Wataru Tsuchiya／Kenzo
Nakagawa
3) Kenzo Nakagawa／Hiroyasu
Nobuyama／Satoshi Morikami
4) Manza Beach Resort
5) 1982(Japan)
993 1) bus stop
2),3) Syuji Torigoe
4) The Gunma Prefectual Office
5) 1981(Japan)
994 1) facilities in a resort／bus
2) Wataru Tsuchiya／Kenzo
Nakagawa
3) Kenzo Nakagawa／Hiroyasu
Nobuyama／Satoshi Morikami
4) Manza Beach Resort
5) 1982(Japan)
995 1) "A Picture Book of
A-I-U-E-O" falling stones
2),3) Yasaburo Kuwayama
4) Typo-Eye Exhibition of "Kami
no Mojikku"
5) 1979(Japan)
996 1) timetable
2),3) Adrian Frutiger
4) Air France
5) (France)
997 1) airport／ground
transport
2) Ernest Lehfeld
3) Ernest Lehfeld／Manuel
Sanchez／Francisco Gallardo／
Jorge Fernandez
4) Mexico Airport
5) 1977-78(Mexico)
6) black yellow(ground)

998 1) ocean exhibition／bus
stop
2) Masaru Katsumi／Akiteru
Nakajima
3) Teruyuki Kunito／Yukio Ota／
Akira Kuroyone
4) Okinawa International Ocean
Exhibition Association
5) 1975(Japan)
6) blue(4PB3.5／12)／
beige(3Y8.5／1)
999 1) parking lot for bus
2),3) PVDI
4) Copek Oil Co., Ltd.
5) 1974(Brazil)
1000 1) bus stop
3) Ruedi Rüegg
5) 1983(Switzerland)
1001 1) bus stop
3) Ruedi Rüegg
5) 1983(Switzerland)
1002 2) Peter Steiner
3) Michael Friedland
4) Canadian Pacific
5) 1983(Canada)
6) blue
1003 1) supermarket／gateway
for carriers
2),3) Takao Yoguchi
4) Chujitsuya
5) 1979(Japan)
1004 1) regional meeting／
fransport
2) Hajime Nakamura／Yasaburo
Kuwayama
3) Yasaburo Kuwayama／Hajime
Ikeda／Norio Ikeda
4) The Regional Meeting of
Jehovah's Witnesses
5) 1980(Japan)
1005 1) transport
2),3) PVDI
5) 1977(Brazil)
1006 1) depertment store／way
for trains
3) Shigeo Fukuda
4) Seibu Depertment Store
5) 1976(Japan)
1007 1) map of
neighborhood／station
2) Akiteru Nakajima
3) Akiteru Nakajima／Kumi
Shirahama／Tamio Takeuchi
4) Art & Graphic
5) 1981(Japan)
1008 1) station
2),3) Syuji Torigoe
4) The Gunma Prefectual Office
5) 1981(Japan)
1009 1) encyclopedia／train
2) Katsuichi Ito
3) Katsuichi Ito Design Studio
4) Tamagawa University
Publishing Department
5) 1979(Japan)
1010 1) exhibition(space
show)／station
2),3) Noriaki Tamura
4) Headquarters／Japan
International Aerospace Show
1979
5) 1979(Japan)
6) sky blue
1011 1) map of
neighborhood／subway station

2) Akiteru Nakajima
3) Akiteru Nakajima／Kumi
Shirahama／Tamio Takeuchi
4) Art & Graphic
5) 1981(Japan)
1012 1) ocean exhibition／
expo. new city-car
2) Masaru Katsumi／Akiteru
Nakajima
3) Teruyuki Kunito／Yukio Ota／
Akira Kuroyone
4) Okinawa International Ocean
Exhibition Association
5) 1975(Japan)
6) blue(4PB3.5／12)／
beige(3Y8.5／1)
1013 1) ocean exhibition／
expo. future-car
2) Masaru Katsumi／Akiteru
Nakajima
3) Teruyuki Kunito／Yukio Ota／
Akira Kuroyone
4) Okinawa International Ocean
Exhibition Association
5) 1975(Japan)
6) fluorescent yellow／
red(5R4／14)
1014 1) "Monomi no To"
centennial
2) Yasaburo Kuwayama
3) Yasaburo Kuwayama／Hajime
Ikeda
4) Jehovah's Witnesses
5) 1979(Japan)
1015 1) transport
2),3) PVDI
5) 1977(Brazil)
1016 3) Ruedi Rüegg
5) 1983(Switzerland)
1017 1) sign in the quarantine
2),3) PVDI
5) 1977(Brazil)
1018 1) train
2) Peter Steiner
3) Michael Friedland
4) Canadian Pacific
5) 1983(Canada)
6) blue
1019 1) freights
2) Peter Steiner
3) Michael Friedland
4) Canadian Pacific
5) 1983(Canada)
6) blue
1020 1) "A Picture Book of
A-I-U-E-O"／train
2),3) Yasaburo Kuwayama
4) Typo-Eye Exhibition of "Kami
no Mojikku"
5) 1979(Japan)
1021 1) "Monomi no To"
centennial
2) Yasaburo Kuwayama
3) Yasaburo Kuwayama／Hajime
Ikeda
4) Jehovah's Witnesses
5) 1979(Japan)
1022 1) sign in quarantine
2),3) PVDI
5) 1977(Brazil)
1023 1) "Shiritori Kanji"
2),3) Yasaburo Kuwayama
4) Typo-Eye Exhibition of "Kami
no Mojikku"
5) 1977(Japan)

6) black
1024 1) ocean exhibition／
sightseeing ship
2) Masaru Katsumi／Akiteru
Nakajima
3) Teruyuki Kunito／Yukio Ota／
Akira Kuroyone
4) Okinawa International Ocean
Exhibition Association
5) 1975(Japan)
6) fluorescent yellow／
red(5R4／14)
1025 2) Peter Steiner
3) Michael Friedland
4) Canadian Pacific
5) 1983(Canada)
6) blue
1026 1) biblical association
game／St. Paul
2) Norio Ikeda
3) Norio Ikeda／Shigeo Ikeda／
So Nakamura
4) Ikedamura Aseduction
5) 1980(Japan)
1027 1) shipbuilding
2),3) Kunihiko Sugiyama
4) Bunri
5) 1979(Japan)
1028 1) ships
2),3) Kunihiko Sugiyama
4) Bunri
5) 1979(Japan)
1029 1) history of the
modernized Japan
2),3) Kunihiko Sugiyama
4) Bunri
5) 1979(Japan)
1030 1) encyclopedia／ship
2) Katsuichi Ito
3) Katsuichi Ito Design Soudio
4) Tamagawa University
Publishing Department
5) 1979(Japan)
1031 1) departure
3) Ruedi Rüegg
5) 1983(Switzerland)
1032 1) map of a realty
dealer／airport
2),3) Akiteru Nakajima
4) Anterope Valley Investment
Company
5) 1976(Japan)
1033 3) Ruedi Rüegg
5) 1983(Switzerland)
1034 1) airport
2) Ernest Lehfeld
3) Ernest Lehfeld／Manuel
Sanchez／Francisco Gallardo／
Jorge Fernandsz
4) Mexico Airport
5) 1977-78(Mexico)
6) black／yellow(ground)
1035 1) airport／departure
2) Ernest Lehfeld
3) Ernest Lehfeld／Manuel
Sanchez／Francisco Gallardo／
Jorge Fernandez
4) Mexico Airport
5) 1977-78(Mexico)
6) black／yellow(ground)
1036 1) airplane
2),3) Kunihiko Sugiyama
4) Bunri
5) 1979(Japan)
1037 1) arrival

3) Ruedi Rüegg
5) 1983(Switzerland)
1038 1) encyclopedia／airplane
2) Katsuichi Ito
3) Katsuichi Ito Design Studio
4) Tamagawa University
Publishing Department
5) 1979(Japan)
1039 2) Peter Steiner
3) Michael Friedland
4) Canadian Pacific
5) 1983(Canada)
6) blue
1040 1) heliport
2) Akiteru Nakajima
3) Akiteru Nakajima／Kumi
Shirahama
4) The Iraqi Government
5) 1981／1982(Japan)
1041 1) timetable
3) Adrian Frutiger
4) Air France
5) (France)
1042 1) "A Picture Book of
A-I-U-E-O"／airplane
2),3) Yasaburo Kuwayama
4) Typo-Eye Exhibition of "Kami
no Mojikku"
5) 1979(Japan)
1043 1) "Monomi no To"
centennial
2) Yasaburo Kuwayama
3) Yasaburo Kuwayama／Hajime
Ikeda
4) Jehovah's Witnesses
5) 1979(Japan)
1044 1) sign in the quarantine
2),3) PVDI
5) 1977(Brazil)
1045 1) "A Picture Book of
A-I-U-E-O"／caretaker
2),3) Yasaburo Kuwayama
4) Typo-Eye Exhibition of "Kami
no Mojikku"
5) 1979(Japan)
1046 1) house
2),3) Ludvik Feller
5) 1983-84(West Germany)
1047 1) bill on the post／realty
2) Yonefusa Yamada
3) Shin Sasaki／Yuko Ishida
4) Toden Kokoku
5) 1982(Japan)
1048 1) "A Picture Book of
A-I-U-E-O"／
2),3) Yasaburo Kuwayama
4) Typo-Eye Exhibition of "Kami
no Mojikku"
5) 1979(Japan)
1049 1) bill on the post／inn
2) Yonefusa Yamada
3) Shin Sasaki／Yuko Ishida
4) Toden Kokoku
5) 1982(Japan)
1050 1) company magazine／
living
2),3) Kunihiko Sugiyama
4) Bunri
5) 1980(Japan)
1051 1) the olympics(trial)／
players' lodgings
2) Tadashi Ikeda
3) Kenichi Miyata／Seiji Masuike
4) 1988 Seoul Olympiad
5) 1982(Japan)

6) black
1052 1) regional meeting／
lodging
2) Hajime Nakamura／Yasaburo
Kuwayama
3) Yasaburo Kuwayama／Hajime
Ikeda／Norio Ikeda
4) The Regional Meeting of
Jehovah's Witnesses
5) 1980(Japan)
1053 1) manufacture of paper
products／the cardboard factory
2),3) Rey R. Dacosta
4) Mendoza Enterprize
5) 1972／1978(Venezuela)
6) green
1054 1) map of a realty
dealer／camp ground
2),3) Akiteru Nakajima
4) Anterope Valley Investment
Company
5) 1976(Japan)
1055 2),3) Ludvik Feller
4) CEDEFOP
5) 1979(West Germany)
1056 1) map of a realty dealer
2),3) Akiteru Nakajima
4) Anterope Valley Investment
Company
5) 1976(Japan)
1057 1) insurance
2),3) Donald Patiwael
5) 1983(Netherland)
1058 1) encyclopedia／house
2) Katsuichi Ito
3) Katsuichi Ito Design Studio
4) Tamagawa University
Publishing Department
5) 1979(Japan)
1059 1) city plan
2),3) Ludvik Feller
4) Johannes Fehse
5) 1971(West Germany)
1060 1) city plan
2),3) Ludvik Feller
4) Johannes Fehse
5) 1971(West Germany)
1061 3) Eduard Prüssen
4) Bergish Gladbach city
5) 1980(West Germany)
6) black
1062 2),3) Ludvik Feller
4) CEDEFOP
5) 1979(West Germany)
1063 1) "A Picture Book of
A-I-U-E-O"／closed
2),3) Yasaburo Kuwayama
4) Typo-Eye Exhibition of "Kami
no Mojikku"
5) 1979(Japan)
1064 1) insurance
2),3) Donald Patiwael
5) 1983(Netherland)
1065 2) Peter Steiner
3) Michael Friedland
4) Canadian Pacific
5) 1983(Canada)
6) blue
1066 1) "A Picture Book of
A-I-U-E-O"／city
2),3) Yasaburo Kuwayama
4) Typo-Eye Exihibition of "Kami
no Mojikku"
5) 1979(Japan)
1067 1) hotel

2) Koji Tasaka
3) Mikado Tatsuzawa／Hiroshi
Mizuguchi
4) Okinawa All Japan Airline
Resort
5) 1983(Japan)
6) blue(CF 8471)
1068 3) Eduard Prüssen
4) Bergish Gladbach City
5) 1980(West Germany)
6) black
1069 1) "Monomi no To"
centennial
2) Yasaburo Kuwayama
3) Yasaburo Kuwayama／Hajime
Ikeda
4) Jehovah's Witnesses
5) 1979(Japan)
1070 1) "Monomi no To"
centennial
2) Yasaburo Kuwayama
3) Yasaburo Kuwayama／Hajime
Ikeda
4) Jehovah's Witnesses
5) 1979(Japan)
1071 1) map／church
2) Teruo Ishikawa
3) Teruo Ishikawa／Yoshiko
Wada
4) Shufu to Seikatsusha"
5) 1982(Japan)
1072 1) sports・public hygienic
service／church
2) Shakespear Design Studio
3) Ronald Shakespear／Raul
Shakespear
4) Buenos Aires Sports Center
5) 1980(Argentina)
1073 1) sports・public hygienic
service／monastery
2) Shakespear Design Studio
3) Ronald Shakespear／Raul
Shakespear
4) Buenos Aires Sports Center
5) 1980(Argentina)
1074 1) hospital／church
2) Shakespear Design Studio
3) Raul Shakespear／Ronald
Shakespear
4) Buenos Aires City Hospital
5) 1970／1980(Argentina)
6) red／blue
1075 1) map of
neighborhood／temple
2) Akiteru Nakajima
3) Akiteru Nakajima／Kumi
Shirahama／Tamio Takeuchi
4) Art & Graphic
5) 1981(Japan)
1076 1) map of
neighrorhood／the temple of
inari
2) Akiteru Nakajima
3) Akiteru Nakajima／Tamio
Takeuchi／Yumi Shirahama
4) Art & Graphic
5) 1981(Japan)
1077 1) "Shiritori Kanji"
2),3) Yasaburo Kuwayama
4) Typo-Eye Exhibition of "Kami
no Mojikku"
5) 1977(Japan)
6) black
1078 1) the ancient Japan
2),3) Kunihiko Sugiyama

4) Bunri
5) 1979(Japan)
1079 1) biblical association
game／nimrod
2) Norio Ikeda
3) Norio Ikeda／Shigeo Ikeda／
So Nakamura
4) Ikedamura Aseduction
5) 1980(Japan)
1080 1) manufacture of paper
products／paper mill
2),3) Rey R. Dacosta
4) Mendoza Enterprize
5) 1972／1973(Venezuela)
6) green
1081 1) sign in a camera
company／indoor storage for
dangerous objects
2) Ken Nara／Akiteru Nakajima
3) Akiteru Nakajima／Kumi
Shirahama／Ryoichi Yamada
4) Canon
5) 1974(Japan)
1082 1) sign in a camera
company／substation
2) Ken Nara／Akiteru Nakajima
3) Akiteru Nakajima／Kumi
Shirahama／Ryoichi Yamada
4) Canon
5) 1974(Japan)
1083 1) manufacture of paper
products／package
2),3) Rey R. Dacosta
4) Mendoza Enterprize
5) 1972／1973(Venezuela)
6) green
1084 1) manufacture of paper
products／paper bag factory
2),3) Rey R. Dacosta
4) Mendoza Enterprize
5) 1972／1973(Venezuela)
6) green
1085 1) map of a realty
dealer／factory
2),3) Akiteru Nakajima
4) Anterope Valley Investment
Company
5) 1976(Japan)
1086 1) city plan
2),3) Ludvik Feller
4) Johannes Fehse
5) 1971(West Germany)
1087 1) text of the preparatory
school
2),3) Kunihiko Sugiyama
4) Yoyogi Seminar
5) (Japan)
1088 1) modernized Japan
2),3) Kunihiko Sugiyama
4) Bunri
5) 1979(Japan)
1089 1) "Monomi no To"
centennial
2) Yasaburo Kuwayama
3) Yasaburo Kuwayama／Hajime
Ikeda
4) Jehovah's Witnesses
5) 1979(Japan)
1090 1) sub textbook
2),3) Kunihiko Sugiyama
4) Bunri
5) (Japan)
1091 1) sub textbook
2),3) Kunihiko Sugiyama
4) Bunri

5) (Japan)
1092 1) chemical company
2),3) Kunihiko Sugiyama
4) Sanso Kagaku
5) (Japan)
1093 1) hydroelectric power station
2),3) Kunihiko Sugiyama
4) Bunri
5) 1979(Japan)
1094 1) travel agency
2) Mace Duncan
3) Mike Quon
4) American Express
5) 1983(U.S.A.)
6) black/white
1095 1) exhibition/the conference of the trade fair in the Berlin exposition
2),3) Ludvik Feller
5) 1981(West Germany)
1096 1) sustainers of human existance
2),3) Kunihiko Sugiyama
4) Bunri
5) 1979(Japan)
1097 1) hospital/staircase
2) Shakespear Design Studio
3) Raul Shakespear/Ronald ShakesPear
4) Buenos Aires City Hospital
5) 1970/1980(Argentina)
6) red/blue
1098 1) coffee shop
2) Akiteru Nakajima
3) Akiteru Nakajima/Kumi Shirahama
4) The Iraqi Government
5) 1981/1982(Japan)
1099 1) hotel(information)
2) Jan Rajlich
3) Jan Rajlich/Jan Rajlich Jr.
4) Morava Hotel
5) 1978(Czechoslovakia)
1100 1) timetable
3) Adrian Frutiger
4) Air France
5) (France)
1101 1) cafeteria
2),3) PVDI
5) 1973(Brazil)
1102 1) sports • public hygienic service/coffee shop
2) Shakespear Design Studio
3) Ronald Shakespear/Raul Shakespear
4) Buenos Aires Sports Center
5) 1980(Argentina)
1103 1) department store
2) Shigeo Fukuda
4) Seibu Department Store
5) 1976(Japan)
1104 1) map of neigbborhood/coffee shop
2) Akiteru Nakajima
3) Akiteru Nakajima/Tamio Takeuchi/Kumi Shirahama
4) Art & Graphic
5) 1981(Japan)
1105 1) ocean exhibition/coffee shop
2) Masaru Katsumi/Akiteru Nakajima
3) Teruyuki Kunito/Akira Kuroyone/Yukio Ota

4) Okinawa International Ocean Exhibition Association
5) 1975(Japan)
1106 3) Ruedi Rüegg
5) 1983(Switzerland)
1107 1) coffee room
2) Shigeru Shimooka
3) Masanobu Watanabe
4) Mitsubishi Motors Co., Ltd. (MMC)
5) 1983(Japan)
6) dark blue(sub-color red)
1108 1) coffee room
2),3) Ichiro Saito
4) Denden Kosha Dojima Buiding
5) 1974(Japan)
1109 3) Ruedi Rüegg
5) 1983(Switzerland)
1110 1) coffee shop
2),3) PVDI
4) Copck Oil Co., Ltd.
5) 1974(Brazil)
1111 1) airport/cafeteria
2) Ernest Lehfeld
3) Ernest Lehfeld/Manuel Sanchez/Francisco Gallardo/Jorge Fernandez
4) Mexio Airport
5) 1977-78(Mexico)
6) black/yellow(ground)
1112 1) bill on the post/coffee shop
2) Yonefusa Yamada
3) Shin Sasaki/Yuko Ishida
4) Toden kokoku
5) 1982(Japan)
1113 1) publication
2),3) Ludvik Feller
5) 1972(West Germany)
1114 1) publication(practical book)/cover & title page
3) Yutaka Hasegawa
4) Shufu to Seikatusha
5) 1982(Japan)
1115 1) prints
3) Akiteru Nakajima
4) Iwaki Glass
5) (Japan)
1116 1) hospital/cafeteria
2) Shakespear Design Studio
3) Raul Shakespear/Ronald Shakespear
4) Buenos Aires City Hospital
5) 1970/1980(Argentina)
6) red/blue
1117 1) hotel
2),3) PVDI
4) Rio Meridian Hotel
5) 1975(Brazil)
1118 1) food/alcohol
2) Akiteru Nakajima
3) Akira Yagi/Takeshi Ogawa/Toru Konno/Hideko Kurihara/Keiko Komazawa
4) Chuo Bijutsu Gakuen Pictorial Course
5) 1980(Japan)
1119 1)
2) Akiteru Nakajima
3) Akiteru Nakajima/Yoichi Moroishi/Kumi Shirahama
4) Hakugen
5) 1978/1980(Japan)
1120 1) timetable

3) Adrian Frutiger
4) Air France
5) (France)
1121 3) Istvan Szekeres
4) Sirvice House
5) 1970(Hungary)
6) black
1122 1) biblical association game
2) Norio Ikeda
3) Norio Ikeda/Shigeo Ikeda/So Nakamura
4) Ikedamura Aseduction
5) 1980(Japan)
1123 1) bar
2),3) PVDI
5) 1973(Brazil)
1124 1) airport/bar
2) Ernest Lehfeld
3) Ernest Lehfeld/Manuel Sanchez/Francisco Gallardo/Jorge Fernandez
4) Mexico Airport
5) 1977-78(Mexico)
6) black/yellow(ground)
1125 1) snack
2),3) PVDI
5) 1973(Brazil)
1126 1) airport
3) Ruedi Rüegg
5) 1983(Switzerland)
1127 1) publication
2),3) Ludvik Feller
5) 1972(West Germany)
1128 1) supermarket
2) Shakespear Design Studio
3) Ronald Shakespear/Raul Shakespear
4) disco supermarket
5) 1982-83(Argentina)
1129 1) hotel
2),3) PVDI
4) Rio Meridian Hotel
5) 1975(Brazil)
1130 1) kiosk
2) Akiteru Nakajima
3) Akiteru Nakajima/Kumi Shirahama
4) The Iraqi Government
5) 1981/1982(Japan)
1131 1) prints
3) Akiteru Nakajima
4) Iwaki Glass
5) (Japan)
1132 1) publication
2),3) Ludvik Feller
5) 1972(West Germany)
1133 1) supermarket
2) Shakespear Design Studio
3) Ronald Shakespear/Roul Shakespear
4) Disco Supermarket
5) 1982-83(Argentina)
1134 1) map of neighborhood/liquor shop
2) Akiteru Nakajima
3) Akiteru Nakajima/Yumi Shirahama/Tamio Takeuchi
4) Art & Graphic
5) 1981(Japan)
1135
2) Akiteru Nakajima
3) Akiteru Nakajima/Yoichi Moroishi/Kumi Shirahama
4) Hakugen

5) 1978/1980(Japan)
1136 1) airport
3) Ruedi Rüegg
5) 1983(Switzerland)
1137 1) prints(greeing cards for summer)
3) Iwao Yamaguchi
4) Design Room Creation
5) 1981(Japan)
1138 1) "Shiritori Kanji"
2),3) Yasaburo Kuwayama
4) Typo Eye Exhibition of "A Picture Book of Letter"
5) 1977(Japan)
6) black
1139 1) map of neighborhood/a tavern
2) Akiteru Nakajima
3) Akiteru Nakajima/Yumi Shirahama/Tamio Takeuchi
4) Art & Graphic
5) 1981(Japan)
1140 1) "A Picture Book of A-I-U-E-O"/Fork Handcrafts
2),3) Yasaburo Kuwayama
4) Typo-Eye Exhibition of "Kami no Mojikku"
5) 1979(Japan)
1141 1) sign in a camera company/a place for emptied bottles
2) Ken Nara/Akiteru Nakajima
3) Akiteru Nakajima/Ryoichi Yamada/Kumi Shirahama
4) Canon
5) 1974(Japan)
1142 1) hotel(Information)
2) Jan Rajlich
3) Jan Rajlich/Jan Rajilich Jr.
4) Hotel Morava
5) 1978(Czechoslovakia)
1143 1) airport
3) Ruedi Rüegg
5) 1983(Switzerland)
1144 1) supermarket
2) Shakespear Design Studio
3) Ronald Shakespear/Raul Shakespear
4) Disco Supermarket
5) 1982-83(Argentina)
1145 1) supermarket
2) Shakespear Design Studio
3) Ronald Shakespear/Raul Shakespear
4) Disco Supermarket
5) 1982-83(Argentina)
1146 1) bill on the post/restaurant
2) Yonefusa Yamada
3) Sin Sasaki/Yuko Ishida
4) Toden Kokoku
5) 1982(Japan)
1147 1) sports • public hygienic service/a room for new-born babies
2) Shakespear Design Studio
3) Ronald Shakespear/Raul Shakespear
4) Buenos Aires Sports Center
5) 1980(Argentina)
1148 3) Ruedi Rüegg
5) 1983(Switzerland)
1149 1) supermarket/nursery
2),3) Takao Yoguchi
4) Chujitsuya

5) 1979(Japan)
1150 1) hospital／pediatrics
2) Shakespear Design Studio
3) Ronald Shakespear／Raul Shakespear
4) Buenos Aires City Hospital
5) 1970／1980(Argentina)
6) red／blue
1151 1) hospital／new-born baby
2) Shakespear Design Studio
3) Ronald Shakespear／Raul Shakespear
4) Buenos Aires City Hospital
5) 1970／1980(Argentina)
6) red／blue
1152 1) biblical association game／Jona
2) Norio Ikeda
3) Norio Ikeda／Shigeo Ikeda／So Nakamura
4) Ikedamura Aseduction
5) 1980(Japan)
1153 1) ceramics
2),3) Kunihiko Sugiyama
4) Bunri
5) 1979(Japan)
1154 1) china
2),3) Kunihiko Sugiyama
4) Bunri
5) 1979(Japan)
1155 1) products／the aquarius
2),3) Shigeji Kobayashi
4) The Lion Sekken Co., Ltd.
5) 1981(Japan)
1156 1) biblical association game／samaritan
2) Norio Ikeda
3) Norio Ikeda／Shigeo Ikeda／So Nakamura
4) Ikedamura Aseduction
5) 1980(Japan)
1157 1) supermarket／nursery
2),3) Takao Yoguchi
4) Chujitsuya
5) 1979(Japan)
1158 1) chemicals
2),3) Kunihiko Sugiyama
4) Bunri
5) 1979(Japan)
1159 1) "Shiritori Kanji"
2),3) Yasaburo Kuwayama
4) Typo-Eye Exhibition of "A Picture Book of Letter"
5) 1977(Japan)
6) Black
1160 1) sign in a camera company／dump for emptied cans
2) Ken Nara／Akiteru NaKajima
3) Akiteru Nakajima／Kumi Shirahama／Yoichi Yamada
4) Canon
5) 1974(Japan)
1161 1) can-plant
2),3) Rey R. Dacosta
4) Mendoza Enterprize
5) 1977(Venezuela)
6) brown
1162 1) regional meeting／emptied can
2) Hajime Nakamura／Yasaburo Kuwayama
3) Yasaburo Kuwayama／Norio Ikeda／Hajime Ikeda

4) The Regional Meeting of Jehovah's Witnesses
5) 1980(Japan)
1163 1) food／to pour to another vessel
2) Akiteru Nakajima
3) Akira Yagi／Takeshi Ogawa／Toru Konno／Hediko Kurihara／Keiko Komazawa
4) Chuo Bijutsu Gakuen Pictorial Course
5) 1980(Japan)
1164 1) food／open the bottom of can
2) Akiteru Nakajima
3) Akira Yagi／Takeshi Ogawa／Toru Konno／Hideko Kurihara／Keiko Komazawa
4) Chuo Bijutsu Gakuen Pictorial Course
5) 1980(Japan)
1165 1) graphic indication of a detergent／quantity(one cap)
2) Akiteru Nakajima
3) Seiko Aoki／Hisako Kataoka／Yoko Kobayashi
4) Chuo Bijutsu Gakuen Pictorial Course
5) 1983(Japan)
1166 1) bill on the post／Japanese soba
2) Yonefusa Yamada
3) Shin Sasaki／Yuko Ishida
4) Toden Kokoku
5) 1982(Japan)
1167 1) bill on the post／chinese foods
2) Yonefusa Yamada
3) Shin Sasaki／Yuko Ishida
4) Toden Kokoku
5) 1982(Japan)
1168 1) regional meeting／soba
2) Hajime Nakamura／Yasaburo Kuwayama
3) Yasaburo Kuwayama／Norio Ikeda／Hajime Ikeda
4) The Regional Meeting of Jehovah's Witnesses
5) 1980(Japan)
1169 1) prints
3) Akiteru Nakajima
4) Iwaki Glass
5) (Japan)
1170 1) "Shiritori Kanji"
2),3) Yasaburo Kuwayama
4) Typo-Eye Exhibition of "A Picture Book of Letter"
5) 1977(Japan)
6) black
1171 1) regional meeting／washing
2) Hajime Nakamura／Yasaburo Kuwahara
3) Yasaburo Kuwayama／Norio Ikeda／Hajime Ikeda
4) The Regional Reeting of Jehovah's Witnesses
5) 1980(Japan)
1172 1) regional meeting
2) Hajime Nakamura／Yasaburo Kuwayama
3) Yasaburo Kuwayama／Norio Ikeda／Hajime Ikeda
4) The Regional Meeting of Jehovah's Witnesses

5) 1980(Japan)
1173 1) map of neighborhood／Chinese restaurant
2) Akiteru Nakajima
3) Akiteru Nakajima／Tamio Takeuchi／Yumi Shirahama
4) Art & Graphic
5) 1981(Japan)
1174 1) "Shiritori Kanji"
2),3) Yasaburo Kuwayama
4) Typo-Eye Exhibition of "A Picture Book of Letter"
5) 1977(Japan)
6) black
1175 1) map of neighborhood／Japanese restaurant
2) Akiteru Nakajima
3) Akiteru Nakajima／Tamio Takeuchi／Yumi Shirahama
4) Art & Graphic
5) 1981(Japan)
1176 1) bill on the post／Japanese food
2) Yonefusa Yamada
3) Shin Sasaki／Yuko Ishida
4) Toden Kokoku
5) 1982(Japan)
1177 1) metalwork
2),3) Kunihiko Sugiyama
4) Bunri
5) 1979(Japan)
1178 1) bill on the post／tea
2) Yonefusa Yamada
3) Shin Sasaki／Yuko Ishida
4) Toden Kokoku
5) 1982(Japan)
1179 1) tea
2) Akiteru Nakajima
3) Akiteru Nakajima／Kumi Shirahama／Yoichi Moroishi
4) Hakugen
5) 1978／1980(Japan)
1180 1) tea
2),3) Ichiro Saito
4) Denden Kosha Dojima Building
5) 1974(Japan)
1181 1) company sign／tea
2) Shigeru Shimooka
3) Masanobu Watanabe
4) Mitsubishi Motors Co., Ltd. (MMC)
5) 1983(Japan)
6) dark blue(sub-color Red)
1182 1) food／to pour hot water
2) Yasuteru Nakajima
3) Akira Yagi／Takeshi Ogawa／Toru Konno／Hideko Kurihara／Keiko Komazawa
4) Chuo Bijutsu Gakuen Pictorial Course
5) 1980(Japan)
1183 1) graphic indication of a detergent／don't pour the boiling water
2) Yasuteru Nakajima
3) Seiko Aoki／Hisako Kataoka／Yoko Kobayashi
4) Chuo Bijutsu Gakuen Pictorial
5) 1983(Japan)
1184 1) biblical association game／esau
2) Norio Ikeda

3) Norio Ikeda／Shigeo Ikeda／So Nakamura
4) Ikedaruma Aseduction
5) 1980(Japan)
1185 1) regional meeting／kitchen work
2) Hajime Nakamura／Yasaburo Kuwayama
3) Yasaburo Kuwayama／Norio Ikeda／Hajime Ikeda
4) The Reigonal Metting of Jehovah's Witnesses
5) 1980(Japan)
1186 1) gas
2),3) Kunihiko Sugiyama
4) Bunri
5) 1979(Japan)
1187 1) publication(guidance of teaching)
2),3) Hiroshi Fukushima
4) Tokyo Shoseki
5) 1979(Japan)
1188 1) publication(guidance of teaching)
2),3) Hiroshi Fukushima
4) Tokyo Shoseki
5) 1979(Japan)
1189 1) assortment of commodities in a supermarket
2),3) Takao Yoguchi
4) Chujitsuya
5) 1977(Japan)
1190 1) supermarket／vinyl bag
2),3) Takao Yoguchi
4) Chujitsuya
5) 1979(Japan)
1191 1) ice cream
2) Akiteru Nakajima
3) Akiteru Nakajima／Yoichi Moroishi／Kumi Shirahama
4) Hakugen
5) 1978／1980(Japan)
1192 1) food
2) Akiteru Nakajima
3) Akiteru Nakajima／Yoichi Moroishi／Kumi Shirahama
4) Hakugen
5) 1978／1980(Japan)
1193 1) supermarket／food
2),3) Takao Yoguchi
4) Chujitsuya
5) 1977(Japan)
1194 1) iron manufacture
2),3) Kunihiko Sugiyama
4) Bunri
5) 1979(Japan)
1195 1) food／to pour
2) Akiteru Nakajima
3) Akira Yagi／Takeshi Ogawa／Toru Konno／Hideko Kurihara／Keiko Komazawa
4) Chuo Bijutsu Gakuen Pictorial Course
5) 1980(Japan)
1196 1) food／to mix up
2) Akiteru Nakajima
3) Akira Yagi／Takeshi Ogawa／Toru Konno／Hideko Kurihara／Keiko Komazawa
4) Chuo Bijutsu Gakuen Pictorial Course
5) 1980(Japan)
1197 1) food／to turn inside out
2) Akiteru Nakajima

3) Akira Yagi／Takeshi Ogawa／
Toru Konno／Hideko Kurihara／
Keiko Komazawa
4) Chuo Bijutsu Gakuen Pictorial
Course
5) 1980(Japan)
1198 1) graphic indication of a
detergent／quantity(one cup)
2) Akiteru Nakajima
3) Seiko Aoki／Hisako
Kataoka／Yoko Kobayashi
4) Chuo Bijutsu Gakuen Pictorial
Course
5) 1983(Japan)
1199 1) supermarket
2),3) Takao Yoguchi
4) Chujitsuya
5) 1977(Japan)
1200 1) bill on the post／sushi
2) Yonefusa Yamada
3) Shin Sasaki／Yuko Ishida
4) Toden Kokoku
5) 1982(Japan)
1201 1) graphic indication of a
detergent／don't spray in
horizontal position
2) Akiteru Nakajima
3) Seiko Aoki／Hisako
Kataoka／Yoko Kobayashi
4) Chuo Bijutsu Gakuen Pictorial
Course
5) 1983(Japan)
1202 1) food
2) Akiteru Nakajima
3) Akira Yagi／Takeshi Ogawa／
Toru Konno／Hideko Kurihara／
Keiko Komazawa
4) Chuo Bijutsu Gakuen Pictorial
Course
5) 1980(Japan)
1203 1) food／to close up tight
2) Akiteru Nakajima
3) Akira Yagi／Takeshi Ogawa／
Toru Konno／Hideko Kurihara／
Keiko Komazawa
4) Chuo Bijutsu Gakuen Pictorial
Course
5) 1980(Japan)
1204 1) the nature of soil and
its transformation
2),3) Kunihiko Sugiyama
4) Bunri
5) 1979(Japan)
1205 1) acid・alkali・salt
2),3) Kunihiko Sugiyama
4) Bunri
5) 1979(Japan)
1206 1) genuine substance and
mixture
2),3) Kunihiko Sugiyama
4) Bunri
5) 1979(Japan)
1207 1) food／to add a
seasoning
2) Akiteru Nakajima
3) Akira Yagi／Takeshi Ogawa／
Toru Konno／Hideko Kurihara／
Keiko Komazawa
4) Chuo Bijutsu Gakuen Pictorial
Course
5) 1980(Japan)
1208
2) Akiteru Nakajima
3) Akiteru Nakajima／Yoichi
Moroishi／Kumi Shirahama

4) Hakugen
5) 1978／1980(Japan)
1209 1) an akebi-craft
2),3) Kunihiko Sugiyama
4) Bunri
5) 1979(Japan)
1210 3) A.G.Chiremanse
5) 1982(Netherlands)
6) white／dark blue
1211 1) ocean exhibition／
restaurant
2) Masaru Katsumi／Akiteru
Nakajima
3) Teruyuki Kunito／Yukio Ota／
Akira Kuroyone
4) Okinawa International Ocean
Exhibition Association
5) 1975(Japan)
6) fluorescent yellow／
red(5R4／14)
1212 1) timetable
3) Adrian Frutiger
4) Air France
5) (France)
1213 1) restaurant
2),3) PVDI
5) 1973(Brazil)
1214 1) restaurant
2),3) PVDI
4) Copek Oil Co., Ltd.
5) 1974(Brazil)
1215 1) restaurant
2) Akiteru Nakajima
3) Akiteru Nakajima／Kumi
Shirahama
4) The Iraqi Government
5) 1981／1982(Japan)
1216 1) dining hall
2),3) Syuji Torigoe
4) The Gunma Prefectural Office
5) 1981(Japan)
1217 1) shopping center／
restaurant
2),3) Syuji Torigoe
4) Tokyu Store
5) 1976(Japan)
1218 1) bill on the post／
restaurant
2) Yonefusa Yamada
3) Sin Sasaki／Yuko Ishida
4) Toden Kokoku
5) 1982(Japan)
1219 1) airport／restaurant
2) Ernest Lehfeld
3) Ernest Lehfeld／Manuel
Sanchez／Francisco Gallardo／
Jorge Fernandez
4) Mexico Airport
5) 1977-78(Mexico)
6) black／yellow(ground)
1220 1) the olympics／dining
hall(trial)
2) Tadashi Ikeda
3) Kenichi Miyata／Seiji Masuike
4) 1988 Seoul Olympiad
5) 1982(Japan)
6) black
1221 1) department store
3) Shigeo Fukuda
4) Seibu Department Store
5) 1976(Japan)
1222 1) restaurant
2),3) Ichiro Saito
4) Denden Kosha Dojima
Biluding

5) 1974(Japan)
1223 1) map of
neighborhood／restaurant
2) Akiteru Nakajima
3) Akiteru Nakajima／Yumi
Shirahama／Tamio Takeuchi
4) Art & Graphic
5) 1981(Japan)
1224 1) company sign
2) Shigeru Shimooka
3) Masanobu Watanabe
4) Mitsubishi Motors Co., Ltd.
(MMC)
5) 1983(Japan)
6) dark blue(sub-color red)
1225 1) hotel(information)
2) Jan Rajlich
3) Jan Rajlich／Jan Rajilich Jr.
4) Hotel Morava
5) 1978(Czechoslovakia)
1226 1) airport
2) Ruedi Rüegg
5) 1983(Switzerland)
1227 1) hotel
2),3) PVDI
4) Rio Meridian Hotel
5) 1975(Brazil)
1228 1) food／to cut
2) Akiteru Nakajima
3) Akira Yagi／Takeshi Ogawa／
Toru Konno／Hideko Kurihara／
Keiko Komazawa
4) Chuo Bijutsu Gakuen Pictorial
Course
5) 1980(Japan)
1229
2) Akiteru Nakajima
3) Akiteru Nakajima／Yoichi
Moroishi／Kumi Shirahama
4) Hakugen
5) 1978／1980(Japan)
1230 1) graphic indication of a
detergent／quantity(a spoonful)
2) Akiteru Nakajima
3) Seiko Aoki／Hisako
Kataoka／Yoko Kobayashi
4) Chuo Bijutsu Gakuen Pictorial
Course
5) 1983(Japan)
1231 1) "A Picture Book of
A-I-U-E-O"／key
2),3) Yasaburo Kuwayama
4) Typo-Eye Exhibition of "Kami
no Mojikku"
5) 1979(Japan)
1232 1) map／coin-locker
2) Teruo Ishikawa
3) Teruo Ishikawa／Yoshiko
Wada
4) Shufu to Seikatsusha
5) 1982(Japan)
1233 1) key
2),3) PVDI
5) 1973(Brazil)
1234 1) bill on the post／hotel
2) Yonefusa Yamada
3) Sin Sasaki／Yuko Ishida
4) Toden Kokoku
5) 1982(Japan)
1235 1) bank
3) Eduardo A. Canovas
5) 1980(Argentina)
6) Dark Green／Green
1236 1) food

2) Akiteru Nakajima
3) Akira Yagi／Takeshi Ogawa／
Toru Konno／Hideko Kurihara／
Keiko Komazawa
4) Chuo Bijutsu Gakuen Pictorial
Course
5) 1980(Japan)
1237 1) map of
neighborhood／barbershop
2) Akiteru Nakajima
3) Akiteru Nakajima／Yumi
Shirahama／Tamio Takeuchi
4) Art & Graphic
5) 1981(Japan)
1238 1) bill on the post／
beauty salon
2) Yonefusa Yanada
3) Shin Sasaki／Yuko Ishida
4) Toden Kokoku
5) 1982(Japan)
1239 1) ocean exhibition／tape
cut room
2) Masaru Katsumi／Akiteru
Nakajima
3) Teruyuki Kunito／Yukio Ota／
Akira Kuroyone
4) Okinawa International Ocean
Exhibition Association
5) 1975(Japan)
6) blue(4PB3.5／12)／
beige(3Y8.5／1)
1240 1) hotel
2),3) PVDI
4) Rio Meridian Hotel
5) 1975(Brazil)
1241 1) bookshop／practical
book
3) Miloš Ćirić
5) 1974(Yugoslavia)
6) red
1242 1) "Monomi no To"
centennial
2) Yasaburo Kuwayama
3) Yasaburo Kuwayama／Hajime
Ikeda
4) Jehovah's Witnesses
5) 1979(Japan)
1243 1) timetable
3) Adrian Frutiger
4) Air France
5) (France)
1244 1) encyclopedia／
livelihood in ancient time
2) Katsuichi Ito
3) Katsuichi Ito Design Studio
4) Tamagawa University
Publishing Department
5) 1979(Japan)
1245 3) Eduard Prüssen
4) Bergish Gladbach
5) 1980(West Germany)
6) black
1246 1) job
2),3) Kunihiko Sugiyama
4) Bunri
5) 1979(Japan)
1247 1) instruments
3) István Szekeres
5) 1975(Hungary)
1248 1) sign in a camera
company／under construction
2) Ken Nara／Akiteru Nakajima
3) Akiteru Nakajima／Ryoich
Yamada／Kumi Shirahama
4) Canon

5) 1974(Japan)

1249 1) sports · public hygienic service／maintenance
2) Shakespear Design Studio
3) Ronald Shakespear／Raul Shakespear
4) Buenos Aires Sports Center
5) 1980(Argentina)

1250 1) instruments
3) Istvan Szekeres
5) 1975(Hungary)

1251 1) instruments
3) Istvan Szekeres
5) 1975(Hungary)

1252 1) laboratory
2),3) Ludvik Feller
4) Bundesinstitut Fur Berufsbildungs-Forschung
5) 1972(West Germany)

1253 1) sign in a camera company／under repairs
2) Ken Nara／Akiteru Nakajima
3) Akiteru Nakajima／Ryoichi Yamada／Kumi Shirahama
4) Canon
5) 1974(Japan)

1254 1) business information
2) Yasaburo Kuwayama
3) Minoru Kamono
4) Maruko Birumen
5) 1977(Japan)

1255 1) company sign
2) Shigeru Shimooka
3) Masanobu Watanabe
4) Mitsubishi Motors Co., Ltd. (MMC)
5) 1983(Japan)
6) dark blue(sub-color Red)

1256 1) sports equipment shop
2),3) Beppe Benenti
5) 1983(Italy)
6) red／yellow

1257 1) special edition／metal-carving
2) Kazunori Okamoto
3) Hiroshi Iseya
4) Diamondsha
5) 1980(Japan)

1258 1) instruments
3) Istvan Szekeres
5) 1975(Hungary)

1259 1) transport
3) Istvan Szekeres
5) 1982(Hungary)
6) dark blue

1260 1) special edition／a weekend carpenter
2) Kazunori Okamoto
3) Hiroshi Iseya
4) Diamondsha
5) 1980(Japan)

1261 1) billon the post／cleaning
2) Yonefusa Yamada
3) Shin Sasaki／Yuko Ishida
4) Toden Kokoku
5) 1982(Japan)

1262 2),3) PVDI
4) Fulnus Electric Center
5) 1972(Brazil)

1263 1) put on the helmet
2),3) PVDI
4) Copek Oil Co., Ltd.
5) 1974(Brazil)

1264 1) sub textbook
2),3) Kunihiko Sugiyama
4) Bunri
5) 1979(Japan)

1265 2),3) PVDI
4) Fulnus Electric Center
5) 1972(Brazil)

1266 1) put on protective glasses
2),3) PVDI
4) Copek Oil Co., Ltd.
5) 1974(Brazil)

1267 1) bill on the post／safety glasses
2) Yonefusa Yamada
3) Shin Sasaki／Yuko Ishida
4) Toden Kokoku
5) 1982(Japan)

1268 1) safety & hygiene／protective glasses
2),3) Tokyo Shibaura Denki Design Department
4) Tokyo Shibaura Denki
5) 1975(Japan)
6) yellow／black(partly white · red)

1269 1) "A Picture Book of A-I-U-E-O"／glasses
2),3) Yasaburo Kuwayama
4) Typo-Eye Exhibition of "Kami no Mojikku"
5) 1979(Japan)

1270 1) safety & hygiene／shilding glasses
2),3) Tokyo Shibaura Denki Design Department
4) Tokyo Shibaura Denki
5) 1975(Japan)
6) yellow／black(partly white · red)

1271 1) put on mask
2),3) PVDI
4) Copek Oil Co., Ltd.
5) 1974(Brazil)

1272 2),3) PVDI
4) Fulnus Electric Center
5) 1972(Brazil)

1273 1) safety & hygiene／protective mask
2),3) Tokyo Shibaura Denki Design Department
4) Tokyo Shibaura Denki
5) 1975(Japan)
6) yellow／black(partly white · red)

1274 1) sign in a camera company／poisonous gas
2) Ken Nara／Akiteru Nakajima
3) Akiteru Nakajima／Ryoichi Yamada／Kumi Shirahama
4) Canon
5) 1974(Japan)

1275 1) sign in a camera company
2) Ken Nara／Akiteru Nakajima
3) Akiteru Nakajima／Ryoichi Yamada／Kumi Shirahama
4) Canon
5) 1974(Japan)

1276 1) ear protection
2),3) PVDI
4) Copek Oil Co., Ltd.
5) 1974(Brazil)

1277 1) jewel shop
2),3) PVDI

5) 1973(Brazil)

1278 1) safety & hygiene／protective clothing
2),3) Tokyo Shibaura Denki Design Department
4) Tokyo Shibaura Denki
5) 1975(Japan)
6) yellow／black(partly white · red)

1279 1) put on gloves
2),3) PVDI
4) Copek Oil Co., Ltd.
5) 1974(Brazil)

1280 1) safety & hygiene／gloves
2),3) Tokyo Shibaura Denki Design Department
4) Tokyo Shibaura Denki
5) 1975(Japan)
6) yellow／black(partly white · red)

1281 1) graphic indication of a detergent／put on gloves
2) Akiteru Nakajima
3) Seiko Aoki／Hisako Kataoka／Yoko Kobayashi
4) Chuo Bijutsu Gakuen Pictorial Course
5) 1983(Japan)

1282 1) safety & hygiene／don't put on gloves
2),3) Tokyo Shibaura Denki Design Department
4) Tokyo Shibaura Denki
5) 1975(Japan)
6) yellow／black(partly white · red)

1283 1) shoe maker
2) Jan Railich
3) Jan Railich Jr.
4) CSVD
5) 1973(Czechoslovakia)

1284 1) safety & hygiene／boots
2),3) Tokyo Shibaura Denki Design Department
4) Tokyo Shibaura Denki
5) 1975(Japan)
6) yellow／black(partly white · red)

1285 1) company sign
2) Shigeru Shimooka
3) Masanobu Watanabe
4) Mitsubishi Motors Co., Ltd. (MMC)
5) 1983(Japan)
6) dark blue(sub-color red)

1286 1) safety & hygiene／safety shoes
2),3) Tokyo Shibaura Denki Design Department
4) Tokyo Shibaura Denki
5) 1975(Japan)
6) yellow／black(partly white · red)

1287 1) safety & hygiene／leggings
2),3) Tokyo Shibaura Denki Design Department
4) Tokyo Shibaura Denki
5) 1975(Japan)
6) yellow／black(partly white · red)

1288 1) company sign
2) Shigeru Shimooka

3) Masanobu Watanabe
4) Mitsubishi Motors Co., Ltd. (MMC)
5) 1983(Japan)
6) dark blue(sub-color red)

1289 1) ocean exhibition／no trespassing
2) Masaru Katsumi／Akiteru Nakajima
3) Teruyuki Kunito／Yukio Ota／Akira Kuroyone
4) Okinawa International Ocean Exhibition Association
5) 1975(Japan)
6) fluorescent yellow／red(5R4／14)

1290
2) Akiteru Nakajima
3) Akiteru Nakajima／Kumi Shirahama
4) The Iraqi Government
5) 1981／82(Japan)

1291 1) laboratory
2),3) Ludvik Feller
4) Bundesinstitut Fur Berufsbildungs-Forschung
5) 1973(West Germany)

1292 1) acceptance
2),3) PVDI
5) 1973(Brazil)

1293 1) Japanese umbrella
2),3) Kunihiko Sugiyama
4) Bunri
5) 1979(Japan)

1294 1) bank
3) Eduardo A.Canovas
4) North Business Bank
5) 1980(Argentina)
6) dark green／green

1295 1) hotel
2),3) PVDI
4) Rio Meridian Hotel
5) 1975(Brazil)

1296 1) weather report board／rain
3) Akira Nakajima
4) Okinawa International Ocean Exhibition Association
5) 1975(Japan)

1297 1) ocean exhibition／expo beach
2) Masaru Katsumi／Akiteru Nakajima
3) Teruyuki Kunito／Yukio Ota／Akira Kuroyone
4) Okinawa International Ocean Exhibition Association
5) 1975(Japan)
6) blue(4PB3. 5／12)／beige(3Y8. 5／1)

1298 1) greeting cards
2),3) Tadashi Mizui
4) Tadashi Mizui
5) 1975(Japan)

1299 1) campaign
2) Kuniharu Masubuchi
3) Emiko Tachiyama／Iseya Hiroshi
4) Mikimoto
5) 1983(Japan)

1300 1) library／umbrella stand
2) Takenobu Igarashi
3) Akiteru Nakajima／Kumi Shirahama

4) Keio Gijuku University
5) 1982(Japan)
1301 1) greeting cards
2),3) Todashi Mizui
4) Tadashi Mizui
5) 1975(Japan)
1302 1) sports • public hygienic service／locker room
2) Shakespear Design Studio
3) Ronald Shakespear／Raul Shakespear
4) Buenos Aires Sports Center
5) 1980(Argentina)
1303 1) hotel(information)
2) Jan Rajlich
3) Jan Rajlich／Jan Rajlich Jr.
4) Hotel Morava
5) 1978(Czechoslovakia)
1304 1) "Shiritori Kanji"
2),3) Yasaburo Kuwayama
4) Typo-Eye Exhibition of "A Picture Book of Letter"
5) 1977(Japan)
6) black
1305 1) texture
2),3) Kunihiko Sugiyama
4) Bunri
5) 1979(Japan)
1306 1) "A Picture Book of A-I-U-E-O"／spool
2),3) Yasaburo Kuwayama
4) Typo-Eye Exhibition of "Kami no Mojikku"
5) 1979(Japan)
1307 1) "A Picture Book of A-I-U-E-O"／woolen yarn
2),3) Yasaburo Kuwayama
4) Typo-Eye Exhibition of "Kami no Mojikku"
5) 1979(Japan)
1308 1) sign in a camera company／instrument of refuge • rope
2) Ken Nara／Akiteru Nakajima
3) Akiteru Nakajima／Ryoichi Yamada／Kumi Shirahama
4) Canon
5) 1974(Japan)
1309 1) a braided rope
2),3) Kunihiko Sugiyama
4) Bunri
5) 1979(Japan)
1310 1) sub textbook
2),3) Kunihiko Sugiyama
4) Bunri
5) 1979(Japan)
1311 1) sub textbook／textile
2),3) Kunihiko Sugiyama
4) Bunri
5) 1979(Japan)
1312 1) regional meeting(check room)
2) Hajime Nakamura／Yasaburo Kuwayama
3) Yasaburo Kuwayama／Hajime Ikeda／Norio Ikeda
4) The Regional Meeting of Jehovah's Witnesses
5) 1980(Japan)
1313 1) travel agency
2) Mace Duncan
3) Mike Quon
4) American Express
5) 1983(U.S.A.)
6) black／white

1314 1) ocean exhibition／booth
2) Masaru Katsumi／Akiteru Nakajima
3) Teruyuki Kunito／Yukio Ota／Akira Kuroyone
4) Okinawa International Ocean Exhibition Association
5) 1975(Japan)
6) blue／beige
1315 1) map／booth
2) Teruo Ishikawa
3) Teruo Ishikawa／Yoshiko Wada
4) Shufu to Seikatsusha
5) 1982(Japan)
1316 1) present
2),3) PVDI
5) 1973(Brazil)
1317 1) "A Picture Book of A-I-U-E-O"／purse
2),3) Yasaburo Kuwayama
4) Typo-Eye Exhibition of "Kami no Mojikku"
5) 1979(Japan)
1318 1) ocean exhibition／check room
2) Masaru Katsumi／Akiteru Nakajima
3) Teruyuki Kunito／Yukio Ota／Akira Kuroyone
4) Okinawa International Ocean Exhibition Association
5) 1975(Japan)
6) blue(4PB3.5／12)／beige(3Y8.5／1)
1319 1) ocean exhibition／a thing left behind
2) Masaru Katsumi／Akiteru Nakajima
3) Teruyuki Kunito／Yukio Ota／Akira Kuroyone
4) Okinawa International Ocean Exhibition Association
5) 1975(Japan)
6) blue(4PB3. 5／12)／beige(3Y8. 5／1)
1320 1) regional meeting／a lost articles
2) Hajime Nakamura／Yasaburo Kuwayama
3) Yasaburo Kuwayama／Hajime Ikeda／Norio Ikeda
4) The Regional Meeting of Jehovah's Witnesscs
5) 1980(Japan)
1321 1) supermarket／checking out at each floor
2),3) Takao Yoguchi
4) Chujitsuya
5) 1979(Japan)
1322 1) supermarket／a place for carts
2),3) Takao Yoguchi
4) Chujitsuya
5) 1979(Japan)
1323 1) pubication(practical book)／cover & title page
3) Yutaka Hasegawa
4) Shufu to Seikatsusha
5) 1982(Japan)
1324 1) regional meeting(check room)
2) Hajime Nakamura／Yasaburo Kuwayama

3) Yasaburo Kuwayama／Hajime Ikeda／Norio Ikeda
4) The Regional Meeting of Jehovah's Witnesses
5) 1980(Japan)
1325 1) travel agency
2) Mace Duncan
3) Mike Quon
4) American Express
5) 1983(U.S.A.)
6) black／white
1326 1) sports • public hygienic service／research
2) Shakespear Design Studio
3) Ronald Shakespear／Raul Shakespear
4) Buenos Aires Sports Center
5) 1980(Argentina)
1327 1) regional meeting
2) Hajime Nakamura／Yasaburo Kuwayama
3) Yasaburo Kuwayama／Hajime Ikeda／Norio Ikeda
4) The Regional Meeting of Jehovah's Witnesses
5) 1980(Japan)
1328 1) hospital／preparation
2) Shakespear Design Studio
3) Ronald Shakespear／Raul Shakespear
4) Buenos Aires City Hospital
5) 1970／1980(Argentina)
6) red／blue
1329 1) sign in a camera company／transport with caution
2) Ken Nara／Akiteru Nakajima
3) Akiteru Nakajima／Ryoich Yamada／Kumi Shirahama
4) Canon
5) 1974(Japan)
1330 1) ocean exhibition／coin-locker
2) Masaru Katsumi／Akiteru Nakajima
3) Teruyuki Kunito／Yukio Ota／Akira Kuroyone
4) Okinawa International Ocean Exhibition Association
5) 1975(Japan)
6) blue(4PB3.5／12)／beige(3Y8.5／1)
1331 1) check room
2),3) Syuji Torigoe
4) The Gunma Prefectual Office
5) 1981(Japan)
1332 1) the olympics／locker room(trial)
2) Tadashi Ikeda
3) Kenichi Miyata／Seiji Masuike
4) 1988 Seoul Olympiad
5) 1982(Japan)
6) black
1333 1) airport
3) Ruedi Rüegg
5) 1983(Switzerland)
1334 1) facilities in a resort
2) Wataru Tsuchiya／Kenzo Nakagawa
3) Kenzo Nakagawa／Hiroyasu Nobuyama／Satoshi Morikami
4) Manza Beach Resort
5) 1982(Japan)
1335 1) airport／check room
2) Ernest Lehfeld
3) Ernest Lehfeld／Manuel

Sanchez／Francisco Gallardo／Jorge Fernandez
4) Mexico Airport
5) 1977-78(Mexico)
6) black／yellow(ground)
1336 1) lost articles station
2),3) Syuji Torigoe
4) The Gunma Prefectual Office
5) 1981(Japan)
1337 1) airport／complaint about baggage
2) Ernest Lehfeld
3) Ernest Lehfeld／Manuel Sanchez／Francisco Gallardo／Jorge Fernandez
4) Mexico Airport
5) 1977-78(Mexico)
6) black／yellow(ground)
1338 1) airport／baggage check
2) Ernest Lehfeld
3) Ernest Lehfeld／Manuel Sanchez／Francisco Gallardo／Jorge Fernandez
4) Mexico Airporo
5) 1977-78(Mexico)
6) black／yellow(ground)
1339 1) airport
3) Ruedi Rüegg
5) 1983(Switzerland)
1340 1) airport
3) Ruedi Rüegg
5) 1983(Switzerland)
1341 1) airport
3) Ruedi Rüegg
5) 1983(Switzerland)
1342 1) airport
3) Ruedi Rüegg
5) 1983(Switzerland)
1343 1) airport
3) Ruedi Rüegg
5) 1983(Switzerland)
1344 1) library／locker
2) Takenobu Igarashi
3) Akiteru Nakajima／Kumi Shirahama
4) Keio Gijuku University
5) 1982(Japan)
1345 1) airport
3) Ruedi Rüegg
5) 1983(Switzerland)
1346 1) sign in a camera company／with wedges
2) Ken Nara／Akiteru Nakajima
3) Akiteru Nakajima／Ryoich Yamada／Kumi Shirahama
4) Canon
5) 1974(Japan)
1347 1) "Shiritori Kanji"
2),3) Yasaburo Kuwayama
4) Typo-Eye Exhibition of "A Picture Book of Letter"
5) 1977(Japan)
6) black
1348 2) Peter Steiner
3) Michael Friedland
4) Canadian Pacific
5) 1983(Canada)
6) blue
1349 1) transport
2),3) PVDI
5) 1977(Brazil)
1350 1) "A Picture Book of A-I-U-E-O"／ring
2),3) Yasaburo Kuwayama
4) Typo-Eye Exhibition of "Kami

no Mojikku"
5) 1979(Japan)

1351 1) food
2) Akiteru Nakajima
3) Akira Yagi／Takeshi Ogawa／Toru Konno／Hideko Kurihara／Keiko Komazawa
4) Chuo Bijutsu Gakuen Pictorial Course
5) 1980(Japan)

1352 1) importation & exportation
2),3) Kunihiko Sugiyama
4) Bunri
5) 1979(Japan)

1353 1) the advancement of national lives and economics
2),3) Kunihiko Sugiyama
4) Bunri
5) 1979(Japan)

1354 1) museum／mining
3) Jiri Rathousky
4) National Technology Museam
5) 1978(Czechoslovakia)

1355 1) sign in a camera company／a place for big emptied cans
2) Ken Nara／Akiteru Nakajima
3) Akiteru Nakajima／Ryoichi Yamada／Kumi Shirahama
4) Canon
5) 1974(Japan)

1356 1) "Shiritori Kanji"
2),3) Yasaburo Kuwayama
4) Typo-Eye Exhibition of "A Picture Book of Letter"
5) 1977(Japan)
6) black

1357 1) sign in a camera company／a place for emptied boxes
2) Ken Nara／Akiteru Nakajima
3) Akiteru Nakajima／Ryoichi Yamada／Kumi Shirahama
4) Canon
5) 1974(Japan)

1358 1) company sign
2) Shigeru Shimooka
3) Masanobu Watanabe
4) Mitsubishi Motors Co., Ltd. (MMC)
5) 1983(Japan)
6) dark blue(sub-color red)

1359 1) sign in a camera company／put in order
2) Ken Nara／Akiteru Nakajima
3) Akiteru Nakajima／Ryoichi Yamada／Kumi Shirahama
4) Canon
5) 1974(Japan)

1360 1) "A Picture Book of A-I-U-E-O"／green
2),3) Yasaburo Kuwayama
4) Typo-Eye Exhibition of "Kami no Mojikku"
5) 1979(Japan)

1361 1) map of neighborhood／a count available for playing tennis
2) Akiteru Nakajima
3) Akiteru Nakajima／Yumi Shirahama／Tamio Takeuchi
4) Art & Graphic
5) 1981(Japan)

1362 1) sports equipment

shop／tennis
2),3) Beppe Benenti
5) 1983(Italy)
6) red／yellow

1363 1) indication of refuge／tennis
2),3) PVDI
5) 1977(Brazil)

1364 1) indication of class／tennis
2) Syunji Niinomi
3) Tetsuharu Mabuchi
4) Tokai Sports
5) 1980(Japan)

1365 1) bill on the post／facilities for playing tennis
2) Yonefusa Yamada
3) Shin Sasaki／Yuko Ishida
4) Toden Kokoku
5) 1982(Japan)

1366 1) map of neighborhood／a room for ping-pong
2) Akiteru Nakajima
3) Akiteru Nakajima／Yumi Shirahama／Tamio Takeuchi
4) Art & Graphic
5) 1981(Japan)

1367 1) indication of refuge／ping-pong
2),3) PVDI
5) 1977(Brazil)

1368 1) map of neighborhood／golf
2) Akiteru Nakajima
3) Akiteru Nakajima／Yumi Shirahama／Tamio Takeuchi
4) Art & Graphic
5) 1981(Japan)

1369 1) golf
2) Syunji Niinomi
3) Tetsuharu Mabuchi
4) Tokai Sports
5) 1980(Japan)

1370 1) bill on the post／facilities for playing golf
2) Yonefusa Yamada
3) Shin Sasaki／Yuko Ishida
4) Toden Kokoku
5) 1982(Japan)

1372 1) sports・public hygienic service／baseball
2) Shakespear Design Studio
3) Ronald Shakespear／Raul Shakespear
4) Buenos Aires Sports Center
5) 1980(Argentina)

1373 1) indication of class／baseball
2) Syunji Niinomi
3) Tetsuharu Mabuchi
4) Tokai Sports
5) 1980(Japan)

1374 1) bill on the post／sports
2) Yonefusa Yamada
3) Shin Sasaki／Yuko Ishida
4) Toden Kokoku
5) 1982(Japan)

1375 1) map of neighborhood／a field available for playing baseball
2) Akiteru Nakajima
3) Akiteru Nakajima／Yumi Shirahama
4) Art & Graphic

5) 1981(Japan)

1376 1) "A Picture Book of A-I-U-E-O"／catching
2),3) Yasaburo Kuwayama
4) Typo-Eye Exhibition of "Kami no Mojikku"
5) 1979(Japan)

1377 1) indication of refuge／soccer
2),3) PVDI
5) 1977(Brazil)

1378 1) sports equipment shop／soccer
2),3) Beppe Benenti
5) 1983(Italy)
6) red／yellow

1379 1) indication of class
2) Syunji Niinomi
3) Tetsuharu Mabuchi
4) Tokai Sports
5) 1980(Japan)

1380 1) indication of refuge／volleyball
2),3) PVDI
5) 1977(Brazil)

1381 1) sports・public hygiencic service／basketball
2) Shakespear Design Studio
3) Ronald Shakespear／Raul Shakespear
4) Buenos Aires Sports Center
5) 1980(Argentina)

1382 1) indication of refuge／basketball
2),3) PVDI
5) 1977(Brazil)

1383 1) sports・public hygienic service／hockey
2) Shakespear Design Studio
3) Ronald Shakespear／Raul Shakespear
4) Buenos Aires Sports Center
5) 1980(Argentina)

1384 1) sports・public hygienic service／water polo
2) Shakespear Design Studio
3) Ronald Shakespear／Raul Shakespear
4) Buenos Aires Spors Center
5) 1980(Argentina)

1385 1) sports・public hygienic service／skateboard
2) Shakespear Design Studio
3) Ronald Shakespear／Raul Shakespear
4) Buenos Aires Sports Center
5) 1980(Argentina)

1386 1) indication of class
2) Syunji Niinomi
3) Tetsuharu Mabuchi
4) Tokai Sports
5) 1980(Japan)

1387 1) map of neiborhood／field available for riding a skateboard
2) Akiteru Nakajima
3) Akiteru Nakajima／Yumi Shirahama／Tamio Takeuchi
4) Art & Graphic
5) 1981(Japan)

1388 1) sports・public hygienic service／roller skate
2) Shakespear Design Studio
3) Ronald Shakespear／Raul Shakespear

5) 1981(Japan)

4) Buenos Aires Sports Center
5) 1980(Argentina)

1389 1) calendar／the archer
2),3) Ludvik Feller
4) Refrex
5) 1971(West Germany)

1390 1) products／the archer
2),3) Shigeji Kobayashi
4) The Lion Sekken Co., Ltd.
5) 1981(Japan)

1391 1) "A Picture Book of A-I-U-E-O"／target
2),3) Yasaburo Kuwayama
4) Typo-Eye Exhibition of "Kami no Mojikku"
5) 1979(Japan)

1392 1) indication of class
2) Syunji Niinomi
3) Tetsuharu Mabuchi
4) Tokai Sports
5) 1980(Japan)

1393 1) encyclopedic yearbook／column "language"
2) Kenzo Nakagawa
3) Hiroyasu Nobuyama
4) Heibonsha
5) 1980(Japan)

1394 1) fight
2),3) Kunihiko Sugiyama
4) Bunri
5) 1979(Japan)

1395 1) indication of class／weight lifting
2) Syunji Niinomi
3) Tetsuharu Mabuchi
4) Tokai Sports
5) 1980(Japan)

1396 1) sports equipment shop／mountaineering
2),3) Beppe Benenti
5) 1983(Italy)
6) red／yellow

1397 1) sports equipment shop／ski
2),3) Beppe Benenti
5) 1983(Italy)
6) red／yellow

1398 1) sports・public hygienic service／athletics
2) Shakespear Design Studio
3) Ronald Shakespear／Raul Shakespear
4) Buenos Aires Sports Center
5) 1980(Argentina)

1399 1) sports goods／table for ping-pong
3) Yoshimitsu Kato
4) Univer Sports
5) 1983(Japan)

1400 1) indication of class
2) Syunji Niinomi
3) Tetsuharu Mabuchi
4) Tokai Sports
5) 1980(Japan)

1401 1) sports equipment shop／shoes
2),3) Beppe Benenti
5) 1983(Italy)
6) red／yellow

1402 1) sports equipment shop
2),3) Beppe Benenti
5) 1983(Italy)
6) red／yellow

1403 1) sports・public hygienic service／yacht

2) Shakespear Design Studio
3) Ronald Shakespear／Raul Shakespear
4) Buenos Aires Sports Center
5) 1980(Argentina)
1404 1) campaign
2) Kuniharu Masubuchi
3) Emiko Tatsuyama／Hiroshi Iseya
4) Mikimoto
5) 1983(Japan)
1405 1) port
2),3) Kunihiko Sugiyama
4) Bunri
5) 1979(Japan)
1406 1) ocean exhibition／expo-port
2) Masaru Katsumi／Akiteru Nakajima
3) Teruyuki Kunito／Yukio Ota／Akira Kuroyone
4) okinawa international Ocean Exhibition Association
5) 1975(Japan)
6) blue(4PB 3.5／12)／beige(3Y 8.5／1)
1407 3) Eduard Prüssen
4) Belgish Bladbach City
5) 1975(West Germany)
6) black
1408
2),3) Shinichi Takahara
4) Taka Design Production
5) 1980(Japan)
1409 1) products／the scales
2),3) Shigeji Kobayashi
4) The Lion Sekken Co., Ltd.
5) 1981(Japan)
1410 1) calendar／the scales
2),3) Ludvik Feller
4) Reflex
5) 1971(West Germany)
1411 1) health center
2),3) Jan Rajlich
5) 1979(Czechoslovakia)
6) blue／red
1412 1) a simple equation
2),3) Kunihiko Sugiyama
4) Bunri
5) 1979(Japan)
1413 1) a simultaneous equation
2),3) Kunihiko Sugiyama
4) Bunri
5) 1979(Japan)
1414 1) work of lever
2),3) Hiroshi Fukushima
4) Tokyo Shoseki
5) 1978(Japan)
1415 1) text of the preparatory school
3) Kunihiko Sugiyama
4) Yoyogi Seminar
5) 1982(Japan)
1416 1) chemical action
2),3) Kunihiko Sugiyama
4) Bunri
5) 1979(Japan)
1417 1) weight and a scale
2),3) Hiroshi Fukushima
4) Tokyo Shoseki
5) 1978(Japan)
1418 1) events(department store)
2),3) Kenzo Nakagawa

4) Isetan Department Store
5) 1975(Japan)
1419 1) sports・public hygienic center／analysis
2) Shakespear Design Studio
3) Ronald Shakespear／Raul Shakespear
4) Buenos Aires Sports Center
5) 1980(Argentina)
1420 1) hospital／analysis
2) Shakespear Design Studio
3) Ronald Shakespear／Raul Shakespear
4) Buenos Aires City Hospital
5) 1970／1980(Argentina)
6) red／blue
1421 1) "Shiritori Kanji"
2),3) Yasaburo Kuwayama
4) Typo-Eye Exhibition of "A Picture Book of Letter"
5) 1977(Japan)
6) black
1422 1) museum
3) Jiri Rathousky
4) National Technology Museam
5) 1978(Czechoslovakia)
1423 1) travel agency
2) Mace Duncan
3) Mike Quon
4) American Express
5) 1983(U.S.A.)
6) black／white
1424 1) map of neighborhood／camera shop
2) Akiteru Nakajima
3) Akiteru Nakajima／Yumi Shirahama／Tamio Takeuchi
4) Art & Graphic
5) 1981(Japan)
1425 1) supermarket／no cameras
2),3) Takao Yoguchi
4) Chujitsuya
5) 1979(Japan)
1426 1) company sign
2) Shigeru Shimooka
3) Masanobu Watanabe
4) Mitsubishi Motors Co., Ltd. (MMC)
5) 1983(Japan)
6) dark blue(sub-color red)
1427 1) no cameras
2) Akiteru Nakajima
3) Akiteru Nakajima／Kumi Shirahama
4) The Iraqi Govenment
5) 1981／1982(Japan)
1428 1) laboratory
2),3) Ludvik Feller
4) Bundesinstitut Fur Berufsbildungs-Forschung
5) 1973(West Germany)
1429 2) Peter Steiner
3) Michael Friedland
4) Canadian Pacific
5) 1983(Canada)
6) blue
1430 1) "Shiritori Kanji"
2),3) Yasaburo Kuwayama
4) Typo-Eye Exhibition of "A Picture Book of Letter"
5) 1977(Japan)
6) black
1431 1) bill on the post／clock

2) Yonefusa Yamada
3) Shin Sasaki／Yuko Ishida
4) Toden Kokoku
5) 1982(Japan)
1432 1) clock
3) Yasaburo Kuwayama／Katsumi Nagata
4) Olympus Kogaku Kogyo
5) 1979(Japan)
1433 1) timetable
3) Adrian Frutiger
4) Air France
5) (France)
1434 1) timer
3) Yasaburo Kuwayama／Katsumi Nagata
4) Olympus Kogaku Kogyo
5) 1979(Japan)
1435 1) medicine
2) F. Linkhorn
3) Mike. Quon
4) Journal
5) 1983(U.S.A.)
6) black／white
1436 1) stopwatch
3) Yasaburo Kuwayama／Katsumi Nagata
4) Olympus Kogaku Kogyo
5) 1979(Japan)
1437 1) telephone／for prints
2) Akiteru Nakajima
3) Akiteru Nakajima／Kumi Shirahama
4) Art & Graphic
5) 1978／1982(Japan)
1438 1) department store
3) Shigeo Fukuda
4) Seibu Department Store
5) 1976(Japan)
1439 1) ocean exhibition／telephone
2) Masaru Katsumi／Akiteru Nakajima
3) Teruyuki Kunito／Yukio Ota／Akira Kuroyone
4) Okinawa International Ocean Exhibition Association
5) 1975(Japan)
6) fluorescent yellow／red(5R4／14)
1440 1) airport／local telephone
2) Ernest Lehfeld
3) Ernest Lehfeld／Manuel Sanchez／Francisco Gallardo／Jorge Fernandez
4) Mexico Airport
5) 1977-78(Mexico)
6) black／yellow(ground)
1441 1) telephone
2) Akiteru Nakajima
3) Akiteru Nakajima／Kumi Shirahama
4) The Iraqi Government
5) 1981／1982(Japan)
1442 1) company sign
2) Shigeru Shimooka
3) Masanobu Watanabe
4) Mitsubishi Motors Co., Ltd. (MMC)
5) 1983(Japan)
6) dark blue(sub-color red)
1443 1) a public telephone
2),3) Ichiro Saito
4) Denden Kosha Dojima Building

5) 1974(Japan)
1444 1) supermarket／a public telephone
2),3) Takao Yoguchi
4) Chujitsuya
5) 1979(Japan)
1445 1) telephone
2),3) PVDI
5) 1973(Brazil)
1446 1) airport／telephone
3) Ruedi Rüegg
5) 1983(Switzerland)
1447 1) indication of refuge／telephone
2),3) PVDI
5) 1977(Brazil)
1448 1) communicator system
3) Velizar Petrov
4) Plant(Telephone)
5) 1983(Bulgaria)
1449 1) communicator system
3) Velizar Petrov
4) Plant(Telephone)
5) 1983(Bulgaria)
1450 1) hotel(Information)
2) Jan Rajlich
3) Jan Rajlich／Jan Rajlich Jr.
4) Hotel Morava
5) 1978(Czechoslovakia)
1451 1) ocean exhibition／Emergency Telephone
2) Masaru Katsumi／Akiteru Nakajima
3) Teruyuki Kunito／Yukio Ota／Akira Kuroyone
4) Okinawa International Ocean Exhibition Association
5) 1975(Japan)
6) blue(4PB 3.5／12)／beige(3Y 8.5／1)
1452 1) airport／international telephone service
2) Ernest Lehfeld
3) Ernest Lehfeld／Manuel Sanchez／Francisco Gallardo／Jorge Fernandez
4) Mexico Airport
5) 1977-78(Mexico)
6) black／yellow(ground)
1453 1) ocean exhibition／international telephone & telegram service
2) Masaru Katsumi／Akiteru Nakajima
3) Teryuki Kunito／Yukio Ota／Akira Kuroyone
4) Okinawa International Ocean Exhibition Association
5) 1975(Japan)
6) fluorescent yellow／red(5R4／14)
1454 1) telephone／prints
2) Akiteru Nakajima
3) Akiteru Nakajima／Kumi Shirahama
4) Art & Graphic
5) 1978／1982(Japan)
1455 1) map of neighborhood／a public telephone
2) Akiteru Nakajima
3) Akiteru Nakajima／Yumi Shirahama／Tamio Takeuchi
4) Art & Graphic
5) 1981(Japan)

1456 1) telephone
2),3) PVDI
4) Copek Oil Co., Ltd.
5) 1974(Brazil)
1457 1) university hospital／
telephone
2),3) PVDI
4) Guanabara Stare University
5) 1974(Brazil)
1458 1) akagi kokutai／
telephone
2),3) Syuji Torigoe
4) The Gunma Prefectural Office
5) 1981(Japan)
1459 1) shopping center／
telephone
2),3) Syuji Torigoe
4) Tokyu Store
5) 1976(Japan)
1460 1) timetable
3) Adrian Frutiger
4) Air France
5) (France)
1461 1) communicator system
3) Velizar Petrov
4) Plant (Telephone)
5) 1983(Bulgaria)
1462 1) communicator system
3) Velizar Petrov
4) Plant (Telephone)
5) 1983(Bulgaria)
1463 1) map／telephone
2) Teruo Ishikawa
3) Teruo Ishikawa／Yoshiko
Wada
4) Shufu to Seikatsusha
5) 1982(Japan)
1464 1) "Monomi no To"
centennial／telephone set
2) Yasaburo Kuwayama
3) Yasaburo Kuwayama／Hajime
Ikeda
4) Jehovah's Witnesses
5) 1979(Japan)
1465 1) publication(practical
book)／cover & title page
3) Yutaka Hasegawa
4) Shufu to Seikatsusha
5) 1982(Japan)
1466 1) prints(catalog)
2),3) Yuich Tanifuji
4) NEC Home Electronics
5) 1983(Japan)
1467 1) telephone service／
accident
3) Asher Kalderon
5) 1983(Israel)
1468 1) facsimile
2) Akiteru Nakajima
3) Akiteru Nakajima／Kumi
Shirahama
4) Art & Graphic
5) 1978／1982(Japan)
1469 1) satellite
2),3) Kunihiko Sugiyama
4) Bunri
5) 1979(Japan)
1470 1) insurance
2),3) Donald Patiwael
5) 1983(Netherlands)
1471 1) agency
2),3) PVDI
4) Empresa Brasileira de
Correios e Telégrafos
5) 1971(Brazil)

1472 1) post
2),3) PVDI
4) Empresa Brasileira de
Correios e Telégrafos
5) 1971(Japan)
1473 1) airport／post
2) Ernest Lehfeld
3) Ernest Lehfeld／Manuel
Sanchez／Francisco Gallardo／
Jorge Fernandez
4) Mexico Airport
5) 1977-78(Mexico)
6) black／yellow(ground)
1474 1) the olympics／post
office(trial)
2) Tadashi Ikeda
3) Kenich Miyata／Seiji Masuike
4) 1988 Seoul Olympiad
5) 1982(Japan)
6) black
1475 1) post
2),3) PVDI
4) Copek Oil co., Ltd.
5) 1974(Brazil)
1476 1) letter pad & envelope
2),3) PVDI
4) Empresa Brasileira de
Correios e Telégrafos
5) 1971(Brazil)
1477 1) ocean exhibition／post
office
2) Masaru Katsumi／Akiteru
Nakajima
3) Teruyuki Kunito／Yukio Ota／
Akira Kuroyone
4) Okinawa International Ocean
Exhibition Association
5) 1975(Japan)
6) blue(4PB3.5／12)／
beige(3Y8.5／1)
1478 1) post
2),3) Syuji Torigoe
4) The Gunma Prefectual Office
5) 1981(Japan)
1479 1) "A Picture Book of
A-I-U-E-O"／letters
2),3) Yasaburo Kuwayama
4) Typo-Eye Exhibition of "Kami
no Mojikku"
5) 1979(Japan)
1480 1) sale of postage stamps
2),3) PVDI
4) Empresa Brasileira de
Correios e Telégrafos
5) 1971(Brazil)
1481 1) overseas postal service
2),3) PVDI
4) Empresa Brasileira de
Correios e Telégrafos
5) 1971(Brazil)
1482 1) domestic postal service
2),3) PVDI
4) Empresa Brasileira de
Correios e Telégrafos
5) 1971(Brazil)
1483 1) airport／telegram
2) Ernest Lehfeld
3) Ernest Lehfeld／Manuel
Sanchez／Francisco Gallardo／
Jorge Fernandez
4) Mexico Airport
5) 1977-78(Mexico)
6) black／yellow(ground)
1484 1) map of
neighborhood／mail box

2) Akiteru Nakajima
3) Akiteru Nakajima／Yumi
Shirahama／Tamio Takeuchi
4) Art & Graphic
5) 1981(Japan)
1485 1) map／mail box
2) Teruo Ishikawa
3) Teruo Ishikawa／Yoshiko
Wada
4) Shufu to Seikatsusha
5) 1982(Japan)
1486 1) "A Picture Book of
A-I-U-E-O"／mail box
2),3) Yasaburo Kuwayama
4) Typo-Eye Exhibition of "Kami
no Mojikku"
5) 1979(Japan)
1487 1) teleplone service／
telegram
3) Asher Kalderon
5) 1983(Israel)
1488 2),3) Ludvik Feller
5) 1983(West Germany)
1489 1) "Shiritori Kanji"
2),3) Yasaburo Kuwayama
4) Typo-Eye Exhibition of "A
Picture Book of Letter"
5) 1977(Japan)
6) black
1490 1) a fire hose
2) Akiteru Nakajima
3) Akiteru Nakajima／Kumi
Shirahama
4) The Iraqi Government
5) 1981／82(Japan)
1491 1) map of
neighborhood／a fire hose
2) Akiteru Nakajima
3) Akiteru Nakajima／
Yumi Shirahama／
Tamio Takeuchi
4) Art & Graphic
5) 1981(Japan)
1492 1) sign in a camera
company／a fire hose
2) Ken Nara／Akiteru Nakajima
3) Akiteru Nakajima／Ryoichi
Yamada／Kumi Shirahama
4) Canon
5) 1974(Japan)
1493 1) airport／water pipe
2) Ernest Lehfeld
3) Ernest Lehfeld／Manuel
Sanchez Francisco Gallardo／
Jorge Fernandez
4) Mexico Airport
5) 1977-78(Mexico)
6) black／yellow(ground)
1494 1) company sign
2) Shigeru Shimooka
3) Masanobu Watanabe
4) Mitsubishi Motors Co., Ltd
(MMC)
5) 1983(Japan)
6) dark blue(sub-color red)
1495 1) water pipe
2),3) PVDI
4) Copek Oil Co., Ltd.
5) 1974(Brazil)
1496 1) a fire hose
2),3) PVDI
4) Fulnus Electric Center
5) 1972(Brazil)
1497 1) hotel
2),3) PVDI

4) Rio Meridian Hotel
5) 1975(Brazil)
1498 1) department store／a
fire extinguisher
3) Shigeo Fukuda
4) Seibu Department Store
5) 1976(Japan)
1499 1) airport／a fire
extinguisher
2) Ernest Lehfeld
3) Ernest Lehfeld／Manuel
Sanchez Francisco Gallald／
Jorge Fernandez
4) Mexico Airport
5) 1977-78(Mexico)
6) black／yellow(ground)
1500 1) shopping center／a fire
extinguisher
2),3) Syuji Torigoe
4) Tokyu Store
5) 1976(Japan)
1501 1) supermarket／a fire
extinguisher
2),3) Tokao Yoguchi
4) Chujitsya
5) 1979(Japan)
1502 1) a fire extinguisher
2),3) Syuji Torigoe
4) The Gunma Prefectural Office
5) 1981(Japan)
1503 1) company sign
3) Shigeru Shimooka
3) Masanobu Watanabe
4) Mitsubishi Motors Co., Ltd.
(MMC)
5) 1983(Japan)
6) dark blue(sub-color red)
1504 1) a fire extinguisher
2),3) PVDI
4) Copek Oil Co., Ltd.
5) 1974(Brazil)
1505 2),3) PVDI
4) Fulnus Electric Center
5) 1972(Brazil)
1506 1) sports・public hygienic
service／oxygen inhaler
2) Shakespear Design Studio
3) Ronald Shakespear／Raul
Shakespear
4) Buenos Aires Sports Center
5) 1980(Argentina)
1507 2),3) PVDI
4) Fulnus Electric Center
5) 1972(Brazil)
1508 2),3) PVDI
4) Copek Oil Co., Ltd.
5) 1974(Brazil)
1509 1) company sign
3) Shigeru Shimooka
3) Masanobu Watanabe
4) Mitsubishi Motors Co., Ltd.
(MMC)
5) 1983(Japan)
6) dark blue(sub-color red)
1510 1) communicator system
3) Velizar Petrov
5) 1983(Bulgaria)
1511 1) alarm
2) Akiteru Nakajima
3) Akiteru Nakajima／Kumi
Shirahama
4) The Iraqi Government
5) 1981／1982(Japan)
1512 1) map of
neighborhood／gas station

2) Akiteru Nakajima
3) Akiteru Nakajima／Yumi Shirahama／Tamio Takeuchi
4) Art & Graphic
5) 1981(Japan)
1513 1) map of neighborhood／under construction
2) Akiteru Nakajima
3) Akiteru Nakajima／Yumi Shirahama／Tamio Takeuchi
4) Art & Graphic
5) 1981(Japan)
1514 1) metalworking industry
2),3) Kunihiko Sugiyama
4) Bunri
5) 1979(Japan)
1515 1) sign in a camera company／an apparatus room
2) Ken Nara／Akiteru Nakajima
3) Akiteru Nakajima／Ryoichi Yamada／Kumi Shirahama
4) Canon
5) 1974(Japan)
1516 1) sign in a camera company／in motion
2) Ken Nara／Akiteru Nakajima
3) Akiteru Nakajima／Ryoichi Yamada／Kumi Shirahama
4) Canon
5) 1974(Japan)
1517 1) transport
3) Istvan Szekeres
5) 1982(Hungary)
6) dark blue
1518 1) museum／mechanical engineering
3) Jiri Rathousky
5) 1978(Czechoslovakia)
1519 1) publication(guidance of feaching)
2),3) Hiroshi Fukushima
4) Tokyo Shoseki
5) 1979(Japan)
1520 1) "Monomi no To" centennial
2) Yasaburo Kuwayama
3) Hajime Ikeda
4) Jehovah's Witnesses
5) 1979(Japan)
1521 1) map of neighborhood／electric appliance shop
2) Akiteru Nakajima
3) Akiteru Nakajima／Yumi Shirahama／Tamio Takeuchi
4) Art & Graphic
5) 1981(Japan)
1522 1) greeting cards
2),3) Tadashi Mizui
4) Tadashi Mizui
5) 1976(Japan)
1523 1) museum／blectricity
3) Jiri Rathousky
5) 1978(Czechoslovakia)
1524 1) map of neighborhood／dry battery
2) Akiteru Nakajima
3) Akiteru Nakajima／Kumi Shirahama／Tamio Takeuchi
4) Art & Graphic
5) 1981(Japan)
1525 1) an electric bulb and dry battery
2),3) Hiroshi Fukushima

4) Tokyo Shoseki
5) 1978(Japan)
1526 1) sign in a camera company／under electrification
2) Ken Nara／Akiteru Nakajima
3) Akiteru Nakajima／Ryoich Yamada／Kumi Shirahama
4) Canan
5) 1974(Japan)
1527 1) electric power
2),3) Kunihiko Sugiyama
4) Bunri
5) 1979(Japan)
1528 1) sign in a camera company／under powertransmission
2) Ken Nara／Akiteru Nakajima
3) Akiteru Nakajima／Ryoichi Yamada／Kumi Shirahama
4) Canon
5) 1974(Japan)
1529 1) company sign
2) Shiberu Shimooka
3) Masanobu Watanabe
4) Mitsubishi Motors Co., Ltd. (MMC)
5) 1983(Japan)
6) dark blue(sub-color red)
1530 1) electric current and electron
2),3) Kunihiko Sugiyama
4) Bunri
5) 1979(Japan)
1531 1) ocean exhibition／electric equipment
2) Masaru Katsumi／Akiteru Nakajima
3) Teruyuki Kunito／Yukio Ota／Akira Kuroyone
4) Okinawa International Ocean Exhibition Association
5) 1975(Japan)
6) florescent yellow／red(5R4 14)
1532 1) museum／atomic energy
3) Jiri Rathousky
5) 1978(Czechoslovakia)
1533 1) electric current and work
2),3) Kunihiko Sugiyama
4) Bunri
5) 1979(Japan)
1534 1) function
2),3) Kunihiko Sugiyama
4) Bunri
5) 1979(Japan)
1535 1) atmospheric pressure and wind blowing
2),3) Kunihiko Sugiyama
4) Bunri
5) 1979(Japan)
1536 1) laboratory
2),3) Ludvik Feller
4) Bundesinstitut Fur Berufsbildungs- Forschung
5) 1972(West Germany)
1537 1) the Machine Industry
2),3) Kunihiko Sugiyama
4) Bunri
5) 1979(Japan)
1538 1) computerization
2),3) Ludvik Feller
5) 1983(West Germany)

1539 1) laboratory
2),3) Ludvik Feller
4) Bundesinstitut Fur Berufsbildungs- Forschung
5) 1972(West Germany)
1540 1) bill on the post／electric appliances
2) Yonefusa Yamada
3) Shin Sasaki／Yuko Ishida
4) Toden Kokoku
5) 1982(Japan)
1541 3) A.G.Chiremanse
5) 1982(Netherlands)
6) white／dark blue
1542 1) "A Picture Book of A-I-U-E-O"／air conditioner
2),3) Yasaburo Kuwayama
4) Typo-Eye Exhibition of "Kami no Mojikku"
5) 1979(Japan)
1543 1) business information／clean up
2) Yasaburo Kuwayama
3) Minoru kamono
4) Maruko Birumen
5) 1977(Japan)
1544 1) transport
3) Istvan Szekeres
5) 1982(Hungary)
6) dark blue
1545 1) energy
2),3) Kunihiko Sugiyama
4) Bunri
5) 1979(Japan)
1546 1) light・heat and work
2),3) Kunihiko Sugiyama
4) Bunri
5) 1979(Japan)
1547 1) ion
2),3) Kunihiko Sugiyama
4) Bunri
5) 1979(Japan)
1548 1) die-casting(the quality of the lionber)speaker
2) Koichi Nishimura
3) Goryo Shimazu
4) Matsushita Tsushin Kogyo
5) 1981(Japan)
1549 1) water-proof(speaker)
2) Koichi Nishimura
3) Yoshimi Segawa
4) Matsushita Tsushin Kogyo
5) 1979(Japan)
1550 1) educational system in electronic engineering
2),3) Ludvik Feller
4) Bnudesinstitut Fur Berufsbildungs-Forschung
5) 1973(West Germany)
1551 2),3) PVDI
4) Fulnus Electric Center
5) 1972(Brazil)
1552 1) cassette running／Reverse
2),3) Koichi Nishimura
4) Matsushita Tsushin Kogyo
5) 1979(Japan)
1553 1) tape recorder
2),3) Yasaburo Kuwayama／Katsumi Nagate
4) Olympus Kogaku Kogyo
5) 1979(Japan)
1554 1) museum／photographs and films

3) Jiri Rathousky
4) National Technology Museum
5) 1978(Czechoslovakia)
1555 1) timetable
3) Adrian Frutiger
4) Air France
5) (France)
1556 1) infomation processing
2),3) Ludvik Feller
5) 1983(West Germany)
1557 1) prints
2),3) Yuichi Tanifuji
4) NEC Home Electronics
5) 1983(Japan)
1558 1) prints
2),3) Yuichi Tanifuji
4) NEC Home Electronics
5) 1983(Japan)
1559 1) prints／door-camera
2),3) Yuichi Tanifuji
4) NEC Home Electronics
5) 1983(Japan)
1560 1) prints／video
2),3) Yuichi Tanifuji
4) NEC Home Electronics
5) 1983(Japan)
1561 1) prints／video-disk
2),3) Yuichi Tanifuji
4) NEC Home Electronics
5) 1983(Japan)
1562 1) prints／audio
2),3) Yuichi Tanifuji
4) NEC Home Electronics
5) 1983(Japan)
1563 1) the olympics／official documentary film(trial)
2) Tadashi Ikeda
3) Kenichi Miyata／Seiji Masuike
4) 1988 Seoul Olympiad
5) 1982(Japan)
6) black
1564 1) publication (column of public relations magazine)
3) Tsuyokatsu Kudo
4) The Saitama Prefecture Office
5) 1980(Japan)
1565 1) ocean exhibition／aprojection room
2) Masaru Katsumi／Akiteru Nakajima
3) Teruyuki Kunito／Yukio Ota／Akira Kuroyone
4) Okinawa International Ocean Exhibition Association
5) 1975(Japan)
6) fluorescent yellow／red(5R4／4)
1566 1) medicine
2) F.Linkhorn
3) Mike Quon
5) 1983(U.S.A.)
6) black／white
1567 1) hospital
2),3) Joe Dieter
4) The John Hopkins Hospital
5) 1982(U.S.A.)
6) navy blue
1568 2) Akiteru Nakajima
3) Akiteru Nakajima／Yoichi Moroishi／Kumi Shirahama
4) Hakugen
5) 1978／1980(Japan)
1569 1) airport／chemist's shop
2) Ernest Lehfeld
3) Arnest Lehfeld／Manuel

Sanchez／Francisco Gallardo／Jorge Fernandez
4) Mexico Airport
5) 1977-78(Mexico)
6) black／yellow(ground)
1570 1) sports／public hygienic service
2) Shakespear Design Studio
3) Ronald Shakespear／Raul Shakespear
4) Buenos Aires Sports Center
5) 1980(Argentina)
1571 1) university hospital／drug store
2),3) PVDI
4) Guanabara State University
5) 1974(Brazil)
1572 1) hospital／drug store
2) Shakespear Design Studio
3) Ronald Shakespear／Raul Shakespear
4) Buenos Aires City Hospital
5) 1970／1980(Argentina)
6) red／blue
1573 1) sports／public hygienic service
2) Shakespear Design Studio
3) Ronald Shakespear／Raul Shakespear
4) Buenos Aires Sports Center
5) 1980(Argentina)
1574 1) a package of injctor-needles
2),3) Kunihiko Sugiyama
4) Hakko Shoji
5) (Japan)
1575 2) Akiteru Nakajima
3) Akiteru Nakajima／Yoichi Moroishi／Kumi Shirahama
4) Hakugen
5) 1978／1980(Japan)
1576 1) hospital／inoculation
2) Shakespear Design Studio
3) Ronald Shakespear／Raul Shakespear
4) Buenos Aires City Hospital
5) 1970／1980(Argentina)
6) red／blue
1577 1) "Monomi no To" centennial／blood transfusion
2) Yasaburo Kuwayama
3) Yasaburo Kuwayama／Hajime Ikeda
4) Jehovah's Witenesses
5) 1979(Japan)
1578 1) hospital
2),3) Joe Dieter
4) The John Hopkins Hospital
5) 1982(U.S.A.)
6) navy blue
1579 1) sports／public hygienic service
2) Shakespear Design Studio
3) Ronald Shakespear／Raul Shakespear
4) Buenos Aires Sports Center
5) 1980(Argentina)
1580 1) hospital／clinic(for outpatients)
2) Shakespear Design Studio
3) Ronald Shakespear／Raul Shakespear
4) Buenos Aires City Hospital
5) 1970／1980(Argentina)
6) red／blue

1581 1) sports／public hygienic service
2) Shakespear Design Studio
3) Ronald Shakespear／Raul Shakespear
4) Buenos Aires Sports Center
5) 1970／1980(Argentina)
1582 1) sign in a camera company／a corrosive Substance
2) Ken Nara／Akiteru Nakajima
3) Akiteru Nakajima／Ryoichi Yamada／Kumi Shirahama
4) Canon
5) 1974(Japan)
1583 1) publication(column of public relations magazine)
3) Tsuyokatsu Kudo
4) The Saitama Prefectual Office
5) 1980(Japan)
1584 1) map of neighborhood／Magazine
2) Akiteru Nakajima
3) Akiteru Nakajima／Yumi Shirahama／Tamio Takcuchi
4) Art & Graphic
5) 1981(Japan)
1585 1) newly built house
2),3) Ludvik Feller
5) 1983／1984(West Germany)
1586 1) publication・print
2),3) Kunihiko Sugiyama
4) Bunri
5) 1979(Japan)
1587 1) bill on the post／books office appliances
2) Yonefusa Yamada
3) Shin Sasaki／Yuko Ishida
4) Toden Kokoku
5) 1982(Japan)
1588 1) events(space show)
2),3) Noriaki Tamura
4) Headquarters Japan International Aerospace Show 1979
5) 1979(Japan)
1589 1) map of neighborhood／bookshop
2) Akiteru Nakajima
3) Akiteru Nakajima／Yumi Shirahama／Tamio Takeuchi
4) Art & Graphic
5) 1981(Japan)
1590 1) regional meeting／branch of documents
2) Hajime Nakamura／Yasaburo Kuwayama
3) Yasaburo Kuwayama／Hajime Ikeda／Norio Ikeda
4) The Regional Meeting of Jehovah's Witnesses
5) 1980(Japan)
1591 1) tv sign／educational program
3) Nikola Nikolov
4) Bulgaria Television
5) 1980-81(Bulgaria)
6) black／white
1592 1) hospital／library
2) Shakespear Design Studio
3) Ronald Shakespear／Raul Shakespear
4) Buenos Aires City Hospital
5) 1970／1980(Argentina)
1593 1) educational system in electronic engineering／a book of

course
2),3) Ludvik Feller
4) Bundesinstitut Fur Berufsbildungs-Forschung
5) 1973(West Germany)
1594 1) educational system in electronic engineering
2),3) Ludvik Feller
4) Bundesinstitut Fur Berufsbildungs!Forschung
5) 1973(West Germany)
1595 1) educational system in electronic engineering
2),3) Ludvik Feller
4) Bundesinstitut Fur Berufsbildungs-Forschung
5) 1973(West Germany)
1596 1) map of neighborhood／library
2) Akiteru Nakajima
3) Akiteru Nakajima／Yumi Shirahama／Tamio Takeuchi
4) Art & Graphic
5) 1981(Japan)
1597 1) sign in a camera company／put the room in order
2) Ken Nara／Akiteru Nakajima
3) Akiteru Nakajima／Ryoichi Yamada／Kumi Shirahama
4) Canon
5) 1974(Japan)
1598 1) arrangement of materials
2),3) Kunihiko Sugiyama
4) Bunri
5) 1979(Japan)
1599 1) hospital
2),3) Joe Dieter
4) The John Hopkins Hospital
5) 1982(U.S.A.)
6) navy blue
1600 1) publication(practical book)／cover & title page
3) Yutaka Hasegawa
4) Shufu to Seikatsusha
5) 1982(Japan)
1601 1) text of the preparatory school／japanese
2),3) Kunihiko Sugiyama
4) Yoyogi Seminar
5) 1982(Japan)
1602 1) hospital／registrar
2) Shakespear Design Studio
3) Ronald Shakespear／Raul Shakespear
4) Buenos Aires City Hospital
5) 1970／1980(Argentina)
6) red／blue
1603 1) office supplies／series of products(pen-stand)
2),3) Yoshihiro Kishimoto
4) Karu Jimuki
5) 1976(Japan)
1604 3) István Szekeres
4) Service House
5) 1970(Hungary)
6) black
1605 1) prints
3) Iwao Yamaguchi
4) Yamachan Kikaku
5) 1979(Japan)
1606 1) sports／public hygienic service
2) Shakespear Design Studio
3) Ronald Shakespear／Raul

Shakespear
4) Buenos Aires Sports Center
5) 1980(Argentina)
1607 1) expression
2),3) Kunihiko Sugiyama
4) Bunri
5) 1979(Japan)
1608 1) tv sign／political criticism
3) Nikola Nikolov
4) Bulgaria Television
5) 1980-81(Bulgaria)
6) black／white
1609 3) István Szekeres
4) Servise House
5) 1970(Hungary)
6) black
1610 1) "A Picture Book of A-I-U-E-O"／brush
2),3) Yasaburo Kuwayama
4) Typo-Eye Exhibition of "Kami no Mojikku"
5) 1979(Japan)
1611 1) Japanese paper
2),3) Kunihiko Sugiyama
4) Bunri
5) 1979(Japan)
1612 1) map of neighborhood／Copying Service
2) Akiteru Nakajima
3) Akiteru Nakajima／Yumi Shirahama／Tamio Takeuchi
4) Art & Graphic
5) 1981(Japan)
1613 1) "A Picture Book of A-I-U-E-O"／colors(paints)
2),3) Yasaburo Kuwayama
4) Typo-Eye Exhibition of "Kami no Mojikku"
5) 1979(Japan)
1614 1) encyclopedia／a painting and handcraft
2) Katsuichi Ito
3) Katsuichi Ito Design Studio
4) Tamagawa University Publishing Department
5) 1979(Japan)
1615 1) "A Picture Book of A-I-U-E-O"／paste
2),3) Yasaburo Kuwayama
4) Typo-Eye Exhibition of "Kami no Mojikku"
5) 1979(Japan)
1616 1) similar figures
2),3) Kunihiko Sugiyama
4) Bunri
5) 1979(Japan)
1617 1) inkstone
2),3) Kunihiko Sugiyama
4) Bunri
5) 1979(Japan)
1618 1) hotel(Information)
2) Jan Rajlich
3) Jan Rajlich／Jan Rajlich Jr.
4) Hotel Morava
5) 1978(Czechoslovakia)
1619 1) text of the preparatory school
2),3) Kunihiko Sugiyama
4) Yoyogi Seminar
5) 1982(Japan)
1620 1) prints(catalog)
2),3) Yuichi Tanifuji
4) NEC Home Electronics
5) 1983(Japan)

1621 1) "A Picture Book of A-I-U-E-O"／stamp
2),3) Yasaburo Kuwayama
4) Typo-Eye Exhibition of "Kami no Mojikku"
5) 1979(Japan)
1622 1) newly built house
2),3) Ludvik Feller
5) 1983／1984(West Germany)
1623 1) publication
2),3) Ludvik Feller
5) 1972(West Germany)
1624 1) smoking room
2) Akiteru Nakajima
3) Akiteru Nakajima／Kumi Shirahama
4) The Iraqi Government
5) 1981／1982(Japan)
1625 1) library／smoking room
2) Takenobu Igarashi
3) Akiteru Nakajima／Kumi Shirahama
4) Keio Gijuku University
5) 1982(Japan)
1626 1) smoking room
2),3) Syuji Torigoe
4) The Gunma Prefectural Office
5) 1981(Japan)
1627 1) supermarket／smoking room
2),3) Takao Yoguchi
4) Chujitsuya
5) 1979(Japan)
1628 1) company sign
2) Shigeru Shimooka
3) Masanobu Watanabe
4) Mitsubishi Motors Co., Ltd. (MMC)
5) 1983(Japan)
6) dark blue(sub-color red)
1629 1) airport／no smoking
3) Ruedi Rüegg
5) 1983(Switzerland)
1630 1) no smoking
2),3) PVDI
4) Fulnus Electric Center
5) 1972(Blasil)
1631 1) hotel／no smoking
2),3) PVDI
4) Rio Meridian Hotel
5) 1975(Brazil)
1632 1) no smoking
2),3) PVDI
4) Copek Oil Co., Ltd.
5) 1974(Brasiq)
1633 1) airport／no smoking
2) Ernest Lehfeld
3) Ernest Lehfeld／Manuel Sanchez／Francisco Gallardo／Jorge Fernandez
4) Mexico Airport
5) 1977-78(Mexico)
6) black／yellow(ground)
1634 1) supermarket／don't throw cigarette ends away
2),3) Takao Yoguchi
4) Chujitsuya
5) 1979(Japan)
1635 1) hospital／no smoking
2) Shakespear Design Studio
3) Ronald Shakespear／Raul Shakespear
4) Buenos Aires City Hospital
5) 1970／1980(Argentina)

6) red／blue
1636 1) map of neighborhood／a tabacco shop
2) Akiteru Nakajima
3) Akiteru Nakajima／Kumi Shirahama／Tamio Takeuchi
4) Art & Graphic
5) 1981(Japan)
1637 1) airport
3) Ruedi Rüegg
5) 1983(Switzerland)
1638 1) airport／a tabacco shop
2) Ernest Lehfeld
3) Ernest Lehfeld／Manuel Sanchez／Francisco Gallardo／Jorge Fernandez
4) Mexico Airport
5) 1977-78(Mexico)
6) black／yellow(ground)
1639 1) map of neighborhood／gift shop
2) Akiteru Nakajima
3) Akiteru Nakajima／／Kumi Shirahama／Tamio Takeuchi
4) Art & Graphic
5) 1981(Japan)
1640 1) airport／gift shop
2) Ernest Lehfeid
3) Ernest Lehfeld／Manuel Sanchez／Francisco Gallardo／Jorge Fernandez
4) Mexico Airport
5) 1977-78(Mexico)
6) black／yellow(ground)
1641 1) stand
2),3) Syuji Torigoe
4) The Gunma Prefectual Office
5) 1981(Japan)
1642 1) the Olympics／stand(trial)
2) Tadashi Ikeda
3) Kenichi Miyata／Seiji Masuike
4) 1988 Seoul Olympiad
5) 1982(Japan)
6) black
1643 1) airport
2) Ruedi Rüegg
5) 1983(Switzerland)
1644 1) encyclopedic yearbook／column "language"
2) Kenzo Nakagawa
3) Kumiko Nagasaki
4) Heibonsha
5) 1980(Japan)
1645 1) sports equipment shop
2),3) Beppe Benenti
5) 1983(Italy)
6) red／yellow
1646 1) sports equipment shop
2),3) Beppe Benenti
5) 1983(Italy)
6) red／yellow
1647 1) "Shiritori Kanji"
2),3) Yasaburo Kuwayama
4) Typo-Eye Exhibition of "A Picture Book of Letter"
5) 1977(Japan)
6) black
1648 1) "Shiritori Kanji"
2),3) Yasaburo Kuwayama
4) Typo-Eye Exhibition of "A Picture Book of Letter"
5) 1977(Japan)
6) black

1649 1) texture
2),3) Kunihiko Sugiyama
4) Bunri
5) 1979(Japan)
1650 1) map of neiborhood／coin-op
2) Akiteru Nakajima
3) Akiteru Nakajima／Kumi Shirahama／Tamio Takeuchi
4) Art & Graphic
5) 1981(Japan)
1651 1) sports equipment shop
2),3) Beppe Benenti
5) 1983(Italy)
6) red／yellow
1652 1) sports equipment shop
2),3) Beppe Benenti
5) 1983(Italy)
6) red／yellow
1653 1) map of neiborhood／cleaners
2) Akiteru Nakajima
3) Akiteru Nakajima／Kumi Shirahama／Tamio Takeuchi
4) Art & Graphic
5) 1981(Japan)
1654 1) sports equipment shop
2),3) Beppe Benenti
5) 1983(Italy)
6) red／yellow
1655 1) Indication of Class
2) Syunji Niinomi
3) Tetsuharu Mabuchi
4) Tokai Sports
5) 1980(Japan)
1656 1) map of neighborhood／haberdashery
2) Akiteru Nakajima
3) Akiteru Nakajima／Yumi Shirahama／Tamio Takeuchi
4) Art & Graphic
5) 1981(Japan)
1657 1) map of neighborhood／draper's shop
2) Akiteru Nakajima
3) Akiteru Nakajima／Yumi Shirahama／Tamio Takeuchi
4) Art & Graphic
5) 1981(Japan)
1658 1) indication of class
2) Syunji Niinomi
3) Tetsuharu Mabuchi
4) Tokai Sports
5) 1980(Japan)
1659 1) bill on the post／boutique
2) Yonefusa Yamada
3) Shin Sasaki／Yuko Ishida
4) Toden Kokoku
5) 1982(Japan)
1660 1) bill on the post／drapery
2) Yonefusa Yamada
3) Shin Sasaki／Yuko Ishida
4) Toden Kokoku
5) 1982(Japan)
1661 1) bill on the post／tailor
2) Yonefusa Yamada
3) Shin Sasaki／Yuko Ishida
4) Toden Kokoku
5) 1982(Japan)
1662 1) bill on the post／haberdashery
2) Yonefusa Yamada
3) Shin Sasaki／Yuko Ishida

4) Toden Kokoku
5) 1982(Japan)
1663 2),3) Shinichi Takahara
4) Taka Design Production
5) 1980(Sapporo)
1664 1) map of neighborhood／bedquilts shop
2) Akiteru Nakajima
3) Akiteru Nakajima／Yumi Shirahama／Tamio Takeuchi
4) Art & Graphic
5) 1981(Japan)
1665 2) Akiteru Nakajima
3) Akiteru Nakajima／Yoichi Moroishi／Kumi Shirahama
4) Hakugen
5) 1978／1980(Japan)
1666 1) salt
2),3) Kunihiko Sugiyama
4) Bunri
5) 1979(Japan)
1667 2) Akiteru Nakajima
3) Akiteru Nakajima／Yoichi Moroishi／Kumi Shirahama
4) Hakugen
5) 1978／1980(Japan)
1668 2) Akiteru Nakajima
3) Akiteru Nakajima／Yoichi Moroishi／Kumi Shirahama
4) Hakugen
5) 1978／1980(Japan)
1669 2) Akiteru Nakajima
3) Akiteru Nakajima／Yoichi Moroishi／Kumi Shirahama
4) Hakugen
5) 1978／1980(Japan)
1670 1) map of neighborhood／butcher's shop
2) Akiteru Nakajima
3) Akiteru Nakajima／Yumi Shirahama／Tamio Takeuchi
4) Art & Graphic
5) 1981(Japan)
1671 1) supermarket
2),3) Takao Yoguchi
4) Chujitsuya
5) 1977(Japan)
1672 1) supermarket
2) Shakespear Design Studio
3) Ronald Shakespear／Raul Shakespear
4) Disco Supermarket
5) 1982-83(Argentinas)
1673 1) airport
3) Ruedi Rücgg
5) 1983(Switzerland)
1674 2) Akiteru Nakajima
3) Akiteru Nakajima／Yoichi Moroishi／Kumi Shirahama
4) Hakugen
5) 1978／1980(Japan)
1675 1) map of neighborhood／confectionary shop
2) Akiteru Nakajima
3) Akiteru Nakajima／Yumi Shirahama／Tamio Takeuchi
4) Art & Graphic
5) 1981(Japan)
1676 1) airport
3) Ruedi Rüegg
5) 1983(Switzerland)
1677 2) Akiteru Nakajima
3) Akiteru Nakajima／Yoichi Moroishi／Kumi Shirahama

4) Hakugen
5) 1978/1980(Japan)
1678 1) map of neighborhood/tenpuraya
2) Akiteru Nakajima
3) Akiteru Nakajima/Yumi Shirahama/Tamio Takeuchi
4) Art & Graphic
5) 1981(Japan)
1679 1) supermarket
2),3) Takao Yoguchi
4) Chujitsuya
5) 1977(Japan)
1680 2) Akiteru Nakajima
3) Akiteru Nakajima/Yoichi Moroishi/Kumi Shirahama
4) Hakugen
5) 1978/1980(Japan)
1681 1) supermarket
2) Shakespear Design Studio
3) Ronald Shakespear/Raul Shakespear
4) Disco Supermarket
5) 1982-83(Argentina)
1682 2) Akiteru Nakajima
3) Akiteru Nakajima/Yoichi Moroishi/Kumi Shirahama
4) Hakugen
5) 1978/1980(Japan)
1683 1) supermarket
2) Shakespear Design Studio
3) Ronald Shakespear/Raul Shakespear
4) Disco Supermarket
5) 1982-83(Argentina)
1684 2) Akiteru Nakajima
3) Akiteru Nakajima/Yoichi Moroishi/Kumi Shirahama
4) Hakugen
5) 1978/1980(Japan)
1685 1) map of neighborhood/bakery
2) Akiteru Nakajima
3) Akiteru Nakajima/Yumi Shirahama/Tamio Takeuchi
4) Art & Graphic
5) 1981(Japan)
1686 1) pot and pan
2) Jan Rajlich
3) Jan Rajlich Jr.
4) CSVD
5) 1973(Czechoslovakia)
1687 1) supermarket
2) Shakespear Design Studio
3) Ronald Shakespear/Raul Shakespear
4) Disco Supermarket
5) 1982-83(Argentina)
1688 1) map of neighborhood/japanese sweet shop
2) Akiteru Nakajima
3) Akiteru Nakajima/Yumi Shirahama/Tamio Takeuchi
4) Art & Graphic
5) 1981(Japan)
1689 1) map of neighborhood/japanese hotchpotch shop
2) Akiteru Nakajima
3) Akiteru Nakajima/Yumi Shirahama/Tamio Takeuchi
4) Art & Graphic
5) 1981(Japan)
1690 1) map of

neighborhood/buckwheat-noodle restaurant
2) Akiteru Nakajima
3) Akiteru Nakajima/Yumi Shirahama/Tamio Takeuchi
4) Art & Graphic
5) 1981(Japan)
1691 1) map of neighborhood/sushi shop
2) Akiteru Nakajima
3) Akiteru Nakajima/Yumi Shirahama/Tamio Takeuchi
4) Art & Graphic
5) 1981(Japan)
1692 1) map/lavatory
2) Teruo Ishikawa
3) Teruo Ishikawa/Yoshiko Wada
4) Shufu to Seikatsusha
5) 1982(Japan)
1693 2) Akiteru Nakajima
3) Akiteru Nakajima/Yoichi Moroishi/Kumi Shirahama
4) Hakugen
5) 1978/1980(Japan)
1694 1) paper・pulp
2),3) Kunihiko Sugiyama
4) Bunri
5) 1979(Japan)
1695 1) lumber
2),3) Kunihiko Sugiyama
4) Bunri
5) 1979(Japan)
1696 1) sports・public hygienic service/a waiting room
2) Shakespear Design Studio
3) Ronald Shakespear/Raul Shakespear
4) Buenos Aires Sports Center
5) 1980(Argentina)
1697 1) hospital/a waiting room
2) Shakespear Design Studio
3) Ronald Shakespear/Raul Shakespear
4) Buenos Aires City Hospital
5) 1970/1980(Argentina)
6) red/blue
1698 1) publication(practical book)/cover & title page
3) Yutaka Hasegawa
4) Shufu to Seikatsusha
5) 1982(Japan)
1699 1) timetable
3) Adrian Frutiger
4) Air France
5) (France)
1700 1) sports/public hygienic service
2) Shakespear Design Studio
3) Ronald Shakespear/Raul Shakespear
4) Buenos Aires Sports Center
5) 1980(Argentina)
1701 1) hospital/ward
2) Shakespear Design Studio
3) Ronald Shakespear/Raul Shakespear
4) Buenos Aires City Hospital
5) 1970/1980(Argentina)
6) red/yellow
1702 1) sign in a camera company/close the door after you
2) Ken Nara/Akiteru Nakajima

3) Akiteru Nakajima/Ryoichi Yamada/Kumi Shirahama
4) Canon
5) 1974(Japan)
1703 1) japanese lacquer ware
2),3) Kunihiko Sugiyama
4) Bunri
5) 1979(Japan)
1704 1) map of neighborhood/a tea dealer's store
2) Akiteru Nakajima
3) Akiteru Nakajima/Yumi Shirahama/Tamio Takeuchi
4) Art & Graphic
5) 1981(Japan)
1705 1) bamboo-craft
2),3) Kunihiko Sugiyama
4) Bunri
5) 1979(Japan)
1706 1) "Shiritori Kanji"
2),3) Yasaburo Kuwayama
4) Typo-Eye Exhibition of "A Picture Book of Letter"
5) 1977(Japan)
6) black
1707 1) "A Picture Book of A-I-U-E-O"/dustpan
2),3) Yasaburo Kuwayama
4) Typo-Eye Exhibition of "Kami no Mojikku"
5) 1979(Japan)
1708 1) sports・public hygienic service/pediatrics
2) Shakespear Design Studio
3) Ronald Shakespear/Raul Shakespear
4) Buenos Aires Sports Center
5) 1980(Argentina)
1709 1) food/refrigeration
2) Akiteru Nakajima
3) Akira Yagi/Takeshi Ogawa/Toru Konno/Hideko Kurihara/Keiko Komazawa
4) Chuo Bijutsu Gakuen Pictorial Course
5) 1980(Japan)
1710 1) special edition/painting
2) Kazunori Okamoto
3) Hiroshi Iseya
4) Diamondsha
5) 1980(Japan)
1711 1) publication
2) Massimo Dradi
3) Ald Travagliati
4) Welcome
5) 1983(Italy)
6) black/white
1712 1) "A Picture Book of A-I-U-E-O"/currency
2),3) Yasaburo Kuwayama
4) Typo-Eye Exhibition of "Kami no Mojikku"
5) 1979(Japan)
1713 1) airport
3) Ruedi Rüegg
5) 1983(Switzerland)
1714 1) map of neighborhood/a cheap store
2) Akiteru Nakajima
3) Akiteru Nakajima/Yumi Shirahama/Tamio Takeuchi
4) Art & Graphic
5) 1981(Japan)

1715 1) food/don's drop
2) Akiteru Nakajima
3) Akira Yagi/Takeshi Ogawa/Toru Konno/Hideko Kurihara/Keiko Komazawa
4) Chuo Bijutsu Gakuen Pictorial Course
5) 1980(Japan)
1716 1) publication(thesaurus)/dice
2),3) Kunihiko Sugiyama
4) Kodansha
5) 1983(Japan)
1717 1) map of neighborhood/mah-jongg house
2) Akiteru Nakajima
3) Akiteru Nakajima/Yumi Shirahama/Tamio Takeuchi
4) Art & Graphic
5) 1981(Japan)
1718 1) encyclopedia/games and toys
2) Katsuichi Ito
3) Katsuichi Ito Design Studio
4) Tamagawa University Publishing Department
5) 1979(Japan)
1719 1) bill on the post/toys
2) Yonefusa Yamada
3) Shin Sasaki/Yuko Ishida
4) Toden Kokoku
5) 1982(Japan)
1720 1) "A Picture Book of A-I-U-E-O"/air pump
2),3) Yasaburo Kuwayama
4) Typo-Eye Exhibition of "Kami no Mojikku"
5) 1979(Japan)
1721 1) indicator
2),3) Syuji Torigoe
4) The Gunma Prefectual Office
5) 1981(Japan)
1722 1) airport/go forward
2) Ernest Lehfeld
3) Ernest Lehfeld/Manuel Sanchez/Francisco Gallardo/Jerbe Fernandez
4) Mexico Airport
5) 1977-78(Mexico)
6) black/yellow(ground)
1723 2),3) PVDI
4) Fulnus Electric Center
5) 1972(Brazil)
1724 1) you may go straight
2),3) PVDI
4) Copek Oil Co., Ltd.
5) 1974(Brazil)
1725 1) educational system in electronic engineering
2),3) Ludvik Feller
4) Bundesinstitut Fur Berufsbildungs-Forschung
5) 1972-1980(Went Germany)
1726 1) hospital/arrow to right
2) Shakespear Design Studio
3) Ronald Shakespear Raul Shakespear
4) Buenos Aires City Hospital
5) 1970/1980(Argentina)
6) red/yellow
1727 1) hotel
2) Jan Rajlich
3) Jan Rajlich/Jan Rajlich Jr.
4) Hotel Morava
5) 1978(Czechoslovakia)

1728 1) laboratory
2),3) Ludvik Feller
4) Bundesinstitut Fur Berufsbildungs-Forschung
5) 1973(West Germany)
1729 1) library／direction
2) Takenobu Igarashi
3) Akiteru Nakajima／Kumi Shirahama
4) Keio Gijuku University
5) 1982(Japan)
1730 1) interior sign
2),3) Yasaburo Kuwayama
4) Pale France
5) 1975(Japan)
1731 1) department store
3) Shigeo Fukuda
4) Seibu Departmennt Store
5) 1976(Japan)
1732 1) ocean exhibition／direction
2) Masaru Katsumi／Akiteru Nakajima
3) Teruyuki Kunito／Yukio Ota／Akira Kuroyone
4) Okinawa International Ocean Exhibition Association
5) 1975(Japan)
6) fluorescent yellow／red(5R4／14)
1733 2),3) Syuji Torigoe
4) The Gunma Prefectural Office
5) 1981(Japan)
1734 1) communicator system
3) Velizar Petrov
4) Plant(Telephone)
5) 1983(Bulgaria)
1735 2),3) PVDI
4) Fulnus Electric Center
5) 1972(Brazil)
1736 1) hotel(information)
2) Jan Rajlich
3) Jan Rajlich／Jan Rajlich Jr.
4) Hotel Morava
5) 1978(Czechoslovakia)
1737 2),3) Syuji Torigoe
4) The Gunma Prefectual Office
5) 1981(Japan)
1738 1) educational system in electronic engineering／quantity
2),3) Ludvik Feller
4) Bundesinstitut Fur Berufsbildungs-Forschung
5) 1972-1980(West Germany)
1739 1) laboratory
2),3) Ludvik Feller
4) Bundesinstitut Fur Berufsbildungs-Forschung
5) 1972(West Germany)
1740 1) ／an inequality
2),3) Kunihiko Sugiyama
4) Bunri
5) 1979(Japan)
1741 1) sign in a camera company／a gate way
2) Ken Nara／Akiteru Nakajima
3) Akiteru Nakajima／Ryoichi Yamada／Kumi Shirahama
4) Canon
5) 1974(Japan)
1742 1) ad magazine／
2),3) Yuji Baba
3) Tokyo Kaijyo Kasai

5) 1977(Japan)
1743 1) map of neighborhood／the house of sweetheart
2) Akiteru Nakajima
3) Akiteru Nakajima／Yumi Shirahama／Tamio Takeuchi
4) Art & Graphic
5) 1981(Japan)
1744 1) medicine／for the heart
3) Akiteru Nakajima
4) Mine Yakuhin
5) 1980(Japan)
1745 1) sports・public hygienic service／cardiology
2) Shakespear Design Studio
3) Ronald Shakespear／Raul Shakespear
4) Buenos Aires Sports Center
5) 1980(Argentina)
1746 1) hospital／cardiology
2) Shakespear Design Studio
3) Ronald Shakespear／Raul Shakespear
4) Buenos Aires City Hospital
5) 1970／1980(Argentina)
6) red／blue
1747 1) company sign
2) Shigeru Shimooka
3) Masanobu Watanabe
4) Mitsubishi Motors Co., Ltd. (MMC)
5) 1983(Japan)
6) dark blue(sub-color red)
1748 1) bookshop／love story
3) Miloš Ćirić
5) 1974(Yugoslavia)
6) Red
1749 1) greeting cards
2),3) Tadashi Mizui
4) Tadashi Mizui
5) 1976(Japan)
1750 1) events(a bargain sale)
2) Jan Rajlich
3) Jan Rajlich Jr.
4) CSVD
5) 1973(Czechoslovakia)
1751 1) map of neighborhood／hospital
2) Akiteru Nakajima
3) Akiteru Nakajima／Yumi Shirahama／Tamio Takeuchi
4) Art & Graphic
5) 1981(Japan)
1752 1) medical treatrent
2),3) PVDI
4) Copek Oil Co., Ltd.
5) 1974(Brazil)
1753 1) bill on the post／Medical Profession
2) Yonefusa Yamada
3) Shin Sasaki／Yuko Ishida
4) Toden Kokoku
5) 1982(Japan)
1754 1) ocean exhibition／a first-aid station
2) Masaru Katsumi／Akitetu Nakajima
3) Teruyuki Kunito／Yukio Ota／Akira Kuroyone
4) Okinawa International Ocean Exhibition Association
5) 1975(Japan)
6) fluorescent yellow／red(5R4／14)

1755 2),3) PVDI
4) Fulnus Electric Center
5) 1972(Brazil)
1756 1) transport
2),3) PVDI
5) 1977(Brazil)
1757 1) insurance
2),3) Donald Patiwael
5) 1983(Netherlands)
1758 1) health center
2),3) Jan Rajlich
5) 1979(Czechoslovakia)
6) blue／red
1759 1) sports・public hygienic service／morgue
2) Shakespear Design Studio
3) Ronald Shakespear／Raul Shakespear
4) Buenos Aires Sports Center
5) 1980(Argentina)
1760 1) interior sign
2),3) Yasaburo Kuwayama
4) Pale France
5) 1975(Japan)
1761 1) timetable
3) Adrian Frutiger
4) Air France
5) France
1762 1) campaign／filter II
2) Kuniharu Masubuchi
3) Emiko Tachiyama／Hiroshi Iseya
4) Mikimoto
5) 1983(Japan)
1763 1) stairs
2),3) Yuji Baba
3) Nippon Broadcasting Company
5) 1978(Japan)
1764 1) events(space show)
2),3) Noriaki Tamura
4) Headquarters Japan International Aerospace Show 1979
5) 1979(Japan)
6) sky blue
1765 1) transport
2),3) PVDI
5) 1977(Brazil)
1766 1) pictogram／for radio, cassette tape recorder, TV set
2) Norihisa Kurose
3) Tadashi Ishikawa／Hideko Sakado
4) Hitachi Scisakujyo
5) 1979(Japan)
1767 1) figure
2),3) PVDI
5) 1973(Brazil)
1768 1) map of neighborhood／all night service
2) Akiteru Nakajima
3) Akiteru Nakajima／Yumi Shirahama／Tamio Takeuchi
4) Art & Graphic
5) 1981(Japan)
1769 1) map of neighborhood／an automatic vending machine
2) Akiteru Nakajima
3) Akiteru Nakajima／Yumi Shirahama／Tamio Takeuchi
4) Art & Graphic
5) 1981(Japan)
1770 1) nature of integral

numbers
2),3) Kunihiko Sugiyama
4) Bunri
5) 1979(Japan)
1771 1) encyclopedia／numbers and figures
2) Katsuichi Ito
3) Katsuichi Ito Design Studio
4) Tamagawa University Publishing Department
5) 1979(Japan)
1772 1) positive number and negative number
2),3) Kunihiko Sugiyama
4) Bunri
5) 1979(Japan)
1773 1) calculation of expressions
2),3) Kunihiko Sugiyama
4) Bunri
5) 1979(Japan)
1774 1) bank
3) Eduardo A. Canovas
5) 1980(Argentina)
6) dark green／green
1775 1) a square root
2),3) Kunihiko Sugiyama
4) Bunri
5) 1979(Japan)
1776 1) text of the preparatory school(chemistry)
2),3) Kunihiko Sugiyama
4) Yoyogi Seminar
5) 1982(Japan)
1777 1) encyclopedia／shops and current coins
2) Katsuichi Ito
3) Katsuichi Ito Design Studio
4) Tamagawa University Publishing Department
5) 1979(Japan)
1778 1) ocean exhibition／bank
2) Masaru Katsumi／Akiteru Nakajima
3) Teruyuki Kunito／Yukio Ota／Akira kuroyone
4) Okinawa International Ocean Exhibition Association
5) 1975(Japan)
6) fluorecent yellow／red(5R4／14)
1779 1) bank
3) Eduardo A. Canavas
5) 1980(Argentina)
6) dark green／green
1780 1) airport／exchange
2) Ernest Lehfeld
3) Ernest Lehfeld／Manuel Sanchez／Francisco Gallardo／Jorge Fernandez
4) Mexico Airport
5) 1977-78(Mexico)
6) black／yellow(ground)
1781 1) encyclopedia
2) Katsuichi Ito
3) Katsuichi Ito Design Studio
4) Tamagawa University Publishing Department
5) 1979(Japan)
1782 1) letters and expression
2),3) Kunihiko Sugiyama
4) Bunri
5) 1979(Japan)
1783 1) map／bus stop
2) Teruo Ishikawa

3) Teruo Ishikawa／Yoshiko Wada
4) Shufu to Seikatsusha
5) 1982(Japan)
1784 1) interior sign
2),3) Yasaburo Kuwayama
4) Pale France
5) 1975(Japan)
1785 1) TV sign／the youth
3) Nikola Nikolov
4) Bulgaria Television
5) 1980-81(Bulgaria)
6) bllack／white
1786 1) east side
2) Akiteru Nakajima
3) Akiteru Nakajima／Kumi Shirahama
4) The Iraqi Government
5) 1981／1982(Japan)
1787 3) Ruedi Rüegg
5) 1983(Switzerland)
1788 1) map／gas station
2) Teruo Ishikawa
3) Teruo Ishikawa／Yoshiko Wada
4) Shufu to Seikatsusha
5) 1982(Japan)
1789 3) Ruedi Rüegg
5) 1983(Switzerland)
1790 1) parking lot
2) Tadashi Ishikawa
3) Tadashi Ishikawa／Hiroko Horimoto
4) Shell Oil Co., Ltd.
5) 1983(Japan)
6) Pontone 312／Pantone 280
1791 1) parking lot
2),3) Syuji Torigoe
4) The Gunma Prefectual Office
5) 1981(Japan)
1792 1) department store
3) Shigeo Fukuda
4) Seibu Department Store
5) 1976(Japan)
1793 1) transport
2),3) PVDI
5) 1977(Brazil)
1794 1) supermarket
2) Shakespear Design Studio
3) Ronald Shakespear／Raul Shakespear
4) Disco Supermarket
5) 1982-83(Argentina)
1795 1) west side
2) Akiteru Nakajima
3) Akiteru Nakajima／Kumi Shirahama
4) The Iraqi Government
5) 1981／1982(Japan)
1796 1) sports・public hygienic service／x-ray
2) Shakespear Design Studio
3) Ronald Shakespear／Raul Shakespear
4) Buenos Aires Sports Center
5) 1980(Argentina)
1797 1) hospital／roentgenograph booth
2) Shakespear Design Studio
3) Ronald Shakespear／Raul Shakespear
4) Buenos Aires City Hospital
5) 1970／1980(Argentina)
6) red／blue
1798 1) transport

2),3) PVDI
5) 1977(Brazil)
1799 1) prints
3) Akiteru Nakajima
4) Iwaki Glass
5) (Japan)
1800 1) sign in a camera company／caution
2) Ken Nara／Akiteru Nakajima
3) Akiteru Nakajima／Ryoichi Yamada／Kumi Shirahama
4) Canon
5) 1974(Japan)
1801 1) bank
3) Eduardo A. Canovas
5) 1980(Argentina)
6) dark green／green

S1 1) airport
2) Ernest Lehfeld
3) Ernest Lehfeld／Manuel Sanchez／Francisco Gallardo／Jorge Fernandez
4) Mexico International Airport
5) 1977-78(Mexico)
6) black／yellow(ground)
((about arrival & departure of passengers))
-1 passenger's Documents(Passport)
-2 Baggage
-3 Check
-4 A waiting room
-5 Sanitation
-6 Complaint about baggage
-7 Customhouse
-8 Domestic／Arrival
-9 Domestic／Departure
-10 International／Arrival
-11 International／Departure
-12 Departure
-13 Arrival
-14 Domestic
-15 International
-16 Transit passenger
-17 Observatory
-18 Airport
((about service for passengers))
-19 Sanitation
-20 Lavatory
-21 ladies Room
-22 mens Room
-23 Bath Chair
-24 Elevator for the physically handicapped
-25 Elevator
-26 Baggage sevice
-27 Information on hotel
-28 Exchange
-29 Land transportation
-30 Land transportation
-31 Land transportation
-32 Rent-a-Car
-33 Parking Lot
((about Communication))
-34 Local telephone service
-35 Call
-36 Overseas call
-37 Information in airport
-38 Telegram
-39 Postal service
(shops & restaurants)
-40 Bar
-41 Restaurant
-42 Cafeteria
-43 Gift shop
-44 Cigarette shop
-45 Flower shop
-46 Chemist's shop
(signs of warning, limitation and emergency)
-47 No transit
-48 No smoking
-49 No mascots
-50 First-Aid(urgency)
-51 An extinguisher
-52 A water pipe
((indicating sign))
-53 To Left
((indicating signs of stairs))
-54 Right upward staircase
-55 Left downward escalator
-56 Right upward escalator

S2 3) Ruedi Rüegg
5) 1983(Switzerland)
((General))
-1～11
((Air Transportation))
-12～17
((Transportation))
-18～25
((Baggage))
-26～34
((Service))
-35 Restaurant
-36 A Drink
-37 A Drink
-38 Coffee
-39 Cake
-40 Snack
-41 Beer
-43 Information
-44 Exchange
-45 Call
-46 Gift Shop
((Sanitation))
-48 Lavatory
-49 ladies Room
-50 mens Room
-51 Shower Bath
-52 Changing Room
-53 ladies Dressing Room
-54 mens Dressing Room
((Health))
-55 Aid
-56 X Rays
((Emergency))
-57 A Firehose
-58 A Fire Exit
((Customhouse))
-59～62
-63 Tabacco
-64 Liquor
((escalator))
-65～71
((Prohibition))
-72～78
S3 2) Peter Steiner
3) Michael Friedland
4) Canadian Pacific
5) 1983(Canada)
6) blue
-1～12
S4 1) quick card
2),3) Akiteru Nakajima
4) Typo-Eye
5) 1984(Japan)
-1 Where is the airport ?
-2 Where is the next stop ?
-3 Where are we flying now ?
-4 Where is the port ?
-5 Where is the station ?
-6 Where is the subway station ?
-7 Where is a taxi stand ?
-8 Where is the bus-stop for ?
-9 Does this bus go to ── ?
-10 How many stops is it till I get to ── ?
-11 Where is here ?
-12 Which direction is north ?
-13 ──, should I go straight ?
-14 Should I turn left (or right)?
-15 ──, please
-16 Could you tell me how to get to ── ?
-17 I think I'm lost.
-18 I lost sight of my

232

companion.
-19 I'd like to change some money, please.
-20 How much is it ?
-21 Can I use this cash-card ?
-22 I'd like to send this letter air mail. (to Japan)
-23 I'd like to send this letter surface mail.
-24 Where is the baggage room ?
-25 Can you carry my bags ?
-26 Where is the elevator ?
-27 Where is the fire exit ?
-28 Where is the restroom ?
-29 Where is the locker room ?
-30 Let me use a rent-a-car.
-31 What time is it now ?
-32 How long does it take to get to ── ?
-33 How much is the one-day's rental ?
-34 I'd like to call Japan.
-35 I'd like to call police.
-36 Please call a doctor.
-37 I'd like a paper, please.
-38 I'd like a magazine.
-39 Please wait for a minute here. I wait here.
-40 Could you show me the way ?
-41 Let's go together.
-42 Let me have something to write on.
-43 Many I use the telephone ?
-44 Where is the telephone booth ?
-45 I want some film.
-46 I'd like to develop this film.
-47 Could you set film in this camera ?
-48 May I take pictures ?
S5 1) telephone service
3) Asher Kalderon
4) Telephon Service
5) 1983(Israel)
-2 A Time Signal
-3 Trouble
-4 Overseas Call
-5 A Fire Station Service
-6 Ambulance
-7 Police Station
-8 Telegram
-9 A call
-10 Inquiry about the arrival
-11 Weather forecast
S6 1) Infomation sign
2),3) PVDI
4) Empresa Brasileira de Correios e Telégrafos
5) 1971(Brazil)
-1 Agency
-2 Letter pad and envelopes
-3 Sale of postage stamps
-4 Style of writing
-5 Domestic postal service
-6 Overseas postal service
-7 Delivery Service
S7 1) laboratory
2),3) Ludvik Feller
4) Bundesinstitut Fur Berufsbildungs-Forschung
5) 1973(West Germany)
-1~8

S8 1) vocational training center
2),3) Ludvik Feller
4) CEDEFOP
5) 1979(West Germany)
-1 Government office
-2 Investigation
-4 Training
-5 Labor market
-6 Vocation
-8 Training for beginners
S9 1) library
2) Takenobu Igarashi
3) Akiteru Nakajima／Kumi Shirahama
4) Keio Gijiku University
5) 1982(Japan)
-1 Direction
-2 Facilities for the physically handicapped
-3 Smoking room
-4 Men
-5 Lavatory
-6 Men
-7 Ladies
-8 Copy
-9 Audio-Visual
-10 Locker
-11 Fire exit
-12 No carrying books in
-13 Inspection
-14 Lounge
-15 No Chatting
-16 Umbrella Stand
S10 1) Association (Insurance Association)
2),3) Bill Wood
4) Association of Administrators (Insurance)
5) 1977(U.S.A.)
6) Black
-1 Internal medicine
-2 Hospital (admission)
-3 Lost job
-4 Child-Birth
-5 Physical handicap
-6 Dentistry
S11 1) medical academy of the army
3) Miloš Ćirić
5) 1977(Yugoslavia)
6) red／blue／green
-1 Man
-2 Doctor
-3 Nurse
-4 Fighter
-5 Officer
-6 Citizen (man)
-7 Citizen (woman)
-8 Group
S12 1) university hospital
2),3) PVDI
4) Gunabara State University
5) 1974(Brazil)
-1 Male patients
-2 Female patients
-3 Chemist's shop
-4 Be quiet
-5 New-Born baby
-6 X-rays
-7 Pediatrics
-8 Reception
S13 1) remedy
3) Asher Kalderon
4) The Dead Sea Hot Spring Building

5) 1983(Israel)
-1 Remedy for limb
-2 Massage by water
-3 Massage under water
-4 Bathing therapy
-5 Main pool
-6 Physio-therapy
-9 Massage
-10 Mud therapy
-11 Rest room for men
-12 Rest room for ledies
-13 Doctor
-14 Nurse
S14 1) sports／public hygienic service
2) Shakespear Design Studio
3) Ronald Shapespear／Raul Shakespear
4) Buenos Aires Sports Center
5) 1980(Argentina)
-1 Cycling
-2 Hockey
-3 Archery
-4 Sailing
-5 Lake
-6 Water polo
-7 Maintenance
-8 Rollerskate
-9 Skate-board
-10 Baseball
-11 Basketball
-12 Tennis
-13 Track-field
-14 Coffee shop
-15 mens room
-16 ladies room
-17 Preparation
-18 Physio-therapy
-19 Nursery
-20 Laboratory
-21 Bed Room
-22 Cardiology
-23 Ophthalmology
-24 Internal medicine
-25 Medicine
-26 Analysis
-27 Inoculation
-28 Handicap
-29 Urology
-30 Blood bank
-31 Obstetics ward
-32 X-rays
-33 Dressing room
-34 Surgery
-35 Pediatrics
-36 Waiting room
-37 Pediatrics
-38 Chemists room
-39 No smoking area
-40 No transit
-41 Registrar
-42 Washing room
-43 General ward
-44 Burn
-45 Otorhinolaryngology
-46 Dermatotogy
-47 Monastery
-48 Church
-49 Mortuary
-50 External wound
-51 Plastic surgery
-52 Dentistry
-53 Recovery room
-54 Gynaecology
-55 Pedtiatrics

-56 Room of new-born babies
-58 First-Aid treatment
-59 Tranquilizer
-60 Oxygen inhaler
-61 Ambulance
-62 Parking lot
-63 Elevator
S15 2) Akiteru Nakajima
3) Akiteru Nakajima／Kumi Shirahama
4) The Iraqi Government
5) 1981／82(Japan)
-1 Direction
-2 Lavatory
-3 Mens Room
-4 Ladies Room
-5 Facilties for the phycically handicapped
-6 Bus
-7 Automobile
-8 Restaurant
-9 Coffee Shop
-10 Cinema
-11 Theater
-12 Lounge
-14 Kiosk
-15 Telephone
-16 Off limits
-17 No smoking
-18 Staircase
-19 Fire exit
-20 Fire stairs
-21 Fire hose
-22 extinguisher
-23 First-Aid station
-24 Shower bath for men
-25 Shower bath for ladies
-26 Information
-27 Heliport
-28 Parking lot
-29 East Side
-30 West Side
-31 Smoking room
-32 Alarm
-33 Stretcher for a first-aid
-34 Don't touch
-35 No fhotography
S16 1) facilities in a resort
2) Wataru Tsuchiya／Kenzo Nakagawa
3) Kenzo Nakagawa／Hiroyasu Nobuyama／Satoshi Morikami
4) Manza Beach Resort
5) 1982(Japan)
-1~16
S17 1) sports
2),3) Jurien Van Der Wal
4) International Olympic Game Cometee
5) 1979(switzerland)
-1 Athletics
-2 Boat
-3 Basketball
-4 Boxing
-5 Canoe
-6 Cycling
-7 Fencing
-8 Association football
-9 Gymnastic
-10 Weight lifting
-11 Handball
-12 Hockey
-13 Judo
-14 Wrestling
-15 Swimming

-16 Modern pentathlon
-17 Horsemanship
-19 Archery
-20 Volleyball
-21 Yachting
S18 1) Akagi Kokutai／facilities
2),3) Shuji Torigoe
4) The Gunma Prefectual Office
5) 1981(Japan)
-1 Mens room
-2 Ladies room
-3 Lavatory
-5 Information office
-6 Off limits
-7 a Rest room
-8 Only for the physically
handicapped
-9 Lost child information office
-10 Seats
-11 First-Aid station
-12 Telephone
-13 Postal service
-14 Restaurant
-15 Booth
-16 Station
-17 Bus stop
-18 Taxi stand
-19 Parking lot
-20 Parking lot for bicycles
-21 Baggage office
-22 Lost-articles office
-23 Smoking room
-24 No smoking
-25 An exitinguisher
-26〜30 Indicator

Yasaburo Kuwayama (About the Editor)

Yasaburo Kuwayama was born in Niigata prefecture, Japan in 1938. He graduated from the Musashino Art University in 1962 and taught typography at Asagaya Academie des Beaux-arts for five years from 1966. In 1969, he established the Kuwayama Design Room. In 1970, he began teaching typography at the Musashino Art university. In 1972, he began serving as an [Examiner of Lettering]. In 1975, he began teaching lettering at the Asahi Culture Center and served as a permanent manager of the Japan Creative Finish Work Association. In 1979, he retired from his posts in : the Musashino Art University, The Organization of Lettering Approval, the Asahi Culture Center, and the Japan Creative Finish Work Association. His retirement from these posts enabled him to create more time for other interests. At present, he is a member of the Association du Typographique Internationale (A. TYP. I), the Japan Typography Association (JTA), the Federation of German Typographers (BOB), the Tokyo Designers Space (TDS), and the Japan Graphic Designer Association (JAGDA). He is a member of the Jehovah Witness Christian faith. His main books include "Lettering & Design", "Typeface Design" and "Graphic Elements of The World."

Appendix

Relative to marks, symbols, and logotypes. there is much room for the development of pictogram design. There are two basic reasons for this :

1) Pictograms are not as established conceptually as marks and symbols, since clients are much more familiar with the latter. This unfamiliarity results in confusion as to what type of pictogram to use to express an idea. The other tendency is to try to project an attractive image as with marks, symbols, logotypes, while not thinking carefully enough about the content or meaning.

2) Time is needed for pictograms to become more widely accepted. This is primarily due to the fact that not many pictograms are activcly in use, but I believe this problem will be remedied with time. Before long the word "pictogram" will become an active part of graphic designers' vocabulary. In fact, a very short time ago the term "graphic design" was quite uncommon. In the past when people thought of designers, they usually thought of just fashion designers. Indeed, the design profession has expanded in scope in a relatively short amount of time.

This book, Pictogram and Sign Design was compiled as a trade paper edition of the orignal version. Unfortunately since page space was limited, I was unable to include many excellent works. For instance, in section 3, "Signs and Letters,"and section 4, "Sets of Pictograms," we were only able to include the most typical pictograms designs.

I am convinced that this new edition will be used by more people than the previous one. I would be delighted if the knowledge and study of pictogram design progressed as a result of the use of this book. It would also be a great pleasure if both active and aspiring designers using this book were to create new pictogram designs ; as undoubtedly they will. I invite and would be happy to receive any comments or inquiries about the pictograms in this book.

Yasaburo Kuwayama (January 1989)

Editor : Yasaburo Kuwayama／Publisher : Kashiwashobo

1985-1991 Works Being Solicited
Marks, Symbols, Logotypes, Pictograms, Signs, Typefaces

Many marks, symbols, logotypes, pictograms and typefaces are designed every year, but what is the role that they play ? In order to find an answer to this question, marks, symbols, logotypes, pictograms, signs and typefaces are being solicited from designers for publication in a book.

Instead of just a record of works, this book will provide abundant material for reference in design, in searching for similar works, and in research. Since publication of an international edition is being planned, this book will undoubtedly benefit design circles throughout the world.

●**Works Solicited**
1. Marks, Symbols
2. Logotypes
3. Pictograms, Signs
4. Typefaces
5. Below you'll find instructions for application to the above mentioned categories.
    * Attach a photograph to works used in a special way or which develop in a special way. For example, those which change or move.
    * Specify special points.

●**Period**
Works designed and used from 1985 to 1991
    * Includes works redesigned during this period

●**Size**
1. Marks, Symbols :　　about 4 cm
2. Logotypes :　　about 9 cm
3. Pictograms, Signs :　　about 3 cm
4. Typefaces :　　Height of one word about 2 cm
    * Other sizes are acceptable.
    * Paste the work on the application slip.
    * When submitting color photographs please use positive film. If black and white film, please send 5×7" prints.
    * Printed matter can be submitted.
    * For works that you want returned, write "R" in red.
    * Attach application slips to examples of the designer's work.
    * In cases where pictograms, signs and typefaces make up sets, paste the works on pasteboard and an application slip on the pasteboard.

●**Category**
Circle one of the following :
1. Marks, symbols
2. Logotypes
3. Pictograms, Signs
4. Typefaces

●**Points to be Noted**
1. Motif or Production Aim (less than 30 words)
2. Business Category
3. Name of the Art Director(s)
4. Name of the Designer(s) (including colleagues)
5. Client
6. Year and Place Designed
7. Color (attach color samples or color proofs)
    * Write in English as much as possible
    * When writing by hand, please write clearly

●**Deadline**
March 1, 1992

●**Send to**
Kuwayama Design Room
1-3-1-501 Higashi Izumi, Komae-shi, Tokyo 201, Japan

    * Ask for or make copies if you want more application slips.
    * No application charge is required, but payment will not be made for works submitted.

*Works will not be returned (color positives will be returned).
*Some works may not be included in the book due to editing considerations.
*There are no qualifications or restrictions on the number of works submitted.
The following works cannot be included in the book.
*Works already included in this series.
*Works with no application slip attached or with inadequate entries on the application slip.
*Works which are inadequate as block copy.

Editor Yasaburo Kuwayama
Member, Japan Typography Association (JTA)
Member, International Typography Association (ATYPI)
Member, Japan Graphic Designers Association (JAGDA)
Member, Tokyo Designers Space (TDS)
Special Member, BDB of West Germany

Publisher Kashiwashobo
1-13-14 Honkomagome, Bunkyo-ku, Tokyo 113
Tel (03) 947-8254

Book Size A4, about 480 pages, 3 to 5 volumes Publication
Date approximately April 1989

Paste Monochrome Work

Application Slip

Circle one of following: 1.Mark, Symbol 2.Logotype 3.Pictogram 4.Typeface

1. Motif or production aim

2. Business Category(or Use Contents)

3. Art Director

4. Designer

5. Client

6. Year and Place Designed

7. Color

*On reverse side, fill applicant's name, address and phone number.